GOD, LOCKE, AND EQUALITY

2003

Are we humans all one another's equals? And if we are, what is this equality based on and what are its implications?

In this concise and engaging book, Jeremy Waldron explores these questions in the company of the seventeenth-century English philosopher John Locke. Waldron believes that Locke provides us with "as well-worked-out a theory of basic equality as we have in the canon of political philosophy." But for us it is a challenging theory because its foundations are unabashedly religious. God has created us equal, says Locke, and a proper grasp of the implications of this equality is inseparable from an understanding of ordinary men and women as creatures of God, created in his image and "made to last during his, not one anothers Pleasure."

The religious foundations of Locke's political thought have been noted before, but they have never been explored more sympathetically, or with greater attention to their implications for modern debates about equality. Jeremy Waldron is one of the world's leading legal and political philosophers, and this book is based on the Carlyle Lectures that he presented in Oxford in 1999. It provides new perspectives on Locke's egalitarianism and the tribute he paid to the status and dignity of the ordinary person; it examines the problems Locke faced in defining the human species for the purposes of his commitment to basic equality; it explores the relation between his egalitarianism and his Christian beliefs; and most important, it offers new interpretations of Locke's views on toleration, slavery, property, aboriginal rights, the Poor Law, the distribution of the franchise, and relations between the sexes.

But this is not just a book about Locke. *God, Locke, and Equality* discusses contemporary approaches to equality as well as rival interpretations of Locke, and this dual agenda gives the whole book an unusual degree of accessibility and intellectual excitement. Indispensable for Locke scholars and for those who study the foundations of equality and the relation between politics and religion, it will be of interest also to philosophers, political theorists, lawyers, and theologians around the world.

GOD, LOCKE, AND EQUALITY

Christian Foundations of John Locke's Political Thought

JEREMY WALDRON

CAMBRIDGE
UNIVERSITY PRESS

PUBLISHED BY THE PRESS SYNDICATE OF THE UNIVERSITY OF CAMBRIDGE
The Pitt Building, Trumpington Street, Cambridge, United Kingdom

CAMBRIDGE UNIVERSITY PRESS
The Edinburgh Building, Cambridge CB2 2RU, UK
40 West 20th Street, New York, NY 10011-4211, USA
477 Williamstown Road, Port Melbourne, VIC 3207, Australia
Ruiz de Alarcón 13, 28014 Madrid, Spain
Dock House, The Waterfront, Cape Town 8001, South Africa

http://www.cambridge.org

First published 2002

Printed in the United Kingdom at the University Press, Cambridge

Typeface Baskerville Monotype 11 /12.5 pt   *System* LaTeX 2$_\varepsilon$ [TB]

A catalogue record for this book is available from the British Library

Library of Congress Cataloguing in Publication data
Waldron, Jeremy.
God, Locke, and equality: Christian foundations of John Locke's political
thought / Jeremy Waldron.
p.   cm.
Includes bibliographical references and index.
ISBN 0 521 81001 9   ISBN 0 521 89057 8 (pbk.)
1. Locke, John, 1632–1704 – Contributions in political science.   2. Locke, John,
1632–1704 – Contributions in the concept of equality.   3. Equality – Religious
aspects – Christianity.   I. Title.
JC153.L87 W34   2002
320.51′2′092 – dc21   2002-022288

ISBN 0 521 81001 9 hardback
ISBN 0 521 89057 8 paperback

To Gwen Taylor,
teacher, friend, and muse
with thanks

Contents

Preface

This book is a revised version of the Carlyle Lectures which I delivered at the University of Oxford in Michaelmas Term 1999, under the title "Christian Equality in the Political Theory of John Locke."

The opportunity to develop and deliver these lectures was most welcome and I am particularly obliged to Larry Siedentop and Mark Philp for the invitation and the arrangements. I am grateful also to the Warden and Fellows of Nuffield College and the Warden and Fellows of All Souls College for office accommodation and living accommodation during my eight weeks in Oxford, and to Suzanne Byrch for administrative arrangements. Thanks also to Gerry Cohen, Cecile Fabre, John Gardner, James Griffin, Bob Hargrave, Tony Honore, Brian Loughman, Dan McDermott, David Miller, Karma Nabulsi, Joseph Raz, Mike Rosen, Alan Ryan, and Andrew Williams for their interest and their comments.

A substantial extract from Chapters 3 and 8 of this book was delivered as the Spring 2000 University Lecture at Columbia University. I want to say "thank you" to President George Rupp and Provost Jonathan Cole for this invitation. It was an honor to be able to present some of these arguments under the great cupola of Columbia's Low Library. The same material was also presented at Political Theory workshops at Johns Hopkins University and the University of Chicago. Participants everywhere have been generous with their comments on this and other work that I have presented on basic equality: I am particularly grateful to Jean Cohen, Jules Coleman, Bill Connolly, Chad Cyrenne, Michael Dorf, Ronald Dworkin, David Estlund, George Fletcher, Robert Gooding-Williams, Kent Greenawalt, David Johnston, Frances Kamm, George Kateb, Ira Katznelson, Philip Kitcher, John Marshall, Alan Musgrave, Thomas Nagel, Graham Oddie, Susan Okin, Thomas Pogge, Gwen Taylor, Susan Wolf, Nicholas Woltersdorff, and Iris Young.

In respect of the revision phase, my greatest debt is to Richard Fisher of Cambridge University Press for his patience and encouragement.

(Thanks, too, to the Press's reviewers, who provided extensive and valuable suggestions.) Ekow Yankah provided research assistance and Chevor Pompey provided secretarial help. I am grateful to Columbia Law School for a summer stipend in 2001 supporting the completion of this work (as well as for the time to present the lectures at Oxford in 1999).

Thanks, finally, to Carol Sanger for her companionship throughout this process, and for her contributions and comments on the text. Those who know her know how lucky I am.

Citations and abbreviations

The major writings of John Locke are frequently cited in the text that follows. Full details are in the bibliography, but the following abbreviations will be used in the text.

1st T   Book I of John Locke, *Two Treatises of Government*, ed. Peter Laslett (Cambridge: Cambridge University Press, 1988), pp. 137–263. My citations to the *First Treatise* are by numbered paragraph.

2nd T   Book II of John Locke, *Two Treatises of Government*, ed. Peter Laslett (Cambridge: Cambridge University Press, 1988), pp. 265–428. My citations to the *Second Treatise* are by numbered paragraph.

E   John Locke, *An Essay Concerning Human Understanding* ed. P. H. Nidditch (Oxford: Clarendon Press, 1971). My citations to the *Essay* are by book, chapter, and section.

LCT   John Locke, *A Letter Concerning Toleration*, ed. James Tully (Indianapolis: Hackett Publishing, 1983). Locke's *Letter Concerning Toleration* is cited by page number.

RC   John Locke, *The Reasonableness of Christianity, as Delivered in the Scriptures* (Bristol: Thoemmes Press, 1997). This is a facsimile of *Reasonableness* from the 1794 edition of Locke's works, reprinted in the series "Key Texts: Classic Studies in the History of Ideas." It is cited by page number.

P&N   John Locke, *A Paraphrase and Notes on the Epistles of St. Paul*, 2 vols., ed. Arthur W. Wainwright (Oxford: Clarendon Press, 1987). This posthumous work of Locke's is cited by volume and page number.

Locke scholars will note that my citations refer to recently published and widely available editions in preference to scholarly editions of

Locke's complete works, most of which are found only in libraries. I have done so because I think it is easier on readers, who are more likely to have these recent editions in front of them. The "Cambridge Texts in the History of Political Thought" series has done much to standardize political theory citations: it is unfortunate, however, that the Locke volumes in this series do not include Locke's 1689 *Letter Concerning Toleration*, and it is a pity too that there is no standard or widely recognized version of *The Reasonableness of Christianity* available for citation. I have done the best I can with these.

Apart from the six works listed above, all other works by Locke and all works by other authors are cited in the footnotes by author and short title. (For some of these, I am afraid, there is no choice but to use ancient library-bound editions.) Readers are referred to the bibliography at the end of the book for full details.

Introduction

My topic is equality: the proposition that humans are all one another's equals – *created* equal, perhaps, or (whether created or not) just *equal*, in some fundamental and compelling sense. What that sense is and what its implications are for law, politics, society, and economy – these are questions I propose to explore in the company of the seventeenth-century English political philosopher John Locke.

I believe that Locke's mature corpus – *An Essay Concerning Human Understanding*, the *Two Treatises of Government*, the four (or rather three-and-a-half) *Letters Concerning Toleration* that he wrote in the 1680s and 1690s, and *The Reasonableness of Christianity* – is as well-worked-out a theory of basic equality as we have in the canon of political philosophy. I shall not try to defend that proposition in this introductory chapter; the whole book may be read as a defense of it. But I want to say something preliminary here, first about what I mean by "basic equality" and, secondly, about my use of political, philosophical, and religious writings from the 1680s and the 1690s in relation to our largely secular interest in this topic at the beginning of the twenty-first century.[1]

I

First, a word about basic equality. In the voluminous modern literature on egalitarianism, there is a tremendous amount on equality as a policy *aim*. Philosophers ask whether we should be aiming for equality of wealth, equality of income, equality of happiness, or equality of opportunity; they ask whether equality is an acceptable aim in itself or code for something

---

[1] The mature writings on which I shall focus are not necessarily consonant with what Locke wrote earlier in his career, and commentators have often ignored this. (As Skinner puts it in "Meaning and Understanding," p. 41, "Locke at thirty is evidently not yet 'Locke.'") And we must be careful not to exaggerate the unity of what I am calling Locke's mature works: this point will be important in Chapter 4, p. 99.

else, like the mitigation of poverty; they ask whether aiming for equality implies an unacceptable leveling; whether, if achieved, it could possibly be stable; how it is related to other social values such as efficiency, liberty, and the rule of law; and so on. A tremendous amount of energy has been devoted to that sort of distributive or policy question in recent political philosophy.[2]

Much less has been devoted to the more abstract philosophical question: "What is the character of our deeper commitment to treating all human beings as equals – a commitment which seems to *underlie* our particular egalitarian aims?" Not "What are its implications?" but "What does this foundational equality amount to?" and "What is it based on?" The difference between these two types of interest in equality is not the difference between prescriptive and descriptive views – equality as aim *versus* equality as a fact or as a descriptive claim. It is between equality as a policy aim, and equality as a background commitment that underlies many different policy positions. (Whether equality in the latter sense requires support from some thesis of the descriptive equality of all humans is a further question, which I will discuss briefly in Chapter 3 and explore in detail elsewhere in some more analytic work on basic equality.)[3]

As I said, although there is plenty of work on equality, there is precious little in the modern literature on the background idea that we humans are, fundamentally, one another's equals. There's a page or two in articles by Bernard Williams, Gregory Vlastos, Stanley Benn, and D. A. Lloyd Thomas, and a few pages towards the end of Rawls's *Theory of Justice.*[4] And that's about it. This is not because the fundamental principle is thought unimportant. On the contrary, much of the work that is being done on equality as an aim presupposes the importance of basic equality. Ronald Dworkin's work on equality provides a fine illustration. Dworkin has done a tremendous amount to explore and articulate the nature of our commitment to equality in the social and economic realm.[5] He has helped us think through the issue of the currency of equality: are we or should we be interested in equality of well-being, equality of primary

---

[2] I have in mind particularly the literature inspired by Dworkin, "What is Equality? 1," and "What is Equality? 2" and Sen, "Equality of What?" See also, for example, Arneson, "Equality and Equality of Opportunity for Welfare"; Dworkin, *Sovereign Virtue*; Frankfurt, "Equality and Respect"; Parfit, *Equality or Priority?*; Raz, *Morality of Freedom*, Ch. 9; and Temkin, *Inequality.*

[3] See below, pp. 68–71.

[4] Williams, "Idea of Equality," pp. 230–39; Benn, "Egalitarianism and the Equal Consideration of Interests," pp. 133–7; Vlastos, "Justice and Equality," pp. 49–60; Lloyd Thomas, "Equality Within The Limits of Reason Alone," pp. 538 ff.; and Rawls, *Theory of Justice*, pp. 504–12. See also Coons and Brennan, *By Nature Equal*, for a survey of the literature on this issue.

[5] See generally Dworkin, *Sovereign Virtue.*

goods, equality of resources generally or equality of basic capacities?[6] He provides a useful account of the relation between equality and market mechanisms, in terms of a distinction between "choice-sensitive" and "luck-sensitive" aspects of social and economic distribution.[7] And he has also developed powerful and interesting arguments about the relation between equality and the "trumping force" associated with moral and constitutional rights.[8] In all of this Dworkin has insisted on attention to the distinction between various articulations of equality, in these and other fields of policy-oriented theorizing, and an underlying principle of equality, which he terms the principle of equal concern and respect. Without that distinction, he says, people will be unable to distinguish between "treatment as an equal" which is fundamental to political morality, and "equal treatment," which may or may not be what the principle of equal concern and respect requires of us in some domain or currency, in some particular set of circumstances.[9] So the distinction between basic equality and equality as an aim is fundamental to Dworkin's work. Yet Dworkin has said next to nothing about the nature and grounding of the principle of equal respect.[10] He has devoted very little energy to the task of considering what that principle amounts to *in itself*, what (if anything) evokes it in the nature of the beings it proposes to treat as equals, and above all, what its denial would involve and what precisely would have to be refuted if this foundational assumption of equality had to be sustained against real-life philosophical opponents.

This is not peculiar to Dworkin. He maintains that it is an obvious and generally accepted truth that governments must treat their citizens as equals, and that no one in the modern world could possibly get away with denying this (though of course they deny particular aspects of egalitarian policy).[11] If he is right – and I think he is – then there is a failure of argument on a very broad front indeed. Among those who make use of some very basic principle of human equality, virtually no one has devoted much energy to explaining what the principle amounts to in itself, nor – as I said – to the task of outlining what the refutation of any serious philosophical denial of basic equality would have to involve.

---

[6] See especially Dworkin, "What is Equality? 1" and "What is Equality? 2."

[7] Dworkin, *A Matter of Principle*, pp. 192 ff., and "What is Equality? 2," pp. 292 ff.

[8] Dworkin, *Taking Rights Seriously*, pp. 272–8, and "Rights as Trumps," pp. 292 ff.

[9] See Dworkin, *Taking Rights Seriously*, p. 227.

[10] The closest he has come to a sustained discussion of these issues is in Dworkin, "In Defense of Equality," but the discussion there is directed mostly at some particular arguments by Jan Narveson, and it is in any case tantalizingly brief.

[11] Dworkin, *Sovereign Virtue*, p. 128.

No doubt part of the reason for reticence here has to do with the unpleasantness or offensiveness of the views – sexist and racist views, for example – that one would have to pretend to take seriously if one wanted to conduct a serious examination of these matters.[12] In philosophy generally one sometimes has to pretend to be a weirdo; one has to pretend to take seriously the possibility that the sun will not rise tomorrow in order to address problems like induction, causation, the regularity of nature, and the reality of the external world. In these areas, unless our speculations appear "cold, and strain'd, and ridiculous" by ordinary standards, we are not doing philosophy.[13] The trouble is that in political philosophy, those ordinary standards may be ordinary *moral* standards. That can make political philosophy, when it turns its attentions to fundamentals, quite an uncomfortable occupation to pursue. As I said: in *general* philosophy, one only has to pretend to be a weirdo or an eccentric. In political philosophy, one has to appear to take seriously positions that in other contexts would be dismissed out of hand as offensive and wrong. Most of us would rather forgo this discomfort, particularly in regard to the testing of a position that most of our peers already seem to accept or take for granted.[14]

By contrast John Locke and his contemporaries in seventeenth-century political theory did not have the luxury of asking themselves whether it might be too distasteful to bother taking seriously the denial of basic human equality. They were *confronted* with such denials, and with

---

[12] Here's an example of the sort of inegalitarian position I mean. In 1907, the Clarendon Press at Oxford published a two-volume treatise on moral philosophy by Hastings Rashdall. The following extract concerns trade-offs between high culture and the amelioration of social and economic conditions:

I will now mention a case in which probably no one will hesitate. It is becoming tolerably obvious at the present day that all improvement in the social condition of the higher races of mankind postulates the exclusion of competition with the lower races. That means that, sooner or later, the lower Well-being – it may be ultimately the very existence – of countless Chinamen or negroes must be sacrificed that a higher life may be possible for a much smaller number of white men. It is impossible to defend the morality of such a policy upon the principle of equal consideration taken by itself and in the most obvious sense of the word. (Rashdall, *The Theory of Good and Evil*, Vol. I, pp. 237–8)

There is not a trace of irony in Rashdall's presentation of this position. Rashdall also appends a footnote: "The exclusion is far more difficult to justify in the case of people like the Japanese, who are equally civilized but have fewer wants than the Western" (ibid., p. 238). My attention was first drawn to this passage by a reference in Haksar, *Equality, Liberty and Perfectionism*, p. 2. Dr. Haksar's whole discussion is very interesting, esp. chs. 2 and 3.

[13] Hume, *Treatise*, Bk. I, Pt. IV, sect. 7, p. 269.

[14] I have heard people say: "Why do we need to explain or defend basic equality? Nobody denies it." But even if that's true, it is still important for philosophers to explore the character and the grounds of propositions we take for granted. See Waldron, "What Plato Would Allow," p. 171.

real political systems built upon them. Some of them – Locke in particular – thought there was no way around such denials, if the political campaigns they were involved in were to succeed at the level of philosophy and ideology. The opponents of equality – not just equality of this or equality of that, but the *basic* equality of all human persons – would have to be dealt with head-on, or else the liberal political enterprise surrendered.

Moreover Locke and his allies faced not just a live enemy on this front, but a formidable one. When Sir Robert Filmer, the great proponent of patriarchalism and the divine right of kings, wrote, in the 1650s, "*that there cannot be any Multitude of Men whatsoever, either great or small, . . . but that in the same Multitude . . . there is one Man amongst them, that in Nature hath a Right to be King of all the rest,*"[15] he was not teasing his audience with a counter-intuitive hypothesis, to liven up a quiet day in a dusty philosophical seminar. He was stating something on which he could reasonably expect implicit agreement from most of the educated and respectable opinion around him, and something that was evidently embodied in aspects of social, familial, political, and ecclesiastical organization that many of his contemporaries believed were or ought to be largely beyond question. It was the contrary position – the principle of equality – that seemed radical, disreputable, beyond reason, valid only as a philosophical hypothesis entertained for the sake of argument in a carefully controlled philosophical environment. Let it loose in politics and in moral belief generally, and there was no telling the harm it would do. It was rather like communism in America in the 1950s. There was no denying that people held this position; but those who held it were widely regarded as unsound and dangerous to the point of incendiary, the last people respectable opinion would rely on for an account of the grounding or the reform of stable and effective political institutions.

Locke, beyond doubt, was one of these equality-radicals. Many are skeptical about this today. But it is important to remember that there was no advantage to Locke – as there might be for a sneaky authoritarian or patriarchialist or bourgeois apologist in the twenty-first century – in pretending to be a partisan of basic equality. Political correctness argued the other way, and Locke knew perfectly well that neither the premise – basic equality – nor the enterprise of figuring out its ramifications was a passport to political or philosophical respectability. But equality was something he took very seriously as a moral and political

---

[15] Quoted at 1st T, 104. Locke says that this is from Filmer's *Observations on Hobbes*, at p. 253, but I have not been able to confirm that reference.

premise. It was not just a preference or a pragmatic rule-of-thumb; nor was it simply a "dictate of reason," like Hobbes's precepts "that no man by deed, word, countenance, or gesture, declare hatred or contempt of another" and "that every man acknowledge another for his equal."[16] Locke accorded basic equality the strongest grounding that a principle could have: it was an axiom of theology, understood as perhaps the most important truth about God's way with the world in regard to the social and political implications of His creation of the human person.[17] God created all of us in what was, morally speaking, "[a] state . . . of equality, wherein all the power and jurisdiction is reciprocal, no one having more than another" (2nd T: 4), all of us lords, all of us kings, each of us "equal to the greatest, and subject to no body" (2nd T: 123). And anything that was said about the power of princes, generals, bishops, teachers, scholars, fathers, husbands, employers, landowners, colonists, or the masters of slaves had to be built upon that basis, and justified with reference to and under the discipline of this truth about basic equality.

In what follows we will see Locke attempting to think through the consequences of this radicalism. And we will watch him respond to the charge of radical unsoundness, sometimes holding fast to what he knew was a counter-intuitive position, sometimes flinching momentarily from his egalitarian commitment, but more often delighting in the fact that he was able to articulate the difference – which we still think it important to articulate – between equality as a premise and some particular egalitarian policy or distribution which he might or might not be in favor of. It would be nice to be able to report that, one way or another, Locke remained steadfast in the basics of his egalitarianism. Unfortunately, I cannot. He flinched at a number of points – most notably in his comments about the default authority of husbands, but also in his doctrine of the bestialization of criminals. But he didn't flinch as often or as pervasively as modern critics suppose. Nor, I shall argue, did he flinch from his egalitarianism in a way that detracts from the truth of the assertion with which I have opened this chapter – that we have in Locke's mature corpus as well-worked-out a theory of basic equality as there is in the canon of political philosophy.

II

Let me say something, secondly, about the historical relation between Locke's ideas and our own, so far as his egalitarianism is concerned.

---

[16] Hobbes, *Leviathan*, Ch. 15, p. 107.
[17] There is an excellent account in John Dunn, *The Political Thought of John Locke*, pp. 96–104.

There are all sorts of things that interest us about equality on which it would be silly and anachronistic to look to John Locke for any help. His writings have nothing to say about affirmative action or universal health insurance or minority culture rights. If we imagine John Locke plonked down among us to talk about equality, we would have to set aside long periods of conversation – conversations that would be marred inevitably by misunderstandings and hurt feelings on both sides – to explain what these issues were and why we thought they were important. And if we were magically transported to England in 1689,[18] it would certainly try the patience of John Locke to have to bring *us* "up to speed" on issues like the Exclusion controversy, freehold suffrage, the right to summon Parliament, and the nature of prerogative authority.

Even if they understood the issues, people on both sides might be puzzled by the terms in which they were debated. We are not accustomed to debate public controversies about equality using Old Testament sources; and Locke, for his part, might be disconcerted by our employment of the technical jargon of modern economic theory – Pareto-optimality and the like. It is not just a matter of unfamiliar words. Even familiar words like "rights," "power," "property," and "civil society" might be occasions for misunderstanding. Locke could not be expected to be familiar with the water that has passed under these terminological bridges since 1689, and we ourselves are often blithely unaware of the tangled history that distinguishes our use of these terms from their use by Locke and his contemporaries.[19]

Nor is it just a matter of different meanings, for between 1689 and 2002 we have to deal with different (though of course not utterly disparate) intellectual worlds. When Locke uses the phrase "Creatures of the same Species and rank" (2nd T: 4) in his discussion of equality, how easy is it for us to remember that he is talking from a world that is not just pre-Darwinian but pre-Linnaean? When he asks us to consider "how much

---

[18] I take 1689 as my benchmark, finessing (I hope) the vexed issue of the date at which the works that interest us – in particular the *Two Treatises* and the *Letter Concerning Toleration* – were written. I have never understood why there is so much interest in the date of composition, rather than the date of publication – i.e. the date at which what is written is actually communicated to an historical audience. The moment of first "uptake" (to use Austin's term in *How to Do Things With Words*) – indeed the moment of first public uptake – is surely what matters in the history of political ideas, rather than the private and uncommunicated moment of first formulation. To think otherwise is to subscribe to a particularly mindless version of the cult of authorial intention, in which actual communication is regarded as a distraction.

[19] See Tuck, *Natural Rights Theories* for a fine account of the tangles associated with the concept of *rights*, from the very beginning. The fact that our use of "rights" is also ridden with confusion and controversy doesn't make it any easier to calibrate our confusions and disagreements with those of seventeenth-century moral and political theory.

numbers of men are to be preferd to largenesse of dominions" (2nd T: 42) in political economy, are we sure we even know how to understand this, let alone disagree with it? When he says, of a state of war, that "there is no appeal but to Heaven" (2nd T: 21), Locke seems to intimate a view about the contingency of the outcome of fighting that is not just different from ours, but incommensurable with it. All those who teach the *Two Treatises* know the difficulty of trying to explain his use of this phrase to a student. Even if we say it is "just" a metaphor, it is a forbidding enough task to explain to a modern student what makes the metaphor *apt*, given Locke's belief that the right side often loses in these "appeals."

So, someone may ask, with all this potential for anachronism and misunderstanding, what could possibly be the point of lining up John Locke alongside an array of twentieth- and twenty-first-century thinkers – say, Bernard Williams, John Rawls, Ronald Dworkin, and Amartya Sen – as a leading theorist of equality? What could possibly be the point of my saying – as I said at the beginning of these introductory remarks – that a body of work first published three hundred years ago is as well-worked-out a theory of basic equality as we have in the canon of political philosophy? In what sense do *we* have it – "we" as modern theorists of equality? With our own peculiar concerns, in what sense is this work by John Locke "ours"?

I am not an historian of ideas, and most of my work on Locke and other thinkers in the canon of political philosophy has proceeded in a way that is largely untroubled by worries like these.[20] But I accept that the question of historical anachronism deserves an answer in the present context. Here's what I want to say to address the historians' concern.

Our thinking about equality is undeniably entangled with the issues of the day, and large parts of it – or, at the very least, large parts of the way we present it – are more or less inseparable from contexts, understandings, and political stakes that would not survive transposition to another time and place. Everyone who argues about equality today knows that. But we are also conscious that part of our discussion addresses something enduring: it addresses the possibility that equality may be grounded on something rather general in human nature and something permanent in its significance for creatures like us. We imagine that even at the level of particular political outcomes, issues of equality and inequality might have to be referred, by way of justification, to a deeper level at which we

---

[20] However, see the discussion in Waldron, *Right to Private Property*, pp. 132–6. See also Waldron, "What Plato Would Allow," pp. 143–7.

argue about what it means to respect one another as equals.[21] And many of us believe that this business of *respecting one another as equals* might have to be referred, in turn, to the idea of something important in or about human nature. That is a possibility reckoned with by all who engage in modern philosophical thinking about equality. Maybe not everyone finally embraces this possibility;[22] but many of us do.

I suspect that in their thinking about equality some three hundred years ago, John Locke and his contemporaries were conscious of much the same duality – the duality between surface issues of equal treatment in politics and economy and a deeper idea of respecting people as equals. On the one hand, they knew that part of their discussion was entangled with the issues of the day – the Exclusion controversy, the Test Acts, the rights of Parliament, and the like – and more or less inseparable from contexts, understandings, and political stakes that would not survive transposition to another time and place. (We have no monopoly on the sensitivity of meaning to context. Locke and his contemporaries were not much less sophisticated, hermeneutically, than we are. They knew there were issues of anachronism and incommensurability in relating their political thinking to that of St. Paul, for example, or Aristotle.) But, on the other hand, they too were conscious of a part of their discussion of equality that asked fundamental and perhaps transcendent questions. They too asked whether there might be a deeper principle requiring us to respect one another as equals, a principle which would require an argument that transcended particular times and particular places and which would have to be grounded on something general in human nature and something permanent in its significance for creatures like us. Like us, Locke and a few of his radical contemporaries thought that was something worth exploring, something worth arguing about.

Now, the fact that Locke was exploring the possibility that humans were *by nature* worthy of respect as one another's equals, not just one another's equals in the politics of late seventeenth-century England, and the fact that we in our modern discussions of justice and rights are exploring the possibility that humans are *by nature* worthy of respect as one another's equals and not just one another's equals in the politics of (say)

---

[21] For this way of stating the distinction, see Dworkin, *Taking Rights Seriously*, pp. 134–6.

[22] Margaret Macdonald rejects it – see Macdonald, "Natural Rights," pp. 36–7. So does Hannah Arendt – see Arendt, *On Revolution*, p. 278 – though for rather different reasons. And we might be more comfortable than Locke is with a philosophical rejection of the foundationalism that seems to be presupposed when a commitment to equality is grounded in a view about human nature. (Cf. Rorty, "Solidarity or Objectivity?" and "Human Rights, Rationality, and Sentimentality.") I will say a little more about this in Chapter 3.

twenty-first-century America – these two facts do not guarantee that we
and Locke are exploring the same issue. Nor does the fact (if it is a fact)
that we are exploring the same issue guarantee that we are exploring it
in ways that are intelligible to one another. But it is not an unreasonable
hypothesis that the issues we are respectively exploring might be close
enough to cast some light on one another. Each is certainly straining to
orient his discussion of equality to something that might be intelligible to
those arguing about equality three hundred years before or three hundred years later: the content of what they are arguing about requires them
to do that. Once we state the issues like this, we see at least how wrong
it is to recoil at the first reproachful mention of anachronism. For one
cannot understand the questions with which we and Locke are respectively wrestling without seeing that their exploration requires us to *risk*
anachronism. I cannot be true to my sense that this issue of the permanent
grounding of basic equality is worth exploring if I say peremptorily that
it is impossible to bring my concept of equality into relation to any place
or time other than my own. And Locke could not have been true to his
determination to explore the basis of "[t]his *equality* of Men, by Nature"
(2nd T: 5) unless he had been prepared to risk such anachronism also.
The sort of fact that basic equality must be grounded on – if it is grounded
upon anything – must be a fact that is discernable in different ages, and
one whose discernability in one age is not inaccessible to another. The
sort of commitment basic equality involves is necessarily a commitment
that is in principle recognizable in all sorts of contexts and circumstances,
for it is precisely a commitment to look beneath the contexts and circumstances that might distinguish one human individual from another and
hold constant an element of enduring respect for the sheer fact of their
underlying humanity. What basic equality generates in the way of social
and political positions may vary from one age to another, and what one
age establishes may be relatively opaque to another. But as an articulate
underlying position, the principle of basic equality predicates itself on
our ability to look through and beyond that. In itself, therefore, the sort of
position we are considering is a reproach to any facile or comprehensive
contextualism.

   We can also put the same point the other way round: if moral and
political claims are utterly inseparable from the historical context in
which they are propounded, if they cannot to any extent be considered
and explored in abstraction from that context, then the claim implicit
in the principle of basic, i.e. *underlying,* human equality is fatuous. If
political and moral claims cannot be abstracted from their context, then

we cannot make sense of the terms in which a claim like Locke's, "[t]*hat All Men by Nature Are Equall*" (2nd T: 54), presents itself. To commit to the exploration of that very claim – written and published in the 1680s – is to commit oneself to explore its relation to, among other things, the claims that *we* make *now* about equality, and to explore the way in which that relation might be mediated by common reference to commonly discernable characteristics that could be seen both in 1689 and in 2002 to be the basis for the way we ought to treat one another in society.

That's the ground on which I am going to proceed. Now, in the chapters that follow, we will have some fun with some of the sillier manifestations of Cambridge-style historicism, particularly with some of the propositions about the relation between historical and philosophical understanding with which Peter Laslett larded his critical edition of the *Two Treatises*. But I don't believe there is anything in what I have said that should dismay those who think it important to study in detail the historical context in which political thinking takes place. The historian's enterprise is not the one I have outlined. But it is not precluded by it; nor need the historian and the political philosopher compete for privilege or priority in this regard. The historian will do well not to underestimate the philosophical agility (by our standards) of a John Locke. He will do well to reflect that a modern philosopher engaging, say, with the *Essay*, might be responding to Locke's ideas more or less as Locke would expect one of his own philosopher-friends to engage with it. (One assumes that Locke and his friends didn't spend their time *contextualizing* each other's conversation, or collating early editions.) And the political philosopher, for his part, will do well not to underestimate the scale and density of the obstacles that stand in the way of representing the thinking of one century – particularly the engaged political thinking of one century – in the categories of another.[23] He should remember that a piece of philosophical writing – even one that purports to address a timeless theme – has a context that may be indispensable for understanding what it says to the timeless theme and what it draws out of it. And the historians are right: it's not enough just to gesture in this direction, if one expects one's engagement with Locke to be more than superficial. The modern political philosopher needs to be constantly alert to the point that text-in-context usually adds up to a richer and more interesting source of ideas for modern deployment, or a richer and more provocative reproach to modern assumptions, than a simple parsing of the text which

---

[23] See also Dunn, *Cunning of Unreason*, pp. 3–47.

pays no more attention to history than is necessary to correct the date
of composition and modernize the spelling.[24] In what follows, I will try
to bear that in mind.

III

The title of my Carlyle Lectures and the sub-title of this book refer to
the *Christian* foundations of Locke's political thought. I am conscious
that there is something vaguely embarrassing, even *bad form*, in this characterization. Why "Christian"? Why not just "*Religious* Foundations of
Equality"? Or why not just "Locke's Theory of Equality"? If, as I said
in section II, I am trying to build bridges between Locke's interest in
basic equality and our own, why emphasize of all things the very aspect
of Locke's thought that is likely to seem most obscure and least congenial to a largely secular body of egalitarian thought in the twenty-first
century?

The historical answer is obvious enough. Locke's mature philosophy
comprised *The Reasonableness of Christianity* as well as the *Essay*, the *Letters
on Toleration*, the *Two Treatises*, and the *Thoughts Concerning Education*. (I shall
include also some references to the posthumously published *Paraphrase
and Notes on the Epistles of St. Paul*.) As a philosopher, Locke was intensely
interested in Christian doctrine, and in the *Reasonableness* he insisted that
most men could not hope to understand the detailed requirements of
the law of nature without the assistance of the teachings and example of
Jesus. The point has not been lost on his most distinguished commentators. John Dunn has argued that the whole frame of discussion in the
Two Treatises of Government is "saturated with Christian assumptions – and
those of a Christianity in which the New Testament counted very much
more than the Old." He wrote in his famous study of Locke:

> Jesus Christ (and Saint Paul) may not appear in person in the text of the *Two
> Treatises* but their presence can hardly be missed when we come upon the norma-
> tive creaturely equality of all men in virtue of their shared species-membership.[25]

Now this is a challenging observation, not least because (as Dunn in-
timates) Jesus and St. Paul are barely mentioned in the actual text of
the *Treatises*. Indeed, one of the things I want to explore is why, in an
argument which appears to be devoted largely to the biblical case for
equality, there is so little from the New Testament.[26] But my interest

---

[24] For a fine statement of this point, see Skinner, *Reason and Rhetoric*, pp. 14–16.
[25] Dunn, *Political Thought of John Locke*, p. 99.   [26] I will address this specifically in Chapter 7.

goes beyond bibliography. I want to ask, not only whether we *can* discern the influence of Christian teaching in Locke's normative doctrine of the "equality of all men in virtue of their shared species-membership," but also whether one can even make sense of a position like Locke's – and a substantive position like Locke's does seem to be what we want so far as basic equality is concerned – apart from the specifically biblical and Christian teaching that he associated with it.

Indeed, I want to go further than that. For Dunn, I suspect, the theological and specifically biblical and Christian aspects of Lockean equality are features of Locke's theory that make it largely irrelevant to our concerns. Teasing out and putting on display the indispensability to Locke's political theory of its theological foundations is a way of confining Locke to the seventeenth century. To paraphrase Dunn's famous title, they are part of "what is dead" in the political thinking of John Locke, part of what explains why the *Two Treatises* and the rest of Locke's work are of mostly antiquarian interest in the history of ideas.[27] If we were to develop an egalitarian political philosophy for our own use, Dunn seems to be saying, it would have quite a different character from Locke's. It would be secular in its foundations – if it had any foundations[28] – and it would not be confined in its appeal, as Locke's theory seemed to be confined in its appeal, to those who were willing to buy into a particular set of Protestant Christian assumptions. I don't mean necessarily that he thinks it would have to be philosophically non-committal in the way that John Rawls has said a political liberalism ought to be.[29] Dunn need not go that far in contrasting what we are looking for with what John Locke thought he had discovered. But the deep philosophical commitments of a modern theory would likely be oriented to secular values such as autonomy or dignity or human flourishing, values that are thought to command our respect quite independently of any conception of the sacred or of our relation to God.

Dunn is probably right about this dissonance between Locke's political philosophy and what most people expect in a theory of equality. For my part, however, I am not so sure. I actually don't think it is clear that we – now – *can* shape and defend an adequate conception of basic human equality apart from some religious foundation.[30] And I think it is quite an

---

[27] Dunn, "What is Living and What is Dead in the Political Theory of John Locke."
[28] Cf. Rorty, "Human Rights, Rationality, and Sentimentality."
[29] Rawls, *Political Liberalism*, pp. 133 ff.
[30] For some recent discussion see Coons and Brennan, *By Nature Equal*.

open question how specific, or sectarian, or scriptural, such a foundation has to be.

We are sometimes quite evasive about this. We tell each other that the principle of equality is just one political position among all the others we hold, and no different from the others in the way that it might be justified. Isaiah Berlin, for example, imagines that there might be a utilitarian defense of basic equality: "One can perfectly well conceive of a society organized on Benthamite or Hobbesian lines ... in which the principle of 'every man to count for one' was rigorously applied for utilitarian reasons."[31] But that is hopelessly confused. Bentham's principle "Every man to count for one, nobody for more than one"[32] is partly *constitutive* of utilitarianism, and so cannot be defended on utilitarian grounds except in a question-begging way. Nor, for the defense of the principle of basic equality, is it enough simply to identify common characteristics that all humans share in common.[33] As we shall see in Chapter 3, that is but a part of the agenda, and though it's difficult it is the easier part: the hard bit is to *defend* the proposition that these characteristics matter sufficiently to be capable of underpinning a commitment that bears the weight that our egalitarianism has to bear. Basic equality is so fundamental to innumerable aspects of our ethical outlook that it requires a special sort of defense – at once transcendent and powerful – so that it can both underpin what are usually taken to be the starting points of public justification and also prevail in the face of the various temptations that invite us to start drawing distinctions between types or grades of human being.

Now, it does not follow from any of this that basic equality *must* be grounded in a religious conception. But the possibility should surely be given serious consideration, if only because generations of our predecessors in this enterprise have been convinced of it. Again, from that fact that theories of basic equality in previous ages have had a religious foundation, it doesn't follow that our egalitarian commitments are inconceivable apart from that heritage. How much we can justify or, to put it provocatively, how much of our egalitarian heritage we can *imitate* with the spare resources of a secular moral vocabulary (not to mention the even more meager vocabulary of a Rawlsian "political" liberalism) remains to be seen.

---

[31] Berlin, "Equality," p. 81; see also ibid., p. 96.

[32] It is surprisingly difficult to find a source for the Bentham slogan. Ritchie observes, in *Natural Rights*, p. 249 n., that the phrase is known from its quotation by J. S. Mill in Chapter V of *Utilitarianism*. "The maxim seems to belong," Ritchie says, "to the unwritten doctrine of the Utilitarian master."

[33] Cf. Rawls, *Theory of Justice*, pp. 504–12 (section 77).

These are questions for us. But it would be quite wrong to assume they were not also questions for Locke. He may have been disposed to offer answers different from those with which we are comfortable (just as he had to deal with challenges that are different from those we are comfortable dealing with). But I shall argue at the end of the book that it is not a case of Locke's assuming, as a matter of background world-view, that *of course* religion must be the basis of equality, and of our assuming, as a matter of a different background world-view, that *of course* it is not. In fact Locke confronted the claim, put forward in his own time, that these fundamental, apparently transcendent positions, could be understood on a purely secular basis. He had grave reservations about these claims, and he conjectured that among his seventeenth-century audience "many are beholden to revelation, who do not acknowledge it" (RC: 145). And I want to ask: is that conjecture so strange to us? I don't think so: I think it shows a Locke confronting more or less exactly the issue *we* have to confront as we consider possible grounds for basic equality. And perhaps it is time someone explored the theological foundations of Locke's egalitarianism on a basis that is sympathetic to his approach or at least not actively hostile to the view that a theory of equality might actually *need* theological foundations. That's what I shall try to do here.

IV

I am conscious, once again, that the historians will see a certain danger in the approach I am taking. To treat Locke's argument as though it were a secular argument, and thus on a par with our patterns of secular argumentation, is one sort of anachronism. To treat Locke's use of religious argumentation (and his reflection upon and hesitation concerning the use of religious argumentation) as though it were on a par with our own worries about the limits of the secular and about the place of religion in our public philosophy may seem more sophisticated; but it too may be anachronistic in its own way. In "What is Living and What is Dead in John Locke," Dunn acknowledges that there are still a great many Christians in the world, and he considers the possibility that Locke's theory "is . . . fully alive for all those who remain such," or at any rate for those who happen to share "Locke's distinctively Protestant religious sensibility."[34] But he concludes that "this resolution at least is definitely quite wrong," because it underestimates the enormous difference in "conceptual structures and

---

[34] Dunn, "What is Living and What is Dead," p. 13.

patterns of argument employed in political understanding by all but the
most intellectually uncouth of present day Christian believers" and the
conceptual structures and patterns of political argument employed by
seventeenth-century Christian thinkers like John Locke.[35]

He has a point. One has only to read the first of Locke's *Two Treatises* to
become aware that we are in a quite different intellectual world from that
of the modern philosopher, even the modern philosopher who is willing
to entertain the possibility that serious moral argument must have a
religious flavor. Every Locke scholar, and not just those of a secular
bent, views the methods and substance of the *First Treatise* as strange and
disconcerting, particularly in the assumption, which seems to pervade
the work (or the half of it we have),[36] that the freedom and equality of
the people of England – perhaps the freedom and equality of people
everywhere – might turn on the precise meaning and accumulation of
biblical verses about the kings, generals, and judges of Israel, the ancient
patriarchs, the endowment of Noah, and the creation of Adam and Eve.
This is not an assumption that would be made in an article in *Philosophy
and Public Affairs*. But nor is it an assumption that one would expect to find
in the pages of a modern journal like *First Things*, or in modern natural
law writing, in the work of John Finnis, for example, or others who take
seriously the religious dimension of moral and political argument.[37] Such
writers certainly would not disparage scripture. But they do not read it,
as Locke reads it in the *First Treatise*, interrogating it minutely for the
precise bearing that it might have on the resolution of quite particular
political issues.

Of course, part of John Locke's interest in the specifically biblical part
of his argument is connected with the determination, driving his work
in the *Two Treatises*, to refute the specific claims of Sir Robert Filmer,
whose *Patriarcha* and other works were republished in the 1670s to provide

---

[35] Ibid.

[36] Locke opens the book with these words (Locke, *Two Treatises*, Preface, p. 137): "*Reader, Thou hast
here the Beginning and End of a Discourse concerning Government; what Fate has otherwise disposed of the Papers
that should have filled up the middle, and were more than all the rest, 'tis not worth while to tell thee.*" One
of the things, I think, that distinguishes *philosophers* interested in Locke's political theory from
historians of ideas is that the former – the philosophers – wake up from time to time screaming
in the middle of night, having dreamed that someone (inevitably someone from Cambridge) has
discovered the long-lost manuscript of the missing half of the *First Treatise* and that we are all
going to have to spend the rest of our professional lives tracing Locke's pursuit of Robert Filmer
through another three hundred pages of "*the Windings and Obscurities which are to be met with in the
several Branches of his wonderful System*" (ibid.).

[37] See, for example, Finnis, *Natural Law and Natural Rights* and Macintyre, *After Virtue*. (*First Things* is
"a monthly journal of religion and public life," published in New York.)

powerful scriptural support for a thesis of basic *in*equality. According to Locke, Filmer "*boasts of, and pretends wholly to build on*" what Locke called "*Scripture-proofs*,"[38] arguments from the Bible "which would perswade all Men, that they are Slaves, and ought to be so" (1st T: 1). Locke needs to prove against Filmer that neither reason nor scripture "hath subjected us to the unlimited Will of another" (1st T: 4). The "reason" part of the argument is mostly presented in the *Second Treatise* (mostly but not wholly for, as we shall see, there are powerful passages of reasoned argument in the *First Treatise* as well); but Locke is not, I think, being ironic when he says that if "*the Assignment of Civil Power is by Divine Institution*," revealed, for example, in the scriptures, then "no Consideration, no Act or Art of Man can divert it from that Person, to whom by this Divine Right, it is assigned, no Necessity or Contrivance can substitute another Person in his room" (1st T: 107). Much later in my book – in Chapter 7 – I will ask what we should make of the fact that Locke devotes much more space to Old Testament passages than Filmer does in the arguments that Locke says he is trying to refute. But whatever the balance of pages, Locke was evidently convinced that he could not sustain his radical egalitarianism without taking on the detail of Filmer's "*Scripture-proofs*."

Now, because Sir Robert Filmer doesn't loom very large in *our* chamber of philosophic or political horrors, it is understandable we are hardly riveted by Locke's patient line-by-line refutation of his scriptural argument. So it is tempting to say that the *First Treatise* is just irrelevant to our modern concerns. This is especially persuasive inasmuch as Filmer's rejection of basic equality consists in what I am going to call a *particularistic* rather than a *general* inegalitarianism. Filmer actually rejected what must have been in his day the most familiar philosophic defense of general inegalitarianism, namely Aristotle's theory of natural slavery. He did so quite firmly at the start of Chapter 2 of *Patriarcha*:

Also Aristotle had another fancy, that those men 'which proved wise of mind were by nature intended to be lords and govern, and those that were strong of body were ordained to obey and be servants' (*Politics*, book I, chapter 2). But this is a dangerous and uncertain rule, and not without some folly. For if a man prove both wise and strong, what will Aristotle have done with him? As he was wise, he could be no servant, as he had strength, he could not be a master. Besides, to speak like a philosopher, nature intends all men to be perfect both in wit and strength. The folly or imbecility proceeds from some error in generation or education, for nature aims at perfection in all her works.[39]

---

[38] Locke, *Two Treatises*, Preface, p. 138.   [39] Filmer, *Patriarcha*, p. 15.

Filmer's primary interest is in identifying specific individuals who have authority over others, rather than classes or types of individual in some general hierarchy.[40] A theory of the divine right of kings is particularistic in this sense inasmuch as it purports to identify particular persons, like Charles Stuart or his brother James, as entitled to monarchical authority. A racist or a sexist theory by contrast would be a *general* inegalitarianism, implying as it does that all humans of a certain type are superior to all humans of some other type. So this too seems to deprive Filmer's theory and its refutation of most of its interest for us. Very few of those today who deny that humans are one another's equals do so on particularistic grounds (for example, because they believe in the divine right of kings established by descent from Adam). There is no modern enterprise in political philosophy for which practicing on Filmer would be an appropriate preparation or exercise.

I don't believe, though, that the particular and the general strands of Locke's answer to Filmer can be disentangled so easily. For one thing, as Locke points out, Filmer is not consistent in his particularism. Filmer purports to be telling us that specific individuals are entitled to be absolute monarchs, by dint of having inherited the crown which God gave to Adam; but much of the time he seems to be arguing for absolute authority in the abstract, an argument that he seems to think does important political work whether we can identify an Adamite heir or not. Locke's attack at this point is one of the most powerful in the book (1st T: 81–3, 105–7, 120–7). And it is not just *ad hominem*; it is also a general meditation on the relation between abstract and practical argumentation in the theory of politics. Unless scripture provides a basis for identifying the Lord's anointed, Locke says,

> the skill used in dressing up Power with all the Splendor and Temptation Absoluteness can add to it . . . will serve only to give a keener edge to Man's Natural Ambition, which of itself is but too keen. What can this do but set Men on the more eagerly to scramble, and so lay a sure and lasting Foundation of endless Contention and Disorder, instead of that Peace and Tranquility, which is the business of Government, and the end of Humane Society. (1st T: 106)

Not only that, but Locke takes the occasion to reflect upon the pragmatics of divine law, and the necessity for human positive law. On the one hand, it is inconceivable that God would have instituted a specific

---

[40] Hence the passage from Filmer that I quoted earlier: "[*T*]*here cannot be any Multitude of Men whatsoever, either great or small . . . but that in the same Multitude . . . there is one Man amongst them, that in Nature hath a Right to be King of all the rest.*" (Quoted by Locke, 1st T: 104.)

monarchy "and yet not to give Rules to mark out, and know that Person by" (1st T: 127).[41] On the other hand, this is just the sort of thing that human law is good at, "since by Positive Laws and Compact, which Divine Institution (if there be any) shuts out, all these endless inextricable Doubts, can be safely provided against" (1st T: 126).

I am quoting these passages not only for their intrinsic interest (which in my view is considerable), but also to dispel the impression, which John Dunn's article might leave us with, that Locke is so different from us that he cites biblical chapter and verse as though it clinched a political argument. That is not so at all: at the very least, Locke like us is interested in the meta-theoretical question of what it would be for a biblical passage to settle, or even to contribute to, a political argument.

Beyond these hermeneutic points, there is also the question of Locke's substantive attitude to the particularism of Filmer's defense of political inequality. Certainly in the *Second Treatise*, Locke's response to Filmer becomes also an attack on *general* inegalitarianism: it becomes a defense of equality against those who purport to order humans generally into ranks, not just a particular child below his particular father and a particular subject below his particular sovereign. His strategy in the *First Treatise*, however, is not confined to taking on Filmer's particularistic inegalitarianism on its own terms. In addition to refuting the particular claims that Filmer makes in respect of Adam and his heirs, Locke also sets out to reproach his particularism with a biblically based *general* egalitarianism, an egalitarianism which holds that nobody in particular could possibly have the authority that Filmer says Adam and his heirs have had because of the relation that God has established among people in general. (The fact that Filmer is not defending inegalitarianism on this general front does not mean that he is invulnerable to attack from this direction.) In general, the *First Treatise* is an indispensable resource in the reconstruction of Locke's theory of equality. My book is about the relation in Locke's thought between basic equality and religious doctrine – and that is *exactly* what the *First Treatise* is devoted to. The *First Treatise* is nothing but a defense of the proposition that humans are, basically, one another's equals; it is a defense of the basis on which the *Second Treatise* proceeds. The affirmative argument in the *First Treatise* has a scriptural aspect, it is true. But it is not just a matter of God's voice having been recorded booming from the heavens, "You are all one another's equals," and that's that. In the *First Treatise*, the argument for general egalitarianism is subtle and complex,

---

[41] See also the discussion in Chapter 5, pp. 138–9.

weaving, as it does, specific biblical passages into the broader fabric of natural law and traditional theology.[42] And it interlaces the particular and the general aspects of that defense in a way that helps enormously in seeing what exactly is going on in the more synoptic argument of the *Second Treatise*. It is worth persevering with it, despite the fact that we have to view Locke's defense there through two prisms – scriptural argumentation and the refutation of particular inegalitarianism – neither of which is familiar or particularly interesting to us.

Secular theorists often assume that they know what a religious argument is like: they present it as a crude prescription from God, backed up with threat of hellfire, derived from general or particular revelation, and they contrast it with the elegant complexity of a philosophical argument by Rawls (say) or Dworkin. With this image in mind, they think it obvious that religious argument should be excluded from public life, and they conclude therefore that we can have very little in common with John Locke or his interlocutors, who seem to have made the opposite assumption – that public reason should be conducted more or less exclusively in these terms. But those who have bothered to make themselves familiar with existing religious-based arguments in modern political theory know that this is mostly a travesty; and I suspect that it might be as caricatural of religious argumentation in Locke's day as it is of religious argumentation in our own. Be that as it may: we should not be in the business of abandoning our capacity to be surprised by styles of argumentation. That, after all, is supposed to be one great advantage of an historically sensitive account: it takes us out of our easy assumptions and challenges what we think an argument of a certain sort *must* be like. Religious arguments are more challenging than most, and for many people they are as foreign when they occur in contemporary political theory as they are when they are found in a seventeenth-century tract. One virtue, then, of devoting all this time and all this space to an analysis and elaboration of Locke's religious case for equality is that it promises not only to deepen our understanding of equality, but also to enrich our sense of what it is like to make a religious argument in politics.

---

[42] Compare for example the use of arguments about *imago dei* in 1st T: 30. See the discussion of this passage in Chapter 2, p. 25.

2

Adam and Eve

In Chapter 1, I suggested that for us the difficulty in undertaking serious philosophical exploration of the idea of basic equality has two sources. There is, first, an awkwardness at the prospect at having to make explicit whatever religious or spiritual assumptions lie behind our conviction that humans are special and that some of the more obvious differences between them are irrelevant to the fundamentals of moral concern and respect. Secondly, we are discomfited at the prospect of having to take seriously, even if only for the sake of clarity and refutation, racist and sexist positions that seem to deny this equality. I am going to take up the first of these awkwardnesses in Chapter 3 and again in Chapter 8. But we also need to face up to the second, to consider and take seriously (at least for the sake of argument) the premises on which racist and sexist doctrines are based.

There is not much in John Locke on the subject of race, and what little there is – so far as it is relevant to issues about the displacement of aboriginal Americans and about the justification of slavery – I shall postpone for consideration until Chapters 5 and 7. I will talk in Chapter 3 about Locke's discussion of the idea of *species*, conducted with reference to the species *Man*, in Books III and IV of the *Essay Concerning Human Understanding*, and in that context we will touch upon an observation or two that Locke made about race.[1] In this chapter, however, I would like to introduce the substance of my discussion of Locke's egalitarianism by focusing on what many regard as the most striking difference within the human species – the difference between men and women.

I

There are many ways of approaching Locke's discussion of sex and gender. What I would like to do is to chart Locke's struggle to free

[1] See below, pp. 62–3.

contemporary thought – indeed to free himself – of the conviction that
a difference as striking as the difference between men and women must
be morally and politically salient in its own right, and that it must also
prefigure and exemplify the general implausibility of human equality as
a starting point for social and political thought. My initial focus will be
on Locke's discussion of Adam and Eve and the circumstances of their
creation and fall, in the *First Treatise*. I have already observed that the
target for the *First Treatise* was the *particular* inegalitarianism of Robert
Filmer, rather than any general categorization of human beings. Locke
wanted to attack the Filmerian view that certain particular men had
the right to rule over the rest. But in the course of his refutation of that
particular inegalitarianism, he necessarily also took on certain propositions that were in his day (and are still sometimes in ours) cited as the
basis of a more *general* inequality. The biblical subordination of Eve to
Adam can be seen as a privileging of Adam in particular and his particular (male) heirs, or it can be seen as a privileging of men generally
over women generally, or husbands generally over wives generally. By
seeking to undercut or diminish Filmer's particular inferences from the
subordination of Eve to Adam, Locke inevitably undercut the appeal of
the two broader positions as well. Now I don't think he was ever entirely
comfortable with this, and the texts I am going to examine show him
in two minds as to the position about women that he wanted ultimately
to adopt. But there is little doubt where his most fundamental premises
were leading him, and the struggle that we can discern in the texts is his
personal struggle to come to terms with the fact that women as much as
men are created in the image of God and endowed with the modicum
of reason that is, for Locke, the criterion of human equality. I believe
that this struggle of Locke's is instructive for our understanding of his
theory of basic equality, and also for our understanding of its theological
foundations. And it is as good a way as any to open up the issues about
equality that will occupy us for the rest of the book.

Let me repeat my description of Locke's endeavor in regard to this
matter of equality between men and women, for it flies in the face of a
number of modern commentaries. There used to be a view – in certain
circles, there still *is* a view – that something as striking as the difference
between the sexes must be morally and politically salient in its own right,
and also that that difference between the sexes foreshadows the general
implausibility of human equality as a starting point for social and political
thought. That view is very deeply rooted, and like all others in our culture,
John Locke felt the force of it. But I believe he struggled in his philosophy
to free himself of this conviction. He certainly sought to demonstrate its

implausibility as a premise for a normative theory of politics. He tried as hard as he could to refute theories that based themselves on it, and he sought to develop an ethics and a politics that had no need of that hypothesis. He did not succeed in this to the satisfaction of modern feminists.[2] I'm not sure he succeeded in it to his own satisfaction: his discussion of men and women, and particularly marriage, has an air of embarrassment about it, an embarrassment perhaps reinforced by his own lack of any first-hand acquaintance with the institution. Indeed the ambivalence and embarrassment is part of the reason I want to begin my discussion of equality with this issue. It is not an easy issue, and setting out the difficulties and inconsistencies in Locke's account helps us understand that basic equality is a demanding principle, one whose adoption can shake up a political theorist quite beyond his expectations.

II

There can be no doubt whatever about John Locke's intention in the *First Treatise* so far as the understanding of Adam and Eve is concerned. That Adam was furnished with God-given political authority over Eve, either by virtue of the circumstances of their creation, or by virtue of their punishment in the Fall, was the first of Filmer's positions on natural inequality that Locke set out to refute.

He tried to refute it in all its manifestations. The first version is a sort of argument from priority. Eve was created after Adam, therefore Adam is boss by virtue of getting in first.[3] Locke is unconvinced. By the same token, he says, Adam was created after all the other animals, after the Lion for example: so "this Argument, will make the Lion have as good a Title to [dominion] as he, and certainly the Ancienter" (1st T: 15). Locke does not say much in response to Filmer's claim that "God created only Adam and of a piece of him made the woman."[4] But later he shows

---

[2] See Lorenne Clark's verdict in "Women and Locke," p. 35: "I conclude, therefore, that Locke's theory does display unequivocally sexist assumptions."

[3] "But perhaps 'twill be said, *Eve* was not made till afterward: Grant it so, What advantage will our A. get by it?" (1st T: 30).

[4] Filmer, "Observations on Mr Hobbes' Leviathan," cited but not discussed by Locke at 1st T: 14. Note, however, the intriguing pun in the final line of this extract from Locke's 1662 "Verses on Queen Catherine," p. 210:

> When the first man without a rivall stood
> Possest of all, and all like him was good:
> Heaven thought that All imperfect, till beside
> 'T had made another self, and given a Bride:
> Empire, and Innocence were there, but yet
> 'Twas Eve made Man, and Paradise compleat.

himself unimpressed by any argument that children are subordinate to their parents because they are created out of their parents' bodily material (1st T: 52–5). If such an argument worked, he says, it would establish the authority of mothers more than fathers, because "the Woman hath an equal share, if not the greater, as nourishing the Child a long time in her own Body out of her own Substance" (1st T: 55). But Locke believed that these body-part arguments did not work at all, and that all credit for and authority arising out of the creation of any human being had to go to "God, who is *the Author and Giver of Life*" (1st T: 55), not to the inadvertent donor of the raw materials. In the *Second Treatise*, the fact that "*Adam* was created a perfect man, his Body and Mind in full possession of their Strength and Reason" shows that he has a responsibility to look after his children, "who are all born Infants, weak and helpless," and "to supply the Defects of this imperfect State, till the Improvement of Growth and Age hath removed them" (2nd T: 56). But the telos and end-point of that responsibility is the child's equality with his parent, not any continuing subordination traceable to the fact that the father was created complete and the infant not. In any case, though Eve may have been made out of a part of Adam, she too was created with her "Body and Mind in full possession of their Strength and Reason." There is just no room here for any inequality based on priority of creation or on ownership of the spare parts used in the process.

The bulk of Locke's argument about Adam and Eve is a response to Filmer's scriptural claim that God gave Adam general plenary authority over everything in His commandment (Genesis 1:28) – "Be fruitful, and multiply, and replenish the earth, and subdue it: and have dominion over the fish of the sea, and over the fowl of the air, and over every living thing that moveth upon the earth." Locke's refutation of this argument of Filmer's is quite devastating on scriptural grounds.

> That this Donation was not made in particular to *Adam*, appears evidently from the words of the Text, it being made to more than one, for it was spoken in the Plural Number, God blessed *them*, and said unto *them*, Have Dominion. God says unto *Adam* and *Eve*, Have Dominion. (1st T: 29)

Since many interpreters think it significant, says Locke, "that these words were not spoken till *Adam* had his Wife, must she not thereby be Lady, as well as he Lord of the World?" (1st T: 29). There then follows a passage of extraordinary importance for the argument about equality:

God in this Donation, gave the World to Mankind in common, and not to *Adam* in particular. The word *Them* in the Text must include the Species of Man, for 'tis certain *Them* can by no means signifie *Adam* alone . . . *They* then were to have Dominion. Who? even those who were to have the *Image* of God, the Individuals of that Species of *Man* that he was going to make, for that *Them* should signifie *Adam* singly, exclusive of the rest, that should be in the World with him, is against both Scripture and all Reason: And it cannot possibly be made Sense, if *Man* in the former part of the *Verse* do not signifie the same with *Them* in the latter, only *Man* there, as is usual, is taken for the Species, and *them* the individuals of that Species . . . God makes him *in his own Image after his own Likeness*, makes him an intellectual Creature, and so capable of Dominion. For wherein soever else the *Image of God* consisted, the intellectual Nature was certainly a part of it, and belong'd to the whole Species. (1st T: 30)

This is the one place in the *Treatise* where Locke associates humankind in general with the Judeo-Christian idea of *imago dei*, the image of God, in a way that makes it absolutely clear that that characterization applies to Eve (the only other member of the species around) as well as to Adam, to women as well as men.

Intriguingly (for us), this passage is also a meditation on pronouns – "[t]he word *Them* in the Text . . . can by no means signifie Adam alone" – and on the meaning of the word "Man" – "*Man* there, as is usual, is taken for the Species, and *them* the individuals of that Species." Now, besides Adam the only other member of the species around at the relevant time is Eve. This whole strident passage of Locke's makes no sense unless we assume that "Them" includes Eve, that "Man" includes "Eve," and that even "him" includes Eve in Locke's comment that "God makes him *in his own Image after his own Likeness*, makes him an intellectual Creature" (1st T: 16). The grant of dominion over the animals, says Locke, "was not to Adam in particular, exclusive of all other Men," and his evidence for this is that God "spoke to Eve also" (1st T: 29). I am laboring this point just because it is so often and so carelessly assumed by modern commentators that by "Man" or "Men" Locke means only males, whereas this whole passage is completely unintelligible unless we assume that females are included also.[5]

What about the role of Eve in the Fall, and the particular sentence God imposed on her, as reported in Genesis 3:16 – "Unto the woman he said, I will greatly multiply thy sorrow and thy conception; in sorrow thou shalt bring forth children; and thy desire shall be to thy husband, and he shall

---

[5] Another passage that is unintelligible unless "Man" includes Eve can be found in Locke, "*Homo ante et post Lapsum*," pp. 320–1.

rule over thee"? Locke's account of this is complicated. First he notes that *both* Adam and Eve are being punished by their offended maker, and that this would be an odd time for God to choose for vesting "Prerogatives and Privileges" in Adam, when He was "Denouncing Judgment, and declaring his Wrath against them both, for their Disobedience" (1st T: 44). Certainly God's words do amount to a curse on Eve "for having been the first and forwardest in the Disobedience" (1st T: 44). And it is a worse curse than Adam suffers: "as a helper in the Temptation, as well as a Partner in the Transgression, *Eve* was laid below him, and so he had accidentally a Superiority over her, for her greater Punishment" (1st T: 44). Yet Adam too had his share in the fall, says Locke, and he suffered along with Eve the most severe punishment of all: the loss of immortality.[6] Adam also suffers the condemnation of having to work for subsistence – "*In the Sweat of thy Face thou shalt eat thy Bread*, says God to him, ver. 19" (1st T: 45) – and Locke notes wryly that Adam is definitely *not* given permission to sit back and let Eve do the spadework, on account of her greater transgression.

Indeed, the subordination of Eve is so much a matter of contingency – so much an optional extra, as it were – that the special curse upon her may be read, Locke suggests, as a prediction rather than a prescription: "God, in this Text, gives not, that I see, any Authority to *Adam* over *Eve*, or to Men over their Wives, but only fortels what should be the Womans Lot, how by his Providence he would order it so" (1st T: 47). Now this is not all that he has to say about the matter as we shall see in a moment, and his introduction of the idea of "Providence" might seem to blur the line between prediction and prescription.[7] But it is worth noting that Locke says about this business of subjection exactly what he says about pain in childbirth. Though Genesis 3:16 predicts pain in childbirth – "in sorrow thou shalt bring forth children" – it does not prohibit anaesthetics; and similarly in the condemnation of Eve to being ruled by her husband,

there is ... no more Law to oblige a Woman to such a Subjection, if the Circumstances either of her Condition or Contract with her Husband should exempt her from it, th[a]n there is, that she should bring forth her Children in Sorrow and Pain, if there could be found a Remedy for it ... (1st T: 47)

---

[6] For a vivid account, see Locke, "*Homo ante et post Lapsum*," p. 321. For an account of their punishment which, like most contemporary Christian accounts, mentions only Adam's transgression, see RC: 4–9.

[7] This is noticed in Butler, "Early Liberal Roots of Feminism," at pp. 142–3. For Locke's broader discussion of the relation between providence, divine appointment, and accident in these matters, see 1st T: 16.

One other point in this connection. Locke's views on the subject of original sin were always controversial – it was one of many grounds on which people accused him of Socinianism.[8] He tended generally to minimize the transmission down the generations from Adam and Eve of either sin or punishment. What was lost in the Fall, he wrote in *The Reasonableness of Christianity*, was immortality. Adam and Eve were created immortal in the image of God; "[b]ut Adam, transgressing the command given him by his heavenly Father, incurred the penalty; forfeited that state of immortality . . . After this, Adam begot children: but they were 'in his own likeness, after his own image;' mortal, like their father" (RC: 106). That, Locke suggests, is a genetic matter (a sort of divine Lysenkoism), or, as he puts it in a note to his paraphrase of Romans 5:12, "[a] mortal father. infected now with death, [was] able to produce noe better than a mortal race" (P&N: ii.524). It is not a *punishment* imposed on all of Adam and Eve's descendants; God cannot be supposed to have committed the injustice of visiting the sins of the father upon the children. And, Locke adds in *The Reasonableness of Christianity*, "[m]uch less can the righteous God be supposed, as a punishment of one sin, wherewith he is displeased, to put man under the necessity of sinning continually" (RC: 6). It seems to follow from this that Locke is not in a position to accept any view about the subordination of women which supposes that they became especially corrupt, all the way down the human line, as a result of the Fall. If Eve sinned, that is true of Eve only. If Eve was subordinated to her husband by her greater transgression, that is true of Eve only. Throughout his work Locke is adamant that punishment is not vicarious: "[E]very one's sin is charged upon himself only" (RC: 7).[9] It would make no sense in the Lockean scheme of things to attribute Eve's particular punishment to all of Eve's female descendants.[10]

Intriguingly, Sir Robert Filmer does not associate political power with the Fall either. Though he was happy to derive what he could from Genesis 3:16, his basic position set out in *The Anarchy of a Limited or Mixed Monarchy* was that Eve was subject to Adam before she sinned. Political

---

[8] See Spellman, *John Locke and the Problem of Depravity*, pp. 104 ff.

[9] This is particularly important in his argument about conquest, in 2nd T: 179 and 182 ("[T]he Father, by his miscarriages and violence, can forfeit but his own Life, but involves not his Children in his guilt or destruction.").

[10] There is a comment in the *First Treatise* about the words of Genesis 3:16 being directed to Eve and "in her, as their representative to all other Women" (1st T: 47), but its seems to be *arguendo* (the passage being prefaced "if we will take them as they were directed . . ."). See footnote 12 in Chapter 7, below, for Locke's theory of representation in regard to the Fall; see also Harris, "The Politics of Christianity."

authority, on Filmer's view, is not at all a post-lapsarian remedy for sin, any more than the legitimate subjection of the angels to God before the fall of Satan.[11] Filmer goes on to acknowledge that Adam would have had no occasion to *coerce* Eve before the Fall, nor even to direct her "in those things which were necessarily and morally to be done." She would be disposed to do those things naturally in her original innocent condition. Yet there were things to be settled in the state of nature – Filmer calls them "things indifferent" (maybe the gardening schedule?) that depended merely on the free will of Adam and Eve – and in these, said Filmer, Eve "might be directed by the power of Adam's command."[12]

Now Locke does not respond directly to that passage of Filmer's, about Adam having a natural power of direction even in paradise over things that are otherwise indifferent. I guess we might expect his response to be that *no one* has a power of direction over things indifferent – that's what natural *freedom* amounts to.[13] But the odd thing is that Locke in fact seems to agree with Filmer. This is where the hesitations and the contradictions begin.

III

Remember I said earlier that Locke suggests we try reading Eve's sub-jection to Adam as a prediction rather than a prescription. But he also says that if you *want* to read it as a divine prescription, the words of Genesis 3:16 "import no more but that Subjection [women] should or-dinarily be in to their Husbands" (1st T: 47). Concerning the subjection of women, he says: "[W]e see that generally the Laws of Mankind and

---

[11] See Filmer, *Anarchy of a Limited or Mixed Monarchy*, p. 145: "Eve was subject to Adam before he sinned; the angels, who are of a pure nature, are subject to God – which confutes their saying who, in disgrace of civil government or power say it was brought in by sin." (I fear that Butler, "Early Liberal Roots of Feminism," p. 138, misreads this as suggesting that the difference between man and woman is comparable to that between God and angel.)

[12] "Government as to coactive power was after sin, because coaction supposeth some disorder, which was not in the state of innocencey: but as for directive power, the condition of human nature requires it, since civil society cannot be imagined without power of government. [F]or although as long as men continued in the state of innocency they might not need the direction of Adam in those things which were necessarily and morally to be done, yet things indifferent – that depended merely on their free will – might be directed by the power of Adam's command." (Filmer, *Anarchy of a Limited or Mixed Monarchy*, p. 145.)

[13] Cf. 2nd T: 4: "[W]e must consider, what State all Men are naturally in, and that is, *a State of perfect Freedom* to order their Actions, and dispose of their Possessions and Persons, as they think fit, within the bounds of the Law of Nature, without asking leave, or depending upon the will of any other Man."

customs of Nations have ordered it so; and there is, I grant, a Foundation in Nature for it" (1st T: 47).

Now *that* is an alarming claim for a theorist of equality: *there is a foundation in nature for the ordinary subjection of a woman to her husband.* And the claim is explicit in Locke's argument in the *Second Treatise* – quite outside of the Adam and Eve context – in some notorious observations that he makes about marriage and about the location of final authority in what he calls "*Conjugal Society.*" The *Second Treatise* passage on this is pretty well-known. It begins with equality of individual rights. The basis of marriage, says Locke, is "a voluntary Compact between Man and Woman" consisting "chiefly in ... a Communion and Right in one another's Bodies." It includes also obligations of "mutual Support, and Assistance" and a "Communion of Interests" uniting their care and affection, and providing of course for their children (2nd T: 78). Intriguingly, in the posthumously published *Paraphrase and Notes on the Epistles of St. Paul*, Locke even produces an argument for reciprocity so far as rights in one another's bodies are concerned. Commenting in a footnote to his paraphrase of 1 Corinthians 7:4,[14] Locke observes:

> The woman (who in all other rights is inferior) has here the same power given her over the mans body, that the man has over hers. The reason whereof is plain. Because if she had not her man, when she had need of him; as well as the man his woman when he had need of her, marriage would be noe remedy against fornication. (P&N: i.199–200)

At any rate, having set up these reciprocal right and duties in the *Second Treatise*, Locke then introduces a sickeningly familiar asymmetry, along the following lines:

> But the Husband and Wife, though they have but one common Concern, yet having different understandings, will unavoidably sometimes have different wills too; it therefore being necessary, that the last Determination, i.e. the Rule, should be placed somewhere, it naturally falls to the Man's share, as the abler and the stronger. (2nd T: 82)

"[N]aturally ... the Man's share, as the abler and the stronger." What does this portend for our project?

It's pretty obvious that this position on marital authority sits uneasily with any principle of basic human equality. But where exactly does the

---

[14] 1 Corinthians 7:4: "The wife hath not power of her own body, but the husband: and likewise also the husband hath not power of his own body, but the wife."

inconsistency lie? It's hard to tell, because the meaning of the passage is unclear. We can read it in two ways. The reference to *strength* – "the abler and the stronger" – might suggest that what we have here is a relationship based on conquest and violence. I don't think that was what Locke meant. It would straightforwardly contradict his contractualist account of marriage. "Conjugal society," he says, "is made by a voluntary compact" (2nd T: 78), and there is no suggestion (as there is in *Leviathan*, for example) that the voluntariness of such an arrangement could be compatible with its being the upshot of coercion.[15] I think that Locke cannot plausibly be read as saying that the husband's matrimonial authority may be established by force, not only because it would embarrass the fundamentals of his contractualist account, but also – perhaps paradoxically – because Locke conceded that although this was likely to happen in fact, its happening in fact did not determine the right of the matter. I have in mind here the distinction between prediction and prescription which we talked about a little while ago.[16] Remember his comment about the prediction of pain in childbirth not prohibiting anaesthetics:

there is here no more Law to oblige a Woman to such a Subjection, if the Circumstances either of her Condition or Contract with her Husband should exempt her from it, th[a]n there is, that she should bring forth her Children in Sorrow and Pain, if there could be found a Remedy for it ... (1st T: 47)

In general Locke was quite careful to distinguish *de facto* probabilities from prescribed or legitimated outcomes. This is a point I shall emphasize several times.[17] In the *Letter Concerning Toleration*, for example, he was adamant that the physical ability of a magistrate to prevail over a subordinated minority didn't make his prevailing right: "You will say, then, the magistrate being the stronger will have his will and carry his point. Without doubt; but the question is not here concerning the doubtfulness of the event, but the rule of right" (LCT: 49). Might is not necessarily right; so the right of male rule is not established by the mere fact of male strength.

---

[15] Cf. Hobbes, *Leviathan*, Ch. 14, p. 97: "Covenants entred into by fear, in the condition of meer Nature, are obligatory." Hobbes of course did not concede that male strength inevitably prevailed: "[T]here is not always that difference of strength or prudence between the man and the woman as that the right can be determined without War" (ibid., Ch. 20, p. 139).

[16] In 1st T: 47, Locke says that Genesis 3:16 – "thy desire shall be to thy husband, and he shall rule over thee" – can be read as a prediction rather than a prescription: "God, in this Text, gives not, that I see, any authority to Adam over Eve, or to Men over their Wives, but only fortels what should be the Womans Lot."

[17] See also the discussion of slavery in Chapter 7, below, pp. 202–3.

(As an aside, let me say that I also don't agree with John Simmons's suggestion that there is anything in common between Locke's argument here about male strength and his argument in the *Second Treatise* about majority rule – "it being necessary to that which is one body to move one way; it is necessary the body should move that way whither the greater force carries it" (2nd T: 96).[18] The only thing in common in the two situations is the need for a decision rule, and as I argued in *The Dignity of Legislation*,[19] the majoritarian argument does not really involve an appeal to physical strength at all.)

However, there is another way of reading this passage about the will of the husband prevailing. It's a more plausible reading, but it still involves a head-on challenge to the principle of basic equality. Locke's suggestion might be that male strength and male ability constitute an *entitlement* to authority – strength and ability in the sense of a superior capacity to carry out the tasks involved in the relationship. It's a distinction of authority based on an allegation about a distinction of merit.

Is this necessarily a problem for basic equality? Even in his most egalitarian moments, Locke does not deny that there are important distinctions in capacity among human beings – and hence functional distinctions in merit. Actually he insists on the point: "Though I have said above, Chap. II. *That all Men by Nature are equal*, I cannot be supposed to understand all sorts of *Equality*: *Age* or *Virtue* may give men a just Precedency: *Excellency of Parts and Merit* may place others above the Common Level" (2nd T: 54). The trouble is that Locke also wants to insist that differences like these are consistent with basic equality *of authority*. The passage just quoted continues:

and yet all this consists with the *Equality*, which all *Men* are in, in respect of Jurisdiction or Dominion one over another; which was the *Equality* I there spoke of, as proper to the Business in hand, being that equal *Right*, that every Man hath, *to his Natural Freedom*, without being subjected to the Will or Authority of any other Man. (2nd T: 54)

But that is exactly what this business about the superior ability of the husband denies. In the passage about husbands and wives, Locke is not just noticing a difference in ability, he is inferring a difference in authority from a difference in the capacities of human beings; and that *is* fundamentally at odds with what he wants to say generally about

---

[18] Simmons, *Lockean Theory of Rights*, p. 174.
[19] Waldron, *Dignity of Legislation*, pp. 136 ff. See also Chapter 5, below, pp. 129–30.

equality. The inconsistency is the more striking because, as far as I can tell, this is the only place in his mature thought where Locke bases entitlement to authority on superior capacity.[20] He does say in a few places that people might *choose* their ruler on the basis of ability.[21] But still, consent is the basis of authority and although the recognition of ability may be a reason for giving consent, it does not trump or override it. Nowhere, except in this passage about husbands and wives, does he say that ability confers authority in default or perhaps even in contradiction of consent.

True, Locke does talk about the power of a parent over a child as based on the difference in their respective capacities. But there the point is that the child really has no will or understanding of its own. In the case of husbands and wives, the passage about the husband's ability is predicated on the assumption that the husband and wife are both rational beings and it is simply a matter of whose will is to prevail: "the Husband and Wife, though they have but one common Concern, yet having different understandings, will unavoidably sometimes have different wills too; it therefore being necessary, that the last Determination, *i.e.* the Rule, should be placed somewhere" (2nd T: 82). The issue is undeniably one of authority, then – authority among beings who are without question supposed to be one another's equals so far as authority is concerned.

IV

I wish this wasn't what Locke said and meant: it would make my life easier as an exponent of his theory of basic equality. But there is no way round it.

The position cannot be saved by saying, "Well, Locke just accepted the custom of his day." Locke was a consistent critic of the customs

[20] He never makes any such claim about the magistrate or about legislative representatives in the *Second Treatise*. In the *Letter Concerning Toleration* he goes to considerable pains to deny that magistracy is best understood in terms of superior ability: "Princes, indeed, are born superior unto other men in power, but in nature equal. Neither the right nor the art of ruling does necessarily carry along with it the certain knowledge of other things" (LCT: 36).

[21] See Locke's discussion in 2nd T: 75 and 105 of adult children's reasons for choosing their fathers as rulers in primeval political society – "He was fittest to be trusted; Paternal affection secured their Property and Interest under his Care . . . If therefore they must have one to rule them . . . who so likely to be the Man as he that was their common Father; unless Negligence, Cruelty, or any other defect of Mind or Body made him unfit for it? But when either the Father died, and left his next Heir, for want of Age, Wisdom, Courage, or any other Qualities, less fit for Rule; or where several Families met, and consented to continue together; There, 'tis not to be doubted, but they used their natural freedom, to set up him, whom they judged the ablest, and most likely, to Rule well over them." (See also the discussion in Chapter 5, below, pp. 134–6.)

of his day on all sorts of topics, and he was well aware of the "gross absurdities" to which "the following of Custom, when Reason has left it, may lead" (2nd T: 157). He was at least as capable of distancing himself from the assumptions of his culture as we are from ours.[22] Moreover, in both *Treatises* he talked about law and custom in regard to men and women, and he made his argument about the "foundation in nature" for male superiority explicitly as a point in addition to that. Or, more precisely, what he said was that there is a natural presumption in favor of husbands that can be displaced either by the contract between husband and wife or by some contrary custom or local law. But even the idea of a defeasible natural presumption here is at odds with basic equality.

Nor can the consistency of Locke's overall position be saved by saying that this is a subordination of wives in the specific circumstance of marriage, not a general proposition about the inequality of women. Strictly speaking, that is true, though Locke's point in the *Treatises* is that the subordination of wives is based on the natural inferiority of women. Elsewhere in his writings, Locke describes women as the "weaker" and "the more timid" sex.[23] He talks also in the *Essay*, of nurses and maids as sources of myth and disinformation.[24] In the footnotes to his paraphrase of 1 Corinthians, Locke talks freely of "the subordination of the sexes," the undesirability of setting "women at liberty from their natural subjection to men," "the confessed superiority and dominion of the man," and "this subordination which god for order's sake had instituted in the world" (P&N: i.222).[25]

In an excellent essay on Locke and feminism, Melissa Butler has observed the "hesitant" tone in which Locke talks about conjugal

---

[22] Lorenne Clark is rightly insistent on this point: "Locke was quite prepared to challenge the deepest principles of English land law" (Clark, "Women and Locke," p. 33).

[23] Locke, *Essays on the Law of Nature*, p. 113; Locke, "Virtue B," p. 288.

[24] Early in the *Essay Concerning Human Understanding*, Locke suggests that "*Doctrines*, that have been derived from no better original, than the Superstition of a Nurse, or the Authority of an old Woman; may, by length of time, and consent of Neighbours, grow up to the dignity of *Principles in Religion or Morality*" (E: 1.3.22). Later he offers this observation about the idea of goblins and sprites: "[L]et but a foolish Maid inculcate these often on the Mind of a Child, and raise them there together, possibly he shall never be able to separate them again so long as he lives, but darkness shall ever afterwards bring with it those frightful *Ideas*" (E: 2.33.10). See also the references in Walker, "Locke Minding Women," pp. 250–2.

[25] One always has to be careful with one's use of Locke's *Paraphrase and Notes on the Epistles* – careful that one is citing Locke and not St. Paul (in Locke's reconstruction of his teachings). Mostly I shall cite only the *footnotes* in this posthumously published work, for it is there that Locke seems to comment in his own voice on the Epistles. (These footnotes amount to substantial commentaries: for example, the footnote from which I have taken the phrases cited in the text runs for three pages.)

inequality.[26] He qualifies it, she says, and he does his best to mitigate it and limit its impact on the rest of the theory. She is right – up to a point. According to Locke, the husband's authority affects only matters of common concern. It does not affect the wife's personal property. It may be offset by the contract between them or by municipal law. And it may be terminated by divorce, "there being no necessity in the nature of the thing, nor to the ends of it, that [this relationship] should always be for Life" (2nd T: 81).[27] And Professor Butler is right in the further point she makes, about Locke's argument that a husband's authority has nothing to do with *political* power. It is, says Locke, at most,

only a Conjugal Power, not Political, the Power that every Husband hath to order the things of private Concernment in his Family, as Proprietor of the Goods and Land there, and to have his Will take place before that of his wife in all things of their common Concernment; but not a Political Power of Life and Death over her, much less over any body else. (1st T: 48)

Still, even this does not really reconcile the position to the principle of basic equality. Locke may insist on a verbal difference between conjugal and political society,[28] and even a difference in content – the husband has no power over the *life* of his lady, whereas the magistrate does. (And we must bear in mind Mary Astell's response: "What tho' a Husband can't deprive a Wife of Life without being responsible to the Law, he may however do what is much more grievous to a generous Mind, render Life miserable.")[29]

The fact is that Locke has built a difference of authority among two adult human wills on the basis of natural differences. And that in itself, being quite at odds with what he says about equality, is enough to cast doubt on the general premise – which is essential to his politics – that no such construction is legitimate. Locke's political theory depends on flattening out the traditional hierarchies within the human species, and

---

[26] Butler, "Early Liberal Roots of Feminism," p. 143.

[27] And Locke continues: "But this reaching but to the things of their common Interest and Property, leaves the Wife in the full and free possession of what by Contract is her peculiar Right, and gives the Husband no more power over her Life than she has over his. The *Power of the Husband* being so far from that of an absolute Monarch, that the *Wife* has in many cases a liberty to *separate* from him; where natural Right, or their Contract allows it; whether that Contract be made by themselves in the state of Nature, or by the Customs or Laws of the Country they live in; and the Children upon Such Separation fall to the Father or Mother's Lot, as such Contract does determine." (2nd T: 82)

[28] Cf. Pateman, *Sexual Contract*, p. 52: "The battle is not over the legitimacy of a husband's conjugal right, but over what to call it."

[29] Astell, *Reflections Upon Marriage*, pp. 17–18; see also Springborg, "Mary Astell," p. 628.

he does that by denying that natural differences among humans give rise to basic differences of authority. Once that is compromised, as it certainly is in this instance, the credibility of the general position is shaken.[30]

v

Carole Pateman believes that a consistent position *is* salvageable if we take seriously the propositions we have just been examining about women and conjugal authority. What we have to realize, says Pateman, is that for Locke the issue of *political* power over women does not arise. In Locke's scheme of things political power is a relation between free and equal individuals; conjugal power on the other hand is a relation between a free individual and a creature that is something less than a free individual. It is a form of "natural subjection" and it is simply unregulated by the equality-oriented principles associated with politics. Hence Pateman's conclusion concerning Locke's discussion of husbands' authority:

> None of this disturbs Locke's picture of the state of nature as a condition "wherein all the Power and Jurisdiction is reciprocal, . . . without Subordination or Subjection." . . . The natural subjection of women, which entails their exclusion from the category of "individual," is irrelevant to Locke's investigation.[31]

In other words, consistency is saved for Locke (according to Pateman) by inferring that when he says all men are equal, he *does* after all mean "men" in the narrow gendered sense. I have a lot of respect for Carole Pateman's work (not just her work on Locke), and I am tempted to concede at least the following: if consistency is to be attributed at all costs to Locke's theory in the *Second Treatise*, then "[w]omen are excluded from the status of 'individual' in the natural condition . . . the attributes of individuals are sexually differentiated; only men naturally have the characteristics of free and equal beings."[32] That will be the price of insisting that the claims about equality have to be reconciled somehow with the claims about superiority: the only way to reconcile them is to read "Men" in "all Men by Nature are equal" (2nd T: 54) as referring only to males.

---

[30] This, by the way, was exactly Mary Astell's critique of Locke in *Reflections Upon Marriage*, p. 17: "[I]f Absolute Sovereignty be not necessary in a State, how comes it to be so in a Family? or if in a Family, why not in a State; since no Reason can be alleg'd for the one that will not hold more strongly for the other."

[31] Pateman, *Sexual Contract*, p. 53.   [32] Ibid., p. 52.

And if we go this far, we won't have to go very much further to infer that John Locke did not believe married women could own property or participate (as property-holders) in politics. Locke insists that no one truly has property in anything which another can rightfully take from her, when he pleases, against her consent (2nd T: 138). It seems to follow then, from the claim that a husband's decisions about family property take precedence over his wife's, that wives cannot really be property-holders at all.[33] Moreover, if there is any question about whether the family property is to be brought under the auspices of civil society in the social contract for its better protection, again it would seem to follow that the husband's will should rightfully prevail so that married woman are not normally to be understood as parties to the social contract in their own right. And so the whole fabric of apparent gender-equality unravels. Locke may have tried to give the impression of arguing against patriarchy, and he may even have pulled the wool over the eyes of a few gullible twentieth-century liberals. But it was all a trick, and feminist commentators are not fooled. They know that this is really a chauvinist wolf in egalitarian clothing.[34]

The position is still not entirely consistent of course. For Locke *does* talk about married women having their own property; in his discussion of just war towards the end of the *Second Treatise*, he insists that even a justly conquered husband does not forfeit his wife's estate: "For as to the Wife's share, whether her own Labour or compact gave her a Title to it, 'tis plain, Her Husband could not forfeit what was hers" (2nd T: 183).[35] In the *First Treatise*, too, Locke will not allow Filmer to evade the force of his insistence that God gave the world to Adam and Eve, not to Adam alone, on the basis of Eve's subordination:

the Grant being to them, *i.e.* spoke to *Eve* also, as many Interpreters think with reason, that these words were not spoken till *Adam* had his Wife, must not she thereby be Lady, as well as he Lord of the World? If it be said that *Eve* was subjected to *Adam*, it seems she was not so subjected to him, as to hinder

---

[33] Cf. Norton, *Founding Mothers*, p. 290: "If property holders by definition could not be subject to the whims of another person, then no wife – no woman – could be the sort of property owner who could participate in the establishment of government."

[34] *Why* Locke should have wanted to conduct this elaborate charade is another question. He had no particular incentive of "political correctness" in this regard. On the contrary, I suspect that in the late seventeenth century his costume of respect for gender-equality would cause him more trouble than the patriarchalism he was supposed to be trying to disguise. But we will let that pass, as we pursue the Pateman interpretation.

[35] Mary Beth Norton mentions this passage in a footnote (Norton, *Founding Mothers*, p. 458 n. 19) but quite understandably does not attempt to reconcile it with her interpretation that "[w]ives by definition owned no property" (ibid., p. 290).

her *Dominion* over the Creatures, or *Property* in them: for shall we say that God ever made a joint Grant to two, and one only was to have the benefit of it? (1st T: 29)

And this is followed by the great passage I quoted earlier (I: 30), to the effect that the word "*Man*" must cover Eve as well – not just as a matter of semantics, but because she too bears the image of God, an intellectual nature, which does not belong to the male sex only.[36] (Even if it were just a matter of the semantics of words like "*Man*," one might think it worth mentioning the passage in the *Essay Concerning Human Understanding* where Locke talks about the way children learn the meaning of that word – generalizing from nurse, and mother and father, and from any "complex idea they had of Peter and James, Mary and Jane."[37] There is no discernable masculine bias in Locke's account of the way the meaning is formed.)

So these inconsistencies remain even if we adopt Carole Pateman's interpretation. And there are others. Since Locke insists explicitly on the contractual (and determinable) nature of marriage, do we not have to infer that women *can* enter into contracts after all? Also what is the status of unmarried women, according to Locke? Subjection to their fathers, brothers, or nearest male relation? Locke makes fun of that position in regard to the authority of Elizabeth I, as he makes fun also of the idea that in England Mary Tudor was subject to *her* husband (1st T: 47). What about widows? What about women who have decided to divorce their husbands? Locke says

The Wife has in many cases a Liberty to *separate* from [the husband]; where natural Right, or their Contract allows it, whether that Contract be made by themselves in the state of Nature, or by the Customs or Laws of the country they live in; and the Children upon such Separation fall to the Father or Mother's lot, as such Contract does determine. (2nd T: 82)

---

[36] The passage is quoted in full, above, at p. 25.

[37] "There is nothing more evident, than that the ideas of the persons children converse with . . . are, like the persons themselves, only particular. The ideas of the nurse and the mother are well framed in their minds; and, like pictures of them there, represent only those individuals. The names they first gave to them are confined to these individuals; and the names of nurse and mamma, the child uses, determine themselves to those persons. Afterwards, when time and a larger acquaintance have made them observe that there are a great many other things in the world, that in some common agreements of shape, and several other qualities, resemble their father and mother, and those persons they have been used to, they frame an idea, which they find those many particulars do partake in; and to that they give, with others, the name man, for example. And thus they come to have a general name, and a general idea. Wherein they make nothing new; but only leave out of the complex idea they had of Peter and James, Mary and Jane, that which is peculiar to each, and retain only what is common to them all." (E: 3.3.7)

Can such a female head of household not enter the social contract, for the better protection of her own and her family's property?

Then there are also some less tangible problems for the Pateman view, from the perspective of the history of ideas. Pateman is certain that, according to Locke, women could not be involved in setting up civil society. I will offer some more detailed comments on this in Chapter 5, when we consider the definition of "the people" in Locke's theory of the constitution of political society. There I shall argue that Locke is precluded by his own logic from saying both that women are subject to natural law and that they are not to be considered as members of the people, for the purposes of the institution of political society.[38] In the meantime, it is worth observing that Pateman offers no explanation of why Locke does not follow Samuel Pufendorf and his own friend James Tyrrell in making this explicit. They spelled it out. Pufendorf said that "states have certainly been formed by men, not women" and this is why the right of the father prevails.[39] Locke said nothing of the sort. But why would he be less forthcoming than Pufendorf if this (as Pateman suggests) was the main point of his argument? James Tyrrell said that "women are commonly unfit for civil business."[40] Again, why would Locke be less forthcoming on this than his friend?[41]

We know Locke was prepared to acknowledge that almost all states have been patriarchal in their actual historical origins. He talks about "how easy it was in the first Ages of the World, . . . for the *Father of the Family* to become the Prince of it" (2nd T: 74). And he says that it was important that people chose someone they naturally loved and trusted as their primeval ruler, for "without such nursing fathers[42] tender and careful of the public weal, all Governments would have sunk under the Weakness and Infirmities of their Infancy" (2nd T: 110). Yet Locke is adamant about inferring *nothing* from this about the appropriate shape or personnel for modern politics, except that it is sometimes a good idea to give political authority to people you trust. With regard to fathers,

---

[38] See below, pp. 120–5.   [39] Pufendorf, *On the Duty of Man and the Citizen*, p. 125.

[40] Tyrrell, *Patriarcha Non Monarcha*, p. 83. (This passage is actually cited in Pateman, *Sexual Contract*, p. 77.) Tyrrell also observed, *Patriarcha Non Monarcha*, p. 83, that "[t]here never was any Government where all the Promiscuous Rabble of Women and Children had Votes, as being not capable of it." (See Butler, "Early Liberal Roots of Feminism," p. 139.)

[41] For the significance of Locke's silences compared with what his contemporaries and predecessors were writing, see Skinner, "Meaning and Understanding," p. 62.

[42] This intriguing phrase is biblical in origin. See Isaiah 49:23: "And kings shall be thy nursing fathers, and their queens thy nursing mothers: they shall bow down to thee with their face toward the earth, and lick up the dust of thy feet; and thou shalt know that I am the Lord: for they shall not be ashamed that wait for me."

husbands, and males generally being appropriate occupants of political office, the conclusion is insistent: "an Argument from what has been, to what should of right be, has no great force" (2nd T: 103).[43] This is quite at variance with the style of argument of those in the seventeenth century whom we *know* held the position that Pateman is attributing to Locke.

Finally we ask: why is Locke at such pains to insist that the Fifth Commandment is a commandment equally to love and respect one's mother as well as one's father, if he held the basically patriarchal view that Pateman attributes to him?[44] In this, as Melissa Butler notes, "Locke broke with one of patriarchy's strongest traditions."[45] His insistence on including mothers as well as fathers is strident and repetitive: it goes on for more than six pages in the *First Treatise*.[46] The Fifth Commandment establishes equality between the parents, says Locke; and he cites a dozen other biblical verses that join "father" and "mother" in the same way.[47] "Nay, the Scripture makes the Authority of *Father and Mother* ... so equal, that in some places it neglects even the Priority of Order, which is thought due to the Father, and the *Mother* is put first, as Lev. 19. 3" (1st T: 61). He rejects out of hand Filmer's suggestion that the man as "the nobler and the principal agent in generation" of children is entitled to the greater benefit of the Fifth Commandment.[48] If anyone has priority it is the woman:

For no body can deny but that the Woman hath an equal share, if not the greater, as nourishing a Child a long time in her own Body out of her own Substance. There it is fashion'd, and from her it receives the Materials and Principles of its Constitution; And it is so hard to imagine the rational Soul should presently Inhabit the yet unformed Embrio, as soon as the Father has done his part in the Act of Generation, that if it must be supposed to derive anything from the Parents, it must certainly owe most to the Mother. (1st T: 55)

---

[43] See also Waldron, "John Locke: Social Contract versus Political Anthropology."

[44] See 1st T: 6, 11, and 60–8. Locke says that if "Honor thy father" is a basis for kingship, then the Law also "enjoyns Obedience to Queens" (1st T: 11), and certainly by including the mother, it "destroys the Sovereignty of one Supream Monarch" (1st T: 65).

[45] Butler, "Early Liberal Roots of Feminism," p. 143.

[46] Would it be unfair to call Pateman's observation that "Locke points out *more than once* that the Fifth Commandment does not refer only to the father of the family" (*Sexual Contract*, p. 52 – my emphasis) a grudging concession? On my count, the point is discussed not just more than once, but *explicitly and at length* in each of twenty different paragraphs of the *Two Treatises*.

[47] 1st T: 61. Indeed this is one of the rare occasions in the *First Treatise* when Locke cites the Gospel – "For God commanded, saying, Honour thy father and mother: and, He that curseth father or mother, let him die the death" (Matthew 15:4). See also 1st T: 66.

[48] Filmer, *Observations on Mr. Hobbes*, p. 192, cited in 1st T: 55.

True, Locke occasionally slips back into describing parental authority as "paternal" authority (2nd T: 170). And since he is arguing against any patriarchialist inference from the rights of a father over his child he often argues explicitly on that ground (2nd T: 69). But as Mary Shanley has pointed out, whenever the issue of mothers' rights was raised, Locke was self-conscious in his insistence that paternal power should be termed *parental*: "For whatever obligation Nature and the right of Generation lays on Children, it must certainly bind them equal to both the concurrent Causes of it" (2nd T: 52).[49]

Of course, none of this actually contradicts the Lockean claim that we are finding problematic – namely, that men and women are unequal on the basis of their own abilities, quite apart from their relation to their children. But still, Locke's emphasis on equal rights for mothers and his dependence on such passages to knock away one of the major platforms of Filmer's patriarchalism does sit rather ill with Carole Pateman's view that Locke himself was a consistent patriarchialist and proud of it.

VI

I have no tidy resolution to offer. Locke's position on the natural subjection of wives *is* an embarrassment for his general theory of equality. And there is not, as Carole Pateman thinks there is, an alternative consistent position – Lockean patriarchalism – into which the claims about the subjection of women fit comfortably. What we are left with is a mess. Bible and nature are cited for the proposition that women are men's inferiors; and Bible and nature are cited for the proposition that women and men are one another's equals, endowed intellectually – both of them – with sense, will, and understanding in the image of God. The combination of the two positions leaves us unclear about how wholeheartedly Locke was prepared to follow through on his convictions about equality in this fraught and contested terrain. They confirm the hunch with which I began, that we what have here is a philosopher struggling *not altogether successfully* to free his own thought as well as the thought of his contemporaries from the idea that something as striking as the difference between the sexes must count in itself as a refutation of basic equality.

[49] Shanley, "Marriage Contract and Social Contract," p. 377.

My theme is the *Christian* foundations of Locke's political thought, and I want to end this chapter by referring again to Locke's notes to his *Paraphrase* of Paul's First Epistle to the Corinthians. I said earlier that those notes contain some of Locke's choicer phrases about the subjection of women. But Locke also made some interesting remarks about the specific argument of 1 Corinthians 11:3–13 about women covering their heads when they pray or prophesy.[50] He refuses to view the passage – he calls it "[t]his about women" – as straightforward. It seems, he says, "as difficult a passage as most in St Pauls Epistles" (P&N: i.220, note a). In his long note he is at pains to interpret Paul's strictures about women covering their heads when they pray or prophesy as referring not to their ordinary participation in a congregation – for he can't imagine that there would be any issue about that – but to the extraordinary "performing of some particular publick action by some one person," a particular woman moved by the Holy Spirit, while the rest of the assembly remained silent (ibid., note c). And he says that although St. Paul was not countenancing the possibility of women taking it upon themselves to be regular "teachers and instructers of the congregation" (ibid., note x) – "This would have had too great an air of standing upon even ground with men" (ibid., note y) – still that background subordination "hinderd not but that by the supernatural gifts of the spirit he might make use of the weaker sex to any extraordinary function when ever he thought fit, as well as he did of men" (ibid., note z).

There is a story that when John Locke himself attended a service led by a woman preacher in 1696, he wrote afterwards to the preacher, Rebecca Collier, congratulating her on her sermon and observing that "[w]omen, indeed, had the honour first to publish the resurrection of the Lord of Love," and why should they not minister again in modern

[50] Here is Locke's paraphrase of 1 Corinthians 3–10 (which we must remember is not necessarily his own view of the matter):

Christ is the head to which every man is subjected, and the man is the head to which every woman is subjected . . . Every man that prayeth or prophesieth . . . in the church for the edifying exhorting and comforting of the congregation haveing his head covered dishonoureth Christ his head, by appearing in a garb not becomeing the authority and dominion which god through Christ has given him over all the things of this world, the covering of the head being a mark of subjection. But on the contrary a woman praying or prophesying in the church with her head uncovered dishonoureth the man who is her head by appearing in a garb that disowns her subjection to him. For to appear bareheaded in publick is all one as to have her hair cut off, which is the garb and dress of the other sex and not of a woman . . . A man indeed ought not to be veyled because he is the image and representative of god in his dominion over the rest of the world, which is one part of the glory of god: But the woman who was made out of the man, made for him, and in subjection to him, is matter of glory to the man. (P&N: i.221–2)

times to "the resurrection of the Spirit of Love?"[51] The question remains unanswered, and it has been suggested that the attribution of this letter to Locke is spurious.[52] Be that as it may, it is perhaps not altogether surprising – and this may be as good a point as any on which to end an inconclusive chapter – to find that among the early readers of Locke's *Paraphrase and Notes on the Epistles of St. Paul* there was one Josiah Martin who read the passages I have just quoted, "and transcrib'd them into my *Common-Place-Book*, thinking they might be of some Service, to vindicate the Doctrine of Friends [i.e. Quakers] concerning Women's *Preaching in the Church*."[53] Martin was impressed by Locke's gloss, and he challenged other readers and "all unprejudiced Persons" to consider

[w]hether the Notes above-cited were not intended to evince and demonstrate, That Women as well as Men had and were to have the Gifts of Prayer and Prophecy . . . and whenever Women were moved or inspired by the Holy Ghost, they had the same Liberty to speak in the Congregation as the Men.[54]

For his part, Martin was convinced that this was what "Judicious *Locke*" meant, and that his sentiments were occasioned by an incident some years earlier:

John Locke being at a Meeting, where a certain North-Country Woman was, who had been travelling on Truth's Account, [sic] was so affected with her Testimony, as to say afterwards in Words to this Effect *That something Divine and Extraordinary affected the Preaching of that Woman*.[55]

This seems to comport with the tenor of the letter Locke allegedly wrote to Rebecca Collier.

I accept that there is nothing probative in any of this. It is perfectly possible to say that women may be preachers – even divinely inspired and extraordinary preachers – and still to believe they are naturally subordinate to men. As I said, I don't think we can attribute a consistent

---

[51] Locke to Rebecca Collier, Nov. 21, 1696, reprinted in Fox Bourne's biography of Locke, p. 453 (cited in Butler, "Early Liberal Roots of Feminism," p. 150).

[52] See the editorial comment in Locke, *Correspondence*, Vol. 5, p. 718.

[53] Martin, *A Letter to the Author of Some Brief Observations*, p. 4.

[54] Ibid., pp. 9–10. (Wainwright's "Bibliography" in Volume 1 of his edition of Locke, *Paraphrase and Notes*, p. 96 indicates that Martin also published in the following year (1717) another book on the subject, with the pithy title: "A Vindication of Women's Preaching, as well from Holy Scripture on Antient Writings as from the Paraphrase and Notes of the Judicious John Locke.")

[55] Martin, *A Letter to the Author of Some Brief Observations*, p. 32.

position to Locke. Still, the impression he left on Josiah Martin is worth remembering. And I hope it is not too much of a concession, on my part, to the historians and the contextualists, to say that the things that strike *us* as evidence that Locke shared his contemporaries' views on the subjection of women did not always or necessarily strike his contemporaries that way.

3

Species and the Shape of Equality

When I was in Oxford in 1982, I heard the Carlyle Lectures delivered that year by Alasdair Macintyre.[1] I remember being very struck by Macintyre's observation that, as he read the *Two Treatises of Government*, the arguments of John Locke concerning basic equality and individual rights were so imbued with religious content that they were not fit, constitutionally, to be taught in the public schools of the United States of America. And maybe he is right: a constitution interpreted in a way that prohibits even a non-sectarian blessing by a rabbi at the beginning of a public high school graduation[2] is certainly in no position to allow students to be instructed in a doctrine of equality or equal protection that takes as its premise the proposition that we are "all the Workmanship of one Omnipotent, and infinitely wise Maker; All the servants of one Sovereign Master, sent into the World by his order and about his business" (2nd T: 6). But I also remember in 1982 balking at this characterization of Macintyre's, fancying myself as an expert on the *Second Treatise*, and arguing (in a paper that I still have, but had the good sense not to try to publish) that the theology could be bracketed out of Locke's theory and that, if it were, a defensible secular conception of equality would remain.

Readers may reasonably assume that, seventeen years later, I would not have given the lectures on which this book is based, under the heading of "Christian Equality in the Political Theory of John Locke," had I not had second thoughts about that bracketing possibility. So let me put the question: Why are we not able to bracket off the theological dimension of Locke's commitment to equality? Why can't we put the religious premises in parentheses – leaving them available for anyone who needs that sort of persuasion, but not presented as an integral part of the package – and

[1] These lectures were later worked up into his book *Whose Justice? Which Rationality?*
[2] *Lee* v. *Weisman*, 505 US 577 (1992).

44

still be left with something recognizably egalitarian in its content, which even an atheist could support?

The hope that some trick like this can be pulled off, the belief that some such bracketing must be possible – if not for Locke's theory, then perhaps for Kant's, or at least for *some* recognizable commitment to equality – this hope is crucial for modern secular liberalism. *Political* liberalism (in Rawls's sense of that phrase) depends absolutely on the success of some such maneuver. Rawls's system definitely requires a premise of equality, a premise strong enough to structure the original position and substantial enough to provide a basis for mutual respect in a well-ordered society;[3] and Rawls's view is that any premise supporting that structure has to stand by itself on the plateau of political values, free of any religious entanglement. Of course, a religious argument for basic equality may be entertained in certain circles in a pluralistic society; but according to the Rawlsian scheme, the very same principle of equality must be conceivable and defensible from a variety of philosophical perspectives, some religious and some not.[4] My approach in the present book indicates that I am doubtful that this Rawlsian strategy will work. What is the basis for these doubts?

I

The hypothesis that we might be able to bracket out the religious content and concentrate on equality itself presupposes that the religious content has a purely *external* relation to the equality principle. By an external relation, I mean a relation that does not go to the meaning of the principle in question. Consider, for example, the relation of some proposition about a commander to the content of his command. A given command with a constant meaning might be conceived of as issued by any number of commanders (and by commanders of quite different kinds). For example, the Sixth Commandment has a content "Thou shalt not kill" which seems logically quite independent of any proposition about whose commandment it was or is, a content which may be debated and responded to quite independently of any issue about what one might call the *preface* to the Decalogue – "I am the Lord thy God, which have brought thee out of the land of Egypt, out of the house of bondage."[5] The latter

---

3 Rawls, *Political Liberalism*, pp. 19 and 109; for the connection to the original position, see ibid., p. 79.
4 For "political" values and the idea of overlapping consensus, see ibid., pp. 133 ff.
5 Exodus 20:2.

material is incontestably religious. But the meaning of the commandment itself does not appear to depend on it. (That's what I mean by an external relation.) Now this is arguably not the case with regard to the Noachide version of the prohibition on killing. The commandment to Noah prohibiting murder cites as a reason the fact that potential victims of murder are made in the image of the person (God) who has issued the commandment.[6] There the religious aspect seems to have an *internal* relation to the commandment, by which I mean a relation that affects or pertains to its content or its meaning.

Someone might object that this confuses content with reasons. A given principle, with a specific content, might be supported by any number of different reasons, each independent of the others, so that if one were taken away the others would remain, and the principle – the *same* principle – would still be supported.[7] So the fact that P is cited as a reason for Q doesn't mean that P is indispensable for understanding the meaning of Q. (For instance, the fact that men are made in the image of God may be interesting, but not indispensable for understanding the Noachide prohibition on murder.) Now this is sometimes true, especially where the reasons in question establish nothing but an instrumental relationship between the principle and some consequentialist value. But I think the Rawlsians overestimate the extent to which it is true generally, particularly in the domain of justice. Abstract principles of justice and rights characteristically need to be filled out and interpreted and it is quite implausible to suppose that this can be done without reference to the reasons that support them. I have argued this elsewhere with regard to John Stuart Mill's "Harm Principle."[8] What counts as "harm" for the purposes of Mill's principle – whether, for example, an acute and painful form of disapproval can count as harm to the disapprover – cannot just be read out of a dictionary. It is necessarily sensitive to the reasons that are given in support of the principle, and no argument for interpreting "harm" one way or the other would be complete without reference to those underlying reasons. I think this is particularly the case where a moral principle involves predicates whose extension is not

---

[6] Genesis 9:6.

[7] Consider, for example, the multifaceted defense of the principle of liberal neutrality in Ackerman, *Social Justice in the Liberal State*, pp. 11–12. Ackerman envisages four possible lines of argument for neutrality, and says it doesn't matter which one we rely on.

[8] Mill, *On Liberty*, Ch. 1, p. 13. See Waldron, "Mill and the Value of Moral Distress," pp. 119–20. See also a similar argument about the meaning of "liberal neutrality," partly responding to the Ackerman approach mentioned in footnote 7 above, in Waldron, "Legislation and Moral Neutrality," pp. 151–3.

given determinately apart from the principle in question. This is true of "harm": there are some paradigm cases, but there are many marginal cases as well, and many different possible ways of drawing lines at the boundaries. No doubt we will have some indeterminate cases wherever the line is drawn. Even so, the extension may be determined in quite different ways or in ways that are quite differently shaped by our sense of why this predicate matters. And our sense of why it matters is unlikely to be separable from our understanding of how and why it features in various normative contexts.

I believe this is also true of the predicate "human" in the principle of basic human equality. I shall argue in this chapter that, in Locke's account, the shape of *human*, the way in which the extension of the predicate "human" is determined, is not in the end separable from the religious reasons that Locke cites in support of basic equality. If someone arrives at what purports to be a principle of human equality on other grounds (e.g., non-religious grounds), there is little reason to believe that that principle will have the same shape or texture as the Lockean principle. It may be better or worse, and more or less robust as a principle; but we should not kid ourselves that we are dealing here with the same principle, arrived at by a different route.

What I am saying here about the reasons that shape our notion of equality is a version of a point sometimes made as a criticism of a certain program of analysis in ethics. Many non-cognitivists assume that moral positions are subjective responses to factual features of the world that can be specified quite independently of the response. They think this is true not just of moral positions like "Causing pain is wrong," where it is clear that we can use the descriptive words "causing pain" to identify the actions concerned in a way that is independent of the particular response (condemnation using the word "wrong"), but also that it is true of moral positions involving "thick" moral concepts, positions like "Honesty is the best policy" and "Courage cannot be taught." The idea is that "thick" concepts like *honesty* and *courage* can be analyzed into descriptive components referring to some fact about the world and evaluative components indicating some attitudinal or prescriptive response to that fact.[9] (So, for example, the term "courage" is supposed to refer descriptively to a certain steadfastness in the face of danger, and to connote evaluatively an attitude of approval to that character-trait.) John McDowell and others have expressed doubts about the general

---

[9] For a recent vote of confidence in this strategy, see Hare, *Sorting Out Ethics*, pp. 60–2.

applicability of this pattern of analysis. What, asks McDowell, makes us so confident that we can always disentangle the descriptive properties from the evaluative response? Why should we think that, corresponding to any value concept, "one can always isolate a genuine feature of the world . . . that is, a feature that is there anyway, independently of anyone's value-experience being as it is," something "left in the world when one peels off the reflection of the appropriate attitude"?[10] The descriptive features underlying a given normative attitude might well seem weird or "shapeless"[11] – who would be interested in *them*, under exactly *that* description? – apart from the attitude which is supposedly a response to them.

I think a version of McDowell's point may apply to the concept *human* embedded in our commitment to equality. When we say that all humans are basically one another's equals, it sounds as if we are taking a descriptive predicate "human" and associating it with a particular prescription or practical orientation. But our concept *human* may be partly shaped by our commitment to equality, and may not be intelligible in a free-standing way, once that commitment is "peeled off," to use McDowell's phrase. Of course even if this is true, more argument would be needed to show that our notion of human is shaped by a specifically religious account of equality. (That argument is what I shall develop in the rest of the chapter, so far as Locke's theory is concerned. I will show that Locke's religious premises help to make sense of or give shape to a certain cluster of human characteristics that are then treated as the basis of equality, a cluster of characteristics that might seem arbitrary, shapeless, even insignificant apart from the religious context.) On its own, however, the shapelessness point deprives the Rawlsians and others who favor the bracketing approach of a quick and easy victory. They cannot say simply that there are facts about humanity to which we might take up egalitarian attitudes (for whatever reason). The facts about humanity to which the egalitarian draws our attention are facts which are shaped by his reasons for committing himself to the principle of basic equality. Take away those particular reasons, and there may not be any "there" there that is reachable by another route.

---

[10] McDowell, "Non-Cognitivism and Rule-Following," p. 144.
[11] The term "shapeless" is used by Simon Blackburn to capture McDowell's point: see Blackburn, "Reply: Rule-Following and Moral Realism," p. 167. Blackburn's response to McDowell concedes the possibility of shapelessness, but denies the imputation that it undermines non-cognitivism: ibid., pp. 166–8. See also Blackburn, *Ruling Passions*, pp. 96–7.

II

All men are equal. There is no basis for any natural subordination among humans. All persons are to be treated with equal concern and respect. These are familiar egalitarian propositions. To whom do they apply? Which particular beings, entities, creatures, animals, get the benefit of this equality? And why? What is the basis of equality? What is it that makes someone a beneficiary of this fundamental egalitarianism? I shall devote the rest of this chapter to an exploration of some of the extraordinary difficulties that John Locke gets into as he tries to answer these questions, difficulties that I think threaten the viability of his whole position in the *Two Treatises*.

The main difficulty is this. In his political works, John Locke asserts as a matter of principle the fundamental equality of *all members of the human species*.[12] Members of this species have a special status, or occupy a special moral position quite unlike that of any other animal. And in this position they are supposed to be one another's equals, in a way that also does not have any parallel for the co-members of any other species. This special status or position of the human species, Locke argues, has enormous consequences for how we think about authority, politics, and morality. But in his philosophy of science and language, in particular in Book III of the *Essay Concerning Human Understanding* (published, if not actually written, in the same year as the *Two Treatises*), Locke comes very close to saying that *there are no such things as species*. He says that species-classification is just a matter of words and that distinctions between species are at best just human conventions (and at worst matters of superstition, confusion, and contestation). Worse still, time and again in that discussion Locke offers up the alleged species-distinction between *man* and the other animals as "Exhibit A" for the purposes of this skepticism.

The danger that this poses to the moral and political argument is enormous. Species-distinctions, Locke says in the *Essay*, are just human conventions. But the special status of humanity and the equality of all members of the human species is asserted in the *Two Treatises* as a matter of natural law. It is fundamental to the whole basis on which Locke proposes to examine and evaluate human conventions. Locke is not a pragmatist, like (say) Richard Rorty, proposing to keep a whole moral system afloat by using some conventional commitments to evaluate others.[13]

---

[12] As John Dunn puts it, Locke's premise is "the normative creaturely equality of all members of the human species" (Dunn, *Political Thought of John Locke*, p. 99).

[13] Cf. Rorty, "Solidarity or Objectivity."

His approach in the *Two Treatises* and in his other political writings is explicitly foundationalist, and the trouble with the argument about species in the *Essay* is that it appears to knock away the foundation on which Locke purports to be building.

III

The discussion about species and species-terms in the *Essay* is not just a matter of a few throwaway lines. It is a sustained discussion that goes on for about thirty pages.[14] Philosophers and epistemologists know this discussion very well; the individuation of species remains an important problem in biology and in the philosophy of biology, just as the general issue of natural kinds is a problem for metaphysics, philosophical logic, and the philosophy of science.[15] Students of Locke's political theory, on the other hand, have mostly ignored this discussion of species, as far as I can tell.[16] They have certainly said precious little about its implications for his theory of equality.

Why have they ignored it? My hunch is that they have failed to notice the difficulty it poses for the application of the equality principle because they have been taught by historians of the Cambridge school – in particular Peter Laslett and his followers – to assume that Locke's politics can and should be studied in more or less complete isolation from the rest of his philosophy. Two or three generations of students have been introduced to the relation between the *Two Treatises* and the *Essay Concerning Human Understanding* by Laslett's claim that "Locke is, perhaps, the least consistent of all the great philosophers, and pointing out the contradictions either within any of his works or between them is no difficult task."[17] The two books were published around the same time, but, in Laslett's view, "the literary continuity between them was about as slight as it could possibly be under such circumstances."[18] Certainly there is no way, he said, that the *Treatises* can be regarded as "an extension into the political field of the general philosophy of the *Essay* . . . The political argument is not presented as a part of a general philosophy, and does not seem to be intended to be read as such."[19] In this respect Locke's corpus is said to

---

[14] See Locke, *Essay*, Bk. III, Ch. 6.
[15] See, for example, Wilkerson, "Species, Essences and the Names of Natural Kinds"; Wilkerson, *Natural Kinds*; and Kitcher, "Species." See also the essays in Wilson (ed.), *Species: New Interdisciplinary Essays*. (I am grateful to Philip Kitcher for a helpful discussion of this literature.)
[16] The exception is Ruth Grant in *John Locke's Liberalism*, pp. 17–21 and 29–31.
[17] Laslett, "Introduction," p. 82.   [18] Ibid., p. 83.   [19] Ibid., pp. 83 and 85.

be quite different in form and tenor from the great philosophical systems of Hobbes, Leibniz, and Spinoza.

I think it is fair to say that this view is no longer as widely accepted among historians of ideas as it used to be. The actual evidence cited for Locke's having contradicted himself was always quite slight – an apparent inconsistency between the *Essay*'s rejection of innate practical principles and a throwaway line about murder in the *Second Treatise*[20] – a line which indicates at worst that Locke is just like most other people in dropping his intellectual standards when it comes to supporting capital punishment.[21] So *that* inconsistency may be superficial and purely verbal. However, the tension that I have mentioned – I am not yet saying that it's a contradiction – between Locke's reliance on the idea of species in the *Treatises* and his skepticism about the idea of species in the *Essay* – is really quite deep and quite disturbing.

Locke himself does not give us much hope that the two positions on species can be reconciled. Indeed, he shows little awareness in either work that they *need* to be reconciled. (I will mention one exceptional passage in the *Essay*, a little later in this chapter.)[22] Moreover, the problem we face is not merely that Locke talks uncritically about species in the *Two Treatises of Government* in a way that the *Essay* appears to undercut; Locke also concedes things in the *Two Treatises* which, when aligned with the nominalist critique of species in the *Essay*, place very severe limits on what he can possibly sustain in the way of a working premise about human equality for the purposes of political theory. We must remember that Locke in his politics was having to argue against the position – which was an active position in his day, even if it is not in ours – that there are different kinds of human being, and they occupy different positions in a hierarchy of authority. Now, if he concedes (as he does) that different humans have different abilities and characteristics – some

---

[20] "And Cain was so fully convinced, that every one had a right to destroy such a criminal, that after the murder of his brother, he cries out, Every one that findeth me, shall slay me; so plain was it writ in the hearts of all mankind" (2nd T: 11).

[21] If Ian Harris is right (Harris, *Mind of John Locke*, p. 31) the *Second Treatise* passage may not be inconsistent with Locke's anti-innatism at all. It depends how we understand "writ in the hearts." Can our reason or our understanding write things in our hearts as the upshot or conclusion of our reasoning?

[22] The exceptional passage is the following: "Nor let any one object, that the names of substances are often to be made use of in morality . . . from which will arise obscurity. For, as to substances, when concerned in moral discourses, their divers natures are not so much inquired into as supposed: e.g. when we say that man is subject to law, we mean nothing by man but a corporeal rational creature: what the real essence or other qualities of that creature are in this case is no way considered" (E: 3.11.16).

with "*Excellency*" and some with deficiencies "*of Parts or Merit*" (2nd T: 54) –
then it looks as though he's going to need some very strong notion that *all
these different types of human nevertheless belong ultimately to the same special species*,
in order to avoid embracing the inference to a natural human hierarchy.
And that's just what the argument about species and species-terms in the
Essay appears to deny him.

So I guess it is understandable that readers who come up against this
difficulty are tempted to take advantage of the myth of a disjunction
between Locke the philosopher and Locke the political pamphleteer,
and to try and immunize the premises of the political account against
the contagion of Locke's philosophical skepticism about species. But I
wish it weren't done so impulsively, so unthinkingly. When I mention the
difficulty I have outlined to historians of ideas of the Cambridge school,
they tend to say quickly that of course they are not surprised (though they
never noticed the difficulty themselves, for it requires reading more than
the first few chapters of the *Essay Concerning Human Understanding*). And
now, having had it drawn to their attention, they say they just *know* in
advance that it's an irresolvable contradiction; they say there's no point
considering how the difficulty might be overcome (and it might be a sin
against historical propriety to even try to overcome it).

Well, I believe they are wrong on both counts. The difficulty ought to
have been noticed earlier, and the only reason it wasn't was the domi-
nance of the view that the detailed arguments of the *Essay* are irrelevant
to Locke's political theory. I shall try to show that it *is* worth spending
time exploring how to overcome it. I must warn the reader, though, that
the exploration is quite complicated; it is not just a matter of noticing the
difficulty and then winching down God to resolve it. But, for all its difficulty, the endeavor is worthwhile as an act of faith in the unity of Locke's
thought. It is also worthwhile as a matter of moral necessity for us. For
even if it were true (which it is not) that Locke kept his politics insulated
from his philosophy, we are not committed in our politics to any such
wall of separation. We want to know what impact a change in our current
thinking about species would have on our moral and political thinking
about humanity and equality. The difficulty about species that Locke
faces up to is a prototype of a difficulty that might face us. How would
we sustain (how should we explicate) our egalitarianism without support from any clear conception of species-differences? I think these are
real questions for anyone who thinks about equality, whether they would
rather keep their philosophy of biology and their political theory in different compartments or not.

IV

The theme of a division of the animal world into species and ranks of species is developed in detail in paragraph 25 of the *First Treatise*. There Locke sets out the ranking of species that he says can be found in chapter 1 of Genesis. "[I]n the Creation of the brute Inhabitants of the Earth, [God] first speaks of them all under one General Name, of *Living Creatures*, and then afterwards divides them into three ranks," namely cattle (or domesticable animals), wild beasts, and reptiles (1st T: 25). Locke also notes a second, slightly different division. He says God divided "the Irrational Animals of the World . . . into three kinds, from the places of their Habitation, viz. *Fishes of the Sea*, *Fowls of the Air*, and *Living Creatures of the Earth*, and these again into *Cattle*, *Wild Beasts*, and *Reptils*" (1st T: 26). His immediate aim in these passages is to establish that neither by God's grant of dominion to Adam and Eve, nor by God's grant of dominion and use to Noah and his sons, is there anything about the subordination of some human beings to other human beings. Everything there is about subordination concerns the relation of men in general to members of the other animal species. The discussion culminates in the great passage I mentioned in Chapter 2 (page 25), where Locke talks about God's decision to "make a Species of Creatures, that should have Dominion over the other Species of this Terrestrial Globe" (1st T: 30). In Chapter 2 we read this as an insistence by Locke that the donation was to Eve as much as to Adam. In the present chapter, however, we are considering the importance that Locke attaches to the dividing line between human and non-human species: since we humans all belong to "the same species and rank . . . there cannot be supposed any such *Subordination* among us . . . as if we were made for one anothers uses, as the inferior ranks of Creatures are for ours."[23]

This conception of a ranking of species is usually interpreted in a way that makes it consonant with the standard theological reading of Locke's politics which John Dunn pioneered in the late 1960s. Commentators assume that Locke, as a child of his times, must have believed in something like Lovejoy's "Great Chain of Being."[24] Dunn begins his chapter

[23] Notice, by the way, that it is not the fact that we are God's workmanship which matters here; the lower animals are His workmanship too. Some of the creatures that God has created *may* legitimately be dominated and exploited by others of his creatures; that's fine. The crucial thing is that such domination and exploitation may not legitimately take place as between members of the human species. The members of that species in particular are singled out because they, in contrast to the members of the other species, are created not just by, but in the image of, God.

[24] In fact, Lovejoy himself made this mistake in *The Great Chain of Being*, pp. 228–9. For a critique see Uzgalis, "The Anti-Essential Locke."

"The Premises of the Argument" with a paraphrase of Locke: "The entire cosmos is the work of God. He created every part of it...with a defined relationship to the purpose of the whole. It is an ordered hierarchy, a 'great chain of being', in which every species has its station, its rank."[25] It is partly on account of *this* aspect of Locke's thought that John Dunn continues to wonder whether the Lockean theory of rights is of anything other than antiquarian interest to us today who accept no such cosmic hierarchy, no such divine-settled architecture or order.[26] If there is anything modern in Locke's account, it is only – as Kirsty McClure has pointed out – Locke's insistence that cosmic hierarchy is interrupted at the boundaries of the human species, and flattened out within those boundaries.[27] But for that very reason, she insists that Locke's human egalitarianism depends crucially on the clarity and intelligibility of the species-boundaries. And that – she assumes – is what Locke's creationism and his adherence to the "great chain of being" idea supply. Moreover, if I may be a little mischievous for a moment, there's a sense in which the historians *need* there to be something like the great chain of being as an unfamiliar axiom of Locke's politics, in order to underwrite the strangeness and thus the philosophical opacity of Locke's work, so far as modern readers are concerned. So long as Locke is interpreted as resting his system on scripturally designated ranks of species in some eternal hierarchy, the historians will never be out of a job. But what I want to explore is the possibility that this antique cosmological apparatus is in fact quite shaky within the context of Locke's own thinking, and shaky in a way that is not at all strange or unfamiliar to us in our *post*-modern hesitations and uncertainties.

v

For Locke's uncertainty, we turn to the *Essay Concerning Human Understanding*. What Locke says there about species is almost entirely at odds with the conception of species-hierarchy that the great chain of being is traditionally thought to involve. It is true that, in the *Essay*, Locke envisages a series of created beings, ascending from the lowest entity to the highest, and maybe "far more *Species* of Creatures above us, than there

---

[25] Dunn, *Political Thought of John Locke*, p. 87; see also Parry, *John Locke*, pp. 20–1. See also McClure, *Judging Rights*, pp. 29 and 76 for the idea of a theologically based "architecture of order" in Locke's work.

[26] For Dunn's views on what is dead in Locke's political theory, see Dunn, "What is Living and What is Dead," esp. pp. 14–15.

[27] McClure, *Judging Rights*, pp. 28 ff.

are beneath" (E: 3.6.12). So the slope is certainly there. But it ascends up from us "by gentle degrees" (E: 3.6.12), not with any sharp punctuation. Indeed, in the same passage Locke insists several times that this chain of being forms a continuous series of entities, rather than a clearly divided series of species:

[I]n all the visible corporeal World, we see no Chasms, or gaps. All . . . down from us, the descent is by easy steps, and a continued series of Things, that in each remove, differ very little one from the other. There are Fishes that have Wings, and are not Strangers to the airy Region: and there are some Birds, that are Inhabitants of the Water; whose Blood is cold as Fishes, and their Flesh so like in taste, that the scrupulous are allow'd them on Fish-days. There are Animals so near of kin both to Birds and Beasts, that they are in the middle between both: Amphibious Animals link the Terrestrial and Aquatique together; Seals live at Land and at Sea, and Porpoises have the warm Blood and Entrails of a Hog; not to mention what is confidently reported of Mermaids, or Sea-men. There are some brutes, that seem to have as much Knowledge and Reason, as some that are called Men: and the Animal and Vegetable Kingdoms, are so nearly join'd, that if you will take the lowest of one, and the highest of the other, there will scarce be perceived any great difference between them; and so on, till we come to the lowest and the most inorganical parts of Matter, we shall find every-where that the several *Species* are linked together, and differ but in almost insensible degrees. (E: 3.6.12)

That's the ontological background according to the *Essay*: different beings, higher and lower beings, but "no Chasms, or gaps" between beings of various *kinds*.

We classify them of course. We language-users have no choice but to confront this continuum with *words*.[28] And since "we have need of general Words" all we can do is, to collect such a number of simple ideas "as by Examination, we find to be united together in Things existing, and thereof to make one complex *Idea*" (E: 3.6.21), and associate them with a sound or sign. "[*T*]he Species of Things to us are nothing but the ranking them under distinct Names, according to the complex Ideas in us" (E: 3.6.8). And Locke does not deny that there are real resemblances: "Nature makes many particular Things, which do agree one with another, in many sensible Qualities, and probably too, in their internal frame and Constitution" (E: 3.6.36). But so far reality is established only at the level of resemblances

---

[28] "[I]t is beyond the Power of humane Capacity to frame and retain distinct *Ideas* of all the particular Things we meet with: every Bird, and Beast Men saw; every Tree, and Plant, that affected the Senses, could not find a place in the most capacious Understanding . . . *Secondly,* If it were possible, it would be useless; because . . . men would in vain heap up Names of particular Things, that would not serve them to communicate their Thoughts" (E: 3.3.2–3).

and differences between particular entities – a resemblance between this particular cat and that particular cat, and a difference between this particular cat and that particular dog. Nothing in nature shows that these resemblances and differences categorize themselves into essences of species. In other words, Locke says that when we move beyond the identification of resemblances among particulars, there is no reason to think that our tendency to organize resemblances into clusters under the auspices of general species-terms reflects anything other than our propensity as language-users to make use of general words. In relation to the use of such general words for kinds or species, we can talk if we like about nominal essences. But that's all they are; as the term "nominal essences" suggests, they are nothing but projections onto nature of our own linguistic habits.

Is the position saved by what Locke says in the *Essay* about "real" essences (as opposed to nominal essences)? What Locke says is this:

> It is true, I have often mentioned *a real Essence*, distinct in Substances from those abstract Ideas of them, which I call their *nominal Essence*. By this *real Essence*, I mean, that real constitution of any Thing, which is the foundation of all those Properties, that are combined in, and are constantly found to co-exist with the *nominal Essence*. (E: 3.6.6)

I think this offers little in the way of assistance for our use of the concept *species* in moral and political theory. We shall see in a moment that Locke's account of real essences is far from straightforward. To the extent that any consistent position emerges in the *Essay*, I believe it is basically a pragmatic one: there can be improvements in our taxonomy – our classifications become less confusing, more useful, or whatever – and the term "real essence" may connote a regulatory ideal, the idea of a sort of limit-case, so far as such improvements are concerned. Now, so long as the basic orientation of such improvement is pragmatic rather than objective, the associated idea of real essence is of no use for politics or morality. The natural law foundations of the political theory are supposed to provide a basis for judging and evaluating the various projects and purposes that people might embark on so far as the classification of human beings is concerned. The opening paragraphs of the *Second Treatise* seem to indicate that the real essence of man or humanity provides a basis for reproaching certain otherwise plausible theories of natural hierarchy. But if the concept *real essence* is expressive of nothing more than the pragmatic idea of an improvement in our nominal classifications, then it cannot do this work. The pragmatic idea of an improvement in our nominal classifications is entirely relative to our purposes in making such classifications; it cannot be used as a basis for judging those purposes.

With this in mind, let's consider what the *Essay Concerning Human Understanding* actually says about real essences. It's a long and complicated discussion,[29] and the gist of Locke's position has to be gathered from a number of scattered passages. It is certainly true that he envisages the possibility of better or worse classifications, more or less skillful observations, and more or less sophisticated correlations between complexes of ideas and an ordered terminology. The usefulness of a given set of nominal essences, he says, "*depends upon the Various Care, Industry, or Fancy of him that makes it*" (E: 3.6.29). We can change and improve our classification of resemblances. We are not just saddled with the products of linguistic history or linguistic stipulation.[30] For example, Locke suggests that resemblances of internal structure are likely to prove scientifically more fertile than the outward resemblances that initially strike us as interesting, because in almost all cases the former – "that Constitution of the parts of Matter, on which these qualities and their union depend" (E: 3.6.6) – seems to explain the latter, rather than the other way round. But because "Languages, in all Countries, have been established long before Sciences" (E: 3.6.25), our nominal associations are invariably between words and *external* similarities – "*obvious appearances*," as Locke puts it – rather than anything science could reveal about the internal constitution of things. So there is definitely room for improvement, and it is worth examining more closely the things we have ranked together under various nominal species-terms. Such examination may well reveal that "many of the Individuals that are ranked into one Sort, called by one common Name, and so received as being of one *Species*, have yet Qualities, depending on their real Constitutions, as far different one from another as from others from which they are accounted to differ *specifically*" (E: 3.6.8).[31] This may lead us to subdivide the class,

---

[29] As Michael Ayers points out, Locke seems to "recognize *both* that there is always something arbitrary about the choice of the nominal essence *and* that it can be done well or badly" (Ayers, *Locke*, p. 75).

[30] Thus Boyd in "Homeostasis, Species, and Higher Taxa," p. 174, may be wrong to attribute to Locke the view "that kinds are established by a sort of *unicameral* linguistic legislation" – people just choosing to impose terms on the world – as opposed to "bicameral legislation, in which the (causal structure of the) world plays a heavy legislative role."

[31] Locke talks, for example, of the "sad Experience" of chemists, vainly searching for qualities in one parcel of a substance which they have found in others of the same name: "For, though they are Bodies of the same *Species*, having the same nominal *Essence*, under the same Name, yet do they often, upon severe ways of examination, betray Qualities so different one from another, as to frustrate the Expectation and Labour of very wary Chymists" (E: 3.6.8).

with a new set of nominal essences, or perhaps even to reorganize our taxonomy on a completely different basis.[32]

It is pretty clear, though, from the language Locke uses, that this process is oriented entirely to pragmatic amelioration of our ability to correlate and explain phenomena. And, as I said, "real essence" serves in his discussion as little more than the limit-idea of such amelioration. For any given set of nominal essences, we are to act on the supposition that it might be improved, and to that extent the set of nominal essences is (so to speak) haunted by the idea of a set of real essences, an idea expressive of our refusal to rest content with the taxonomy we happen to have at any given time. There is, accordingly, no question of our saying, "At last, we have hold of the real essence of sulphur or the real essence of man; now we can act on the basis of that, rather than on the basis of some (nominal) approximation to the real essence." Real essence doesn't work like that in Locke.

Sometimes Locke presents the unavailability to us of objective real essences as a reflection of the limitations on our knowledge. He says "I would fain know why a shock[33] and a hound are not as distinct species as a spaniel and an elephant" and "so it must remain till somebody can show us" a difference of kind as between the two differences (E: 3.6.38). He suggests that the reason we are unable to rank, sort, and denominate things "by their *real Essences* [is] because we know them not" (E: 3.6.9).

The Workmanship of the All-wise, and Powerful God, in the great Fabrick of the Universe, and every part thereof . . . exceeds the Capacity and Comprehension of the most inquisitive and intelligent Man . . . Therefore we in vain pretend to range Things into sorts, and dispose them into certain Classes, under Names, by their *real Essences*, that are so far from our discovery or comprehension. A blind Man may as soon sort Things by Their Colours . . . (E: 3.6.9)

That's what he says some of the time. But most of the time what he says indicates that we should not characterize our ignorance in this regard as though there *were* real species, only ones to which we do not have epistemic access. He says that "the *supposition of Essences, that cannot be known*; and the making of them nevertheless to be that, which distinguishes the Species of Things, *is so wholly useless*, and unserviceable to any part of our Knowledge, that that alone were sufficient to make us lay it by" (E: 3.3.17). In fact, our talk of real essences is not backed up by any independent assurance "that Nature, in the production of Things,

---

[32] Bear in mind that Locke wrote about the difficulty of species-distinctions more than seventy years before Carl Linnaeus published his most famous work, *Philosophia Botanica*, in 1751.

[33] A shock is a dog with floppy hair, like a spaniel.

always designs them to partake of certain regulated established essences"
(E: 3.6.14.) And without such an assurance, it is simply a distraction. Even
if we were to succeed in examining the inner workings of things scientifically, there's no particular reason to think that we will find different
kinds of inner workings – with clear boundaries, "gaps, and Chasms" –
at that level either. We may find resemblances, but, as Michael Ayers
emphasizes several times in his excellent account of Locke on species,
"[r]esemblances do not draw lines."[34]

And there are also logical difficulties in the quest for real essences.
Given the importance of nominal essences to language-users like us,
it is not clear what arriving at real essences would amount to. The
very inquiry is necessarily bound up with the characteristics of our own
ideas and associations: "what difference in the real internal Constitution
makes a specifick difference, it is in vain to enquire; whilst *our measures
of Species* be, as they *are, only our abstract* Ideas" (E: 3.6.22). Even on the
most optimistic assumptions, what we use the term "real essence" to
refer to is still going to be an arbitrary matter of which resemblances –
but now which *internal* resemblances – strike us as worth marking with
words.[35] Locke seems to suggest that the idea of real essence is tied to
the idea of nominal essence as the idea of cause is tied to the idea of
effect: he says the real essence is "the foundation of all those Properties, that are combined in, and are constantly found to co-exist with the
nominal Essence" (E: 3.6.6). This seems to hold the real essence hostage
to the arbitrariness of the nominal essence (as though the real essence
of man might have to include the internal cause of his being without
feathers).

VI

In general, we seem to have here a pretty thorough-going anti-realism,
so far as species are concerned. It is evident, says Locke, "that *Men make
sorts of Things*. For it being different Essences alone, that make different
Species, 'tis plain that they who make those abstract *Ideas* which are the
nominal Essences do thereby make the *Species*, or sort" (E: 3.6.35). There
are, as I reported, genuine resemblances, on Locke's account. But they
do not cluster naturally into anything equivalent to our differentiations
of natural kinds. "[*T*]*he boundaries of the Species . . . are made by Men*; since
the Essences of the *Species*, distinguished by different Names, are . . . of
Man's making" (E: 3.6.37). And Locke does not flinch from applying this

---

[34] Ayers, *Locke*, p. 68. See also Grant, *John Locke's Liberalism*, p. 17.   [35] See ibid., pp. 464–5.

skepticism about species to the species-word to which he attaches such importance in the *Two Treatises of Government* – "that which of all others we are the most intimately acquainted with" (E: 3.6.26), the species-word "man" or "human." The discussion of "man" is pervasive in the *Essay*'s chapter on species-terms, and each of the moves that I have outlined in the previous section is applied cheerfully to that term in particular.

Let's begin with the point that the putative boundaries between humans and other animals are blurred in a number of ways. Fetuses are sometimes oddly shaped, familiarly shaped humans often vary enormously in their rational abilities, some allegedly non-human animals have been rumored to have the power of speech, humans have been known to interbreed with apes (Locke alleges), and so on:

> There are Creatures in the World, that have shapes like ours, but are hairy, and want Language, and Reason. There are Naturals amongst us, that have perfectly our shape, but want Reason, and some of them Language too. There are Creatures, as 'tis said, (*sit fides penes authorem*, but there appears no contradiction that there should be such), that, with Language and Reason and a shape in other Things agreeing with ours, have hairy Tails; others where the Males have no Beards, and others where the Females have. (E: 3.6.22)

What are we to make of this array? The fact is, says Locke, that you are likely to get disagreement among people as to how to draw the boundaries of the species: "[I]f several Men were to be asked, concerning some odly shaped *Foetus*, as soon as born, whether it were a Man, or no, 'tis past doubt, one should meet with different Answers" (E: 3.6.27). This could not happen, he says, if our species-conceptions "were exactly copied from precise Boundaries Set by Nature" (E: 3.6.27).

For most of us, he says, "the Idea in our *Minds*, of which the Sound Man in our Mouths is the Sign, is nothing else but of an Animal of such a certain Form" (E: 2.27.8), based on the external shape, size, appearance, and mobility of the human frame.[36]

> I think I may be confident, that, whoever should see a Creature of his own Shape . . . though it had no more reason all its Life, than a *Cat* or a *Parrot*, would call him still a *Man*; or whoever should hear a *Cat* or a *Parrot* discourse, reason, and philosophize, would call or think it nothing but a *Cat* or a *Parrot*; and say, the one was a dull irrational *Man*, and the other a very intelligent rational *Parrot*. (E: 2.27.8).

---

[36] Elsewhere, however, Locke says that mere static bodily form simply cannot be the sole basis of our concept *man*: "That the body is the grosse structure of a man which may be seen and handled I think will not be questioned. But these solid sensible parts thus put together are noe more a man than Polinchinelle is a man. Sense and motion are as necessary to the being of a man as bulke and shape" (P&N: ii.677).

Some people, he concedes, may add a criterion of rationality: they understand by "man" not just a featherless biped, but a rational animal. But then what we have are two rival classifications – so that, as Locke says in the *Essay*, the same individual will be a true man to the one classifier which is not so to the other (E: 3.6.26)[37] – and nothing by which the rivalry can be judged. Maybe an account of the insides of the beings in question would make us judge differently: "No body will doubt, that the Wheels, or Springs (if I may so say) within, are different in a rational Man, and a changeling" (E:3.6.39). We can certainly imagine that more detailed inquiry would enhance our knowledge and we can postulate for ourselves the limit-idea of such knowledge:

[H]ad we such a Knowledge of That Constitution of *Man*, from which his Faculties of Moving, Sensation, and Reasoning, and other Powers flow; and on which his so regular shape depends, as 'tis possible Angels have, and 'tis certain his Maker has, we should have a quite other *Idea* of his *Essence*, than what now is contained in our Definition of that *Species*, be it what it will: and our *Idea* of any individual *Man* would be as far different from what it is now, as is his, who knows all the Springs and Wheels and other contrivances within, of the famous Clock at *Strasburg*, from that which a gazing Country-man has of it, who barely sees the motion of the Hand, and hears the Clock strike, and observes only some of the outward appearances. (E: 3.6.3)

But again, which internal features caught our attention would be a matter of which were inherently interesting to us, or else which external appearances we wanted to understand the causality of. Either way, it is our interests that would dictate what revisions we made in (what we called) the essence of man.[38] Our views about real essences would not be the source of our interests, nor would they be capable of regulating them.

As he considers the implications of this skepticism in the *Essay*, Locke does not present them as confined to the arena of philosophical speculation or biological taxonomy. "Who would undertake to resolve," he asks, "what *Species* that Monster was of, which is mentioned by *Licetus*

---

[37] "It could not possibly be that the abstract *Idea*, to which the name *Man* is given, should be different in several Men, if it were of Nature's making; and that to one it should be *Animal rationale*, and to another, *Animal implume bipes latis unguibus*. He that annexes the name *Man*, to a complex *Idea*, made up of Sense and spontaneous Motion, join'd to a Body of such a shape, has thereby one Essence of the *Species Man*: And he that, upon further examination, adds rationality, has another Essence of the *Species* he calls *Man*" (E: 3.6.26).

[38] "But whether one or both these differences be essential or specifical, is only to be known to us by their agreement, or disagreement with the complex *Idea* that the name *Man* stands for: For by that alone can it be determined whether one, or both, or neither of those be a Man, or no" (E: 3.6.39).

(*lib*. i. *c*. 3), with a Man's Head and Hog's Body?...Had the upper part, to the middle, been of humane shape, and all below Swine; Had it been Murther to destroy it?" (E: 3.6.27). Similarly, when he talks about fetal monstrosities, Locke says that there is a question about whether the entity is entitled to baptism – that is, to the spiritual status of humanity.

[N]one of the Definitions of the word *Man*, which we yet have ... are so perfect and exact as to satisfy a considerate inquisitive Person; much less to obtain a general Consent, and to be that which men would every where stick by, in the Decision of Cases, and determining of Life and Death, Baptism or No Baptism, in Productions that might happen. (E: 3.6.27)

And of course spiritual status is exactly what's at stake in the opening paragraphs of the *Second Treatise*. Once again, I think this shows the absurdity of the Laslett suggestion that we have, on the one hand, Locke the philosopher (uninterested in normative implications) and, on the other hand, Locke the political theorist (uninterested in philosophy). The *Essay* shows us someone exercised by this difficulty about species wearing both his hats.[39]

Let us turn, then, to the implications for the moral and political philosophy. On the face of it, the implications of Locke's skepticism about species are pretty serious. If the boundaries of species are made by men and not given by our Creator in the nature of things, and if the human conventions that establish those boundaries are contestable and contested, then, as Locke says, "the same individual will be a true *Man* to the one [party], which is not so to the other" (E: 3.6.26). On the one hand, we have a moral theory premised on claims such as this – "there [is] nothing more evident, than that Creatures of the same species ... should also be equal one amongst another without Subordination or Subjection" (2nd T: 4) – and this – "there cannot be supposed any such *Subordination* among us, that may Authorize us to destroy one another, as if we were made for one anothers uses, as the inferior ranks of Creatures are for ours" (2nd T: 6). On the other hand, we have a contestable definition of which creatures get the benefit of this status and which don't. And Locke's comment in Book IV of the *Essay*, on how an English child might "prove" that *a negro is not a man*, is really quite disconcerting in

---

[39] See also Grant, *John Locke's Liberalism*, p. 29: "Locke shows both the difficulty of defining species of substances, particularly the human species, and the legislative or political problems that may result from this difficulty in his repeated discussion of changelings and monsters and how they ought to be treated."

this regard.[40] One would have thought it was the task of Locke's theory of natural law to resolve such disputes, and tell us whether the negro in Book IV of the *Essay* ought to get the benefit of the *Second Treatise* doctrine of equality. If he is supposed to get the benefit of it, then the natural law theory would provide a basis for criticizing and overthrowing any conventions or nominal definitions that treat him as sub-human. But it turns out that the natural law theory uses terms (like "species") that are defined by their conventional content. Far from affording a basis for the evaluation of our conventions, Locke's natural law premises seem to be at the mercy of them.

I guess it might be thought that by rejecting essentialism, Locke is undercutting those theories of human inequality that depend on "essentializing" superficial characteristics like skin color or sex organs. Kathy Squadrito says, for example, that Locke's rejection of external form as real essence means that he doesn't really think there is an important difference between men and women.[41] But this is naive. Quite apart from the question of whether sex-differences are more than skin deep, the point about Locke's anti-essentialism is that it leaves the field wide open for anyone to draw the boundaries of humanity wherever he likes. This looks benign against the background of some tacit assumption that the default position is a set of very generous boundaries, and that it is only essentialism – i.e. the drawing of essentialist lines – within those boundaries that is to be discredited. But Locke's skepticism really does discredit the whole enterprise. It leaves him with no naturalistic basis whatsoever for distinguishing those creatures one is allowed to hunt, exploit, enslave, or eat from those that must not be treated in any of these ways. Maybe this should boost the morale of anti-speciesist defenders of animal rights; but it is hardly calculated to cheer those who think there is something special about humans and human equality.

In any case, even if essentialism is seen by some as a source of evil, so that they are cheered by its demolition,[42] we need to remember that

---

[40] E: 4.7.16: "[A] Child having framed the *Idea* of a *Man*, it is probable that his *Idea* is just like that Picture, which the Painter makes of the visible Appearances joyned together; and such a Complication of *Ideas* together in his Understanding makes up the single complex *Idea* which he calls *Man*, whereof White or Flesh-colour in *England* being one, the Child can demonstrate to you, that *a Negro Is Not a Man*, because White-colour was one of the constant simple *Ideas* of the complex *Idea* he calls *Man*."

[41] Squadrito, "Locke on the Equality of the Sexes," p. 9.

[42] I have in mind the use of "essentialism" as a pejorative term in critical race theory and feminist jurisprudence. See, for example, Harris, "Race and Essentialism in Feminist Legal Theory," and Wong, "The Anti-essentialism versus Essentialism Debate."

essentialism is not the only basis on which people discriminate against and ill-treat one another. For consider again the argument developed in Chapter 2. Locke bases a difference in authority upon (what he believes is) a natural difference in ability between men and women. We reproached that on the grounds that Locke is also supposed to have committed himself to a fundamental principle of equality: members of the same species are naturally equal in authority, whatever the other differences between them. But now that species-based notion has collapsed, and there is nothing with which to reproach Locke's sexism. We may of course contest his claim about the particular difference; and we do. Still it is undeniable that there are *some* differences of *"Excellency of Parts and Merit"* among the individuals we regard as human; and without the natural-law notion of species, Locke seems to have deprived himself of the resource he needs to limit what we make of these differences in social and political life.[43]

So there's the difficulty. My strategy in this chapter is to show the indispensability for Locke's theory of equality of the religious aspect of his argument in paragraph 6 of the *Second Treatise*. But we can't just winch down the religious stuff – *deus ex machina* – whenever it suits us. It is important to see that, at the stage of the argument we have reached, neither God nor scripture can supply the deficiency of science, so far as the species-extension of Locke's principle of equality is concerned. Divine command gives rise to the problem; divine command cannot solve it. The species-difficulty arises because even if God *has* announced that all humans are created equal and commanded us to treat them as such, we still face the problem of defining the class of beings, the species-members, who are supposed to get the benefit of that commandment.

Let me develop this a little further. In biblical revelation, the only direct intimation of a basis for the distinction of the human species is descent from Adam. However, Locke is very doubtful whether that can do the work. His doubts arise, first, from the possibility of cross-overs between humans and other animals:

---

[43] I think H. M. Bracken states the position correctly in "Essence, Accident and Race," p. 84:

> Locke's discussion of substance constitutes an attack on the model of essential properties... It then becomes possible to treat any or no property as essential. Within the revised framework, it becomes much more difficult to distinguish men from the other animals. The older model had the advantage of trying to formulate what was essential to man. In so doing it provided a modest conceptual barrier to treating race, colours, religion, or sex as other than accidental.

> Whether this is the key (as Bracken thinks it is) to Locke's views on slavery and the exclusion of Catholics is, however, another matter; for these issues, see below, Chapters 7 and 8. (I am grateful to Robert Gooding-Williams for this reference.)

Nor let any one say, that the power of propagation in animals by the mixture of Male and Female . . . keeps the supposed real *Species* distinct and entire . . . for if History lie not, women have conceived by Drills;[44] and what real *Species*, by that measure, such a Production will be in Nature, will be a new Question; and we have Reason to think this is not impossible. . . . I once saw a Creature, that was the issue of a Cat and a Rat, and had the plain Marks of both about it; wherein Nature appeared to have followed the Pattern of neither sort alone, but to have jumbled them both together. (E: 3.6.23)

Secondly, they arise from the fact that monsters sometimes emerge even from the pure Adamic line:

how far Men determine of the sorts of Animals, rather by their Shape, than Descent, is very visible; since it has been more than once debated, whether several humane *Foetus* should be preserved, or received to Baptism or no, only because of the difference of their outward Configuration, from the ordinary Make of Children, without knowing whether they were not as capable of Reason, as Infants cast in another Mould. (E: 3.6.26)

Anyway, a purely genealogical basis for equality and inequality would be practically inadequate. Even for scientific purposes it would be unsatisfactory: "[I]f the *Species* of Animals and Plants are to be distinguished only by propagation, must I go to the *Indies* to see the Sire and Dam of the one, and the Plant from which the Seed was gather'd that produced the other, to know whether this be a Tiger or that Tea?" (E: 3.6.23). Locke says in his political philosophy that any basis for inequality must be *evident*, *clear*, and *manifest*.[45] The point is connected with his insistence towards the end of the *First Treatise* that one cannot obey *the idea* of an authority (1st T: 81). One needs to have some ready and reliable way of identifying who, in particular, the authority is. It's a point Locke makes again and again:

The great Question which in all Ages has disturbed Mankind, and brought on them the greatest part of those Mischiefs which have ruin'd Cities, depopulated Countries, and disordered the Peace of the World, has been, Not whether there be Power in the World, nor whence it came, but who should have it . . . For if this remain disputable, all the rest will be to very little purpose. (1st T: 106)[46]

A theory of natural political inequality is no good "if there be no Marks to know him by, and distinguish him, that hath Right to Rule from other

---

[44] A kind of ape, like a mandrill.
[45] Thus he qualifies his account of natural equality as follows: "unless the Lord and Master of them all should, by any *manifest Declaration* of His Will, set one above another, and confer on him, by an *evident and clear appointment, an undoubted Right* to Dominion and Sovereignty" (2nd T: 6, my emphasis).
[46] See also 1st T: 81–4, 104–6, and 119–28.

men" (1st T: 81). It's not just a matter of identification, it is also a matter of
settling men's consciences and reconciling them to their subordination.[47]
And exactly the same applies to a principle of equality. One's allegiance
to the principle of human equality is as nothing until one has a way of
delineating who the putative equals are.

VII

So what is to be done? I think that in order to make Locke's account of
equality in the *Two Treatises* consistent with his discussion in Book III of the
Essay, we have to forget about real essences, and abandon the emphasis
on species altogether. I think we should focus instead on what Locke *is*
prepared to concede – namely, real resemblances between particulars:
"Nature makes many particular things, which do agree one with another
in many sensible qualities" (E: 3.6.36).[48] We have to make do with that.
We must ask which resemblances are actually doing the crucial work
in Locke's account of equality, whether they afford a basis for a natural
kind or not. That will give us his definition of humanity, at least for moral
purposes.

What would the Lockean doctrine of equality look like if we ap-
proached it in this spirit? Well, if we read out any reference to species and
focus only on characteristics, the crucial passages from the beginning of
the *Second Treatise* read as follows:

[T]here [is] nothing more evident than that Creatures . . . promiscuously born to
all the same advantages of Nature, and the use of the same faculties, should also
be equal one amongst another without Subordination or Subjection . . . [B]eing
furnished with like Faculties . . . there cannot be supposed any such *Subordination*
among us, that may Authorize us to destroy one another, as if we were made
for one anothers uses, as . . . creatures [who do not share such faculties] are for
ours. (2nd T: 4 and 6)

---

[47] See 1st T: 10: "Our A— [Filmer] having placed such a mighty Power in *Adam*, and upon that
supposition, founded all Government, and all Power of Princes, it is reasonable to expect, that
he should have proved this with Arguments clear and evident, suitable to the weightiness of the
Cause. That since Men had nothing else left them, they might in Slavery have such undeniable
Proofs of its Necessity, that their Consciences might be convinced, and oblige them to Submit
peaceably to that Absolute Dominion, which their Governors had a Right to exercise over
them."

[48] The contrast between a real-resemblance approach and a real-essence approach is repeated in
E: 3.6.37: "I do not deny, but Nature, in the constant production of particular Beings, makes
them not always new and various, but very much alike and of kin to one another: But I think it
is nevertheless true, that *the boundaries of Species, whereby Men sort them, are made by Men*."

The emphasis now is on characteristics not on species or ranks of species. The domain of equality will simply be the domain of relevant similarity – i.e. the possession of faculties that can be regarded as the same or (relevantly) similar. The change may seem slight, except when you remember that the species-words "man" and "human" are no longer put to any work at all. Our heuristic now is emphatically *not* to survey the class of beings we are inclined to call human and *come up with* some likeness in their faculties that will, as it were, *do the job* so far as a basis for equality is concerned. Instead we have to start from the idea of a similarity among faculties that would be robust enough to sustain the sort of equality thesis Locke wants, and then actually *look and see* what class of creatures that applies to, i.e. what class of creatures comes within the range of the relevant similarity.

This is not just my bright idea for the reconstruction of Locke's position. It is what Locke himself says, in the only passage in the *Essay* where he ever really considers the implications for morality of his skepticism about species.[49] He says this:

Nor let any one object, that the names of Substances are often to be made use of in Morality... from which will arise Obscurity. For as to Substances, when concerned in moral Discourses, their divers Natures are not so much enquir'd into as supposed; v.g. when we say that *Man is subject to Law*: we mean nothing by *Man*, but a corporeal rational Creature: What the real Essence or other Qualities of that Creature are in this Case, is no way considered. And therefore, whether a Child or Changeling be a *Man*, in a physical Sense, may amongst the Naturalists be as disputable as it will, it concerns not at all the *moral Man*, as I may call him, which is this immovable unchangeable *Idea, a corporeal rational Being.* (E: 3.11.16)

And he says too that he is willing to follow this resemblance where it leads.

[W]ere there a Monkey, or any other Creature to be found, that had the use of Reason, to such a degree, as to be able to understand general Signs, and to deduce Consequences about general *Ideas*, he would no doubt be subject to Law, and, in that Sense, be a Man, how much soever he differ'd in Shape from others of that Name. (E: 3.11.16)

In other words, Locke is going to finesse the whole problem of biological taxonomy – all this "pudder ... about essences" (E: 3.5.16) – by focusing moral attention not on species, but on the complex property of *corporeal*

---

[49] This passage is also cited by Grant in *John Locke's Liberalism*, p. 30.

rationality. If the moralist can secure that idea (as the basis of a fundamentally relevant resemblance among certain individuals), then the detail of the issue about species can be left as a purely speculative problem for the naturalists and philosophers.[50]

Notice yet again how John Locke's care in this regard makes nonsense of the Laslett thesis that he wrote his philosophy wearing an entirely different hat, without regard to its implications for political theory. In the passage just cited, Locke is raising (and answering) questions about the implications of his philosophical position for morals and politics. He does not aim to seal off the one discussion from the other. By showing a philosophical difference between species and real resemblance, he puts himself in a position to explore in a philosophically rigorous way the possibility that morality requires only the latter, not the former.

VIII

Before going any further, I want to pause and consider the philosophical character of the position we have saddled Locke with. We began by noticing that he seemed to associate the principle of basic equality with membership of the human species. But species and species-membership turned out to be an unstable basis for equality, given Locke's skepticism about real essences. So now we have him associating basic equality, not with species-membership, but with a certain real resemblance – *corporeal rationality* – which a number of creatures of various shapes and sizes might possess, and in virtue of which they might loosely be termed "men" (in both a gender-neutral and non-speciesist sense).

In a moment we will turn to the difficulty of pinning down exactly the degree or type of rationality that Locke has in mind here. But first, I want to ask: what exactly is the relation supposed to be between possession of this property (however we end up defining it) and the normative consequences associated with equality? It's a question we could ask as well about the initial species-oriented position, or about rationality, or about any account of what we are supposed to have in common in terms of faculties and capabilities. All such accounts identify something like a descriptive property (or kind) or a cluster of properties, D; and from the fact that two given individuals both exhibit D, it is supposed to follow, as a normative or prescriptive matter, that they are to be treated as

---

[50] The argument is analogous to Locke's discussion of personal identity: we can't see our way through that issue either until we see that "Person," which looks like a species term, is in fact "a forensic" term, and works in a somewhat different way.

one another's equals. If we call this prescriptive consequence P, then we may ask: what exactly is the logical relation supposed to be between D and P?

Matthew Kramer has argued that Locke deserves to be chastised for jumping from the descriptive to the prescriptive, for what he calls an illicit *is/ought* cross-over.[51]

> From the fact that people were generally alike in strength and capabilities, he concluded that people were morally alike in that no one could properly enjoy nonconsensual control over fellow human agents . . . He focused on similarities among human agents in regard to key observable traits. And he drew from his observations a general norm for human life . . . Even if one adopts the view that people's overall capabilities were uniform by and large, one can certainly refuse to credit the deduction by which Locke held that people's rights and privileges of autonomy in their interactions with one another should have been uniform.[52]

But I don't think we should read Locke this way at all. I don't think he is attempting to commit the naturalistic fallacy by *inferring* our normative equality from some factual similarity. He says in the *Second Treatise* that the connection is "evident" (2nd T: 4), but that this is not the same as saying that it is logically implied is indicated by his going on to add that creatures who share the relevant descriptive property might still be unequal if God had so ordained it.

There is a difference between saying that the truth of a descriptive statement (*a* has property D) implies a prescription (*a* ought to be treated in manner P), and saying that P supervenes upon D. Supervenience implies that if *a* is to be treated differently from *b*, then there must be some other difference between *a* and *b* on which that prescriptive difference supervenes. This is arguably a feature of all moral discourse, not just of moral discourse that attempts to commit the naturalistic fallacy or to bridge the is/ought gap.[53] Of course, if P supervenes upon D, and there is no attempt to establish a relation of implication between them, then there must be some other way of explaining their relation. We must be able to say *why* the fact that *a* has D and *b* doesn't is a reason for treating *a* in accordance with P but not *b*. That explanation will normally be itself a moral proposition, and of course it too will need to be defended.

---

[51] Kramer, *John Locke and the Origins of Private Property*, p. 43.   [52] Ibid., pp. 38, 39, and 43.
[53] The best account of supervenience in the moral context remains Hare, *Language of Morals*, pp. 80 ff. But see also Blackburn, *Essays in Quasi-Realism*, pp. 130–48.

Now in the case of equality, we know that we are getting near the
rock-bottom of moral justification. It may well be that there is no other
explanation of the difference in the way it is appropriate to treat *a* and *b*
than an appeal to a principle "Anything which is D should be treated
in manner P." That principle may be regarded as self-evident (which,
again, is not the same as saying that D implies P). Or there may be
some further account of the relation between them, although, as I have
stressed throughout, that is unlikely to be an ordinary or mundane moral
account (for example a utilitarian account) since the P in question, in
the case of basic equality, is one of the fundamental presuppositions of
utilitarian reasoning.

There is more to say about all this, but I cannot pursue it now.[54] Just
one additional thought. If P is a principle of equality, then the supervenience relation is complicated. Strictly speaking, if *a* is to be treated the
same as *b*, supervenience does not require that there be any descriptive
property that they share. Supervenience *would* have to be invoked to explain why *b*, but not *c*, should be treated the same as *a*; there must be
some relevant difference between *b* and *c*. And if we say that *a* but not *c*
is to be treated the same as *b*, we will presumably point also to a relevant
difference between *a* and *c*. And it is likely that that difference will be the
same as the difference we thought relevant between *b* and *c*; so that it
will follow, indirectly, that *a* and *b* do have something in common. (But
these last two steps are not logically necessary, and it is not unimaginable
that one could defend a principle of equality without them.)

Elsewhere I have considered the possibility that one might defend a
principle of human equality, without prejudice to the question of whether
non-human animals are our equals. One says: humans, at any rate, are
one another's equals, whatever the relation between humans and other
primates or humans and dolphins, etc. But of course to do this, one has
to have some sense of who it is one is defending equality among: one
has to have at least an intuitive idea of the class of humans, and one
has to be able to explain or defend one's confidence that individuals
in this class, at any rate, are one another's equals. I suspect that that
is almost always going to involve pointing to some descriptive property
or cluster of properties that individuals in this class share, and that was
doubly important for John Locke, since, as we have seen, for philosophical
reasons he was not prepared to say that we are in possession of a secure
or intuitive grasp of the class of humans. So there will almost always be

---

[54] See Waldron, "Three Essays on Basic Equality."

some descriptive characteristic, D, in play here. Where this differs from the naturalism, however, for which Kramer wrongly chastises Locke, is that it is taken to be a further question why D should be relevant to equality.

IX

Let me return now to the main line of argument, and focus on the characteristic that seems to interest Locke. The key, he says, is *corporeal rationality*. That equality (and indeed the issue of humanity, in the moral sense) would depend upon rationality is a perfectly familiar position. It makes sense in relation to issues of authority and jurisdiction, which, on Locke's account, constitute the domain of basic equality. Our being regarded as one another's equals has to do with the way we can think, reason, and act. I will come back to this shortly, for it is the primary domain within which the equality claim has to be articulated and defended.

It is intriguing, though, that *corporeality* is also invoked – "*a corporeal rational Being*" (E: 3.11.16). Locke is not talking now about the corporeality of any particular form or species, but corporeality as such, which I take to mean the mere fact of embodiment. Why would this be? This little point, I believe, is quite unintelligible apart from the moral theology. Locke speculates that there are all sorts of rational beings in the cosmos – probably "more *Species* [!] of intelligent Creatures above us, than there are of sensible and material below us" (E: 3.6.12) – but there is an important distinction between the moral standing of those that are corporeal and those like angels, for instance, that are not. Though Locke was not a believer in original sin, I think he accepted that the moral circumstances – if you like, the moral predicament – of a rational being that was *embodied* are of quite a different order than the moral circumstances of a disembodied spirit.[55] (This is something like Kant's distinction in the *Groundwork* between beings whose reason infallibly determines their will, and beings whose will may vary from the requirements of reason – i.e. beings for whom imperatives are necessary.)[56]

Let us turn now to the rationality criterion. In the *First Treatise*, Locke said that God made man "in his own Image after his own Likeness . . . an intellectual Creature . . . For wherein soever else the *Image of God* consisted, the intellectual Nature was certainly a part of it, and belong'd to the whole Species" (1st T: 30). Unfortunately, however, *imago dei* does

---

55 See also the distinction in Locke's *Paraphrase* between *animal man* and *spiritual man* (P&N: i.177).
56 Kant, *Grounding*, pp. 23–4 (4: 412–13).

not solve the following problem. On the one hand, non-human animals have minds, at least to the extent of having and acting on ideas and combinations of ideas (E: 2.11.5–7). Since they are "not bare Machins (as some would have them), we cannot deny them to have some Reason" (E: 2.11.11). On the other hand, those we are accustomed to calling human vary enormously in their intellectual capacities. If the *imago dei* idea is supposed to help us, it has to help us make discriminations along this spectrum – not necessarily now in a way that is guided by some spurious concept of species – but discriminations nevertheless, which will enable us to resist the temptation to treat all beings who are less intellectually able than we are (or than we think we are) as something less than our equals, without giving up some version of the distinction Locke relies on in the *Second Treatise* between animals that are and animals that are not "made for one anothers uses" (2nd T: 6). Taken literally, *imago dei* is not going to help with this. For even if we (that is, you and I, dear Reader) can confidently think of ourselves as created in the image of God, there is no denying that we are a rather *blurred* image – intellectually as well as spiritually.[57] And the intellectual differences between us would seem to be important in this regard, indicating that some of us are less blurred than others in the image of God that we present. By itself *imago dei* goes no way towards answering our threshold question: how blurred may the image be, exactly, before it ceases to count in the relevant respect?

The difficulty at this stage of the argument is quite general. A principle of basic equality requires a binary distinction – (i) those who are one another's equals, and (ii) those who are not the equals of the members of class (i) – and reason or rationality is not really a binary concept. There are degrees of rationality, both among those we are pre-theoretically inclined to call humans and in a broader class of animals that includes apes and dolphins, dogs and cats, as well as those we call humans. On this gradual scale, who gets the benefit of equality? Or why is it not more sensible to abandon equality and take as the basic premise of moral and political philosophy the idea of a proportionate response to each entity's particular location on the scale?

Once again, it is Locke himself who provides the raw material for this skeptical, anti-egalitarian approach. We can discern, he says, enormous differences in reason and rational ability among those we are accustomed to call human. There is, for example, the human fetus, which, Locke

---

[57] See Spellman, *John Locke and the Problem of Depravity*, pp. 104 ff.

says, "*differs not much from the State of a Vegetable . . .* [There are] few signs of a soul accustomed to much thinking in a new-born child" (E: 2.1.21). And something similar is true of humans at the end of their lives:

Take one, in whom decrepit old Age has blotted out the Memory of his past Knowledge and clearly wiped out the *Ideas* his Mind was formerly stored with; and has, by destroying his Sight, Hearing, and Smell . . . stopp'd up almost all the Passages for new ones to enter; or, if there be some of the Inlets yet half open, the Impressions made are scarce perceived, or not at all retained. How far such an one . . . is in his Knowledge, and intellectual Faculties above the Condition of a Cockle, or an Oyster, I leave to be considered. (E: 2.9.14)

Locke continues, "if a man had passed Sixty Years in such a State . . . I wonder what difference there would have been, in any intellectual Perfections, between him, and the lowest degree of Animals" (E: 2.9.14).

Now among the very grossest differences in mental capacity, Locke is evidently not committed to any thesis of equality. That is, he is not committed to following our nominal conception of humanity where it leads, and to drawing a rationality-line that will include all whom we pre-theoretically describe as human. In the case of "defects that may happen out of the ordinary course of nature," lunacy, idiocy, and so on, he is quite clear: such a being "is never capable of being a free man, [and] is never [to be] let loose to the disposure of his own will (because he . . . has not understanding, its proper guide)" (2nd T: 60). Infants are a slightly different case, and I will say more about this in Chapter 5.[58] In their case, however, Locke's argument is that they are to be treated as beings destined for equality, though not our equals at present.

But even in the ordinary run of things, even without the contrast between "*Westminster-hall* or the *Exchange* on the one hand, [and] *Alms-Houses* or *Bedlam* on the other" (E: 4.20.5), there are intellectual differences that seem to leave us all at sea, once we abandon the notion of species. There are some who fall short of lunacy but suffer nevertheless from some deficiency in the mind – for instance, "[t]hat it moves slowly, and *retrieves not the ideas,* that it has . . . *quick enough* to serve the mind upon occasion" (E: 2.10.8). There is what Locke calls "the obstinacy of a worthy man, who yields not to the evidence of reason, though laid before him as clear as day-light" (E: 2.33.2). This, he says, may perhaps be considered a form of madness, for although everyone uses his mind in this way on some occasions, we ought to wonder whether one who "should on all occasions argue or do as in some cases he constantly does, would not

---

[58] See below, pp. 110–14.

be thought fitter for *Bedlam*, than Civil Conversation" (E: 2.33.4). And finally there are the familiar distinctions between the wise and the silly, those who have attended to and those who have neglected their mental cultivation, the lazy and the assiduous, the learned and the illiterate, the philosophical and the intuitive, and so on.[59] If we start paying attention to these differences, then we are going to find that, having let go of the species-concept of humanity, there is nothing much to hang on to so far as social and political equality is concerned. If there is, as Locke says, "a difference of degrees in Men's Understandings ... to so great a latitude, that one may, without doing injury to Mankind, affirm that there is a greater distance between some Men and others in this respect than between some Men and some Beasts" (E: 4.20.5), then how can we work with or justify any notion of basic equality? Against a background of this sort of variation, how are we supposed to set the sharp divides or maintain the thresholds on this scale that the idea of equality appears to presuppose?

Locke is sometimes tempted by the position – which I guess his radical empiricism leaves open – that, considered as *tabulae rasae*, our minds are all the same, and that the intellectual differences between us are simply a matter of input and exercise. In a late work, *Of the Conduct of the Understanding*, he speculated that "[a]s it is in the body, so it is in the mind; practice makes it what it is, and most even of those excellences which are looked on as natural endowments will be found, when enquired into more narrowly, to be the product of exercise."[60] But such a possibility cannot do all the work.[61] For as Locke also said, in the same book,

There is, it is visible, great variety in men's understandings, and their natural constitutions put so wide a difference between some men in this respect, that art and industry would never be able to master; and their very natures seem to want a foundation to raise on it which other men easily attain unto.[62]

We are back where we were in the discussion of essences. Whether we look at the outward workings of the human mind, or at "the Wheels, or Springs ... within" (E: 3.6.39), whether we look at individuals as they

---

[59] E: 1.4.15: "[T]he wise and considerate Men of the World, by a right and careful employment of their Thoughts and Reason, attained true Notions in this, as well as other things; whilst the lazy and inconsiderate part of Men, making far the greater number, took up their Notions by chance, from common Tradition and vulgar Conceptions, without much beating their Heads about them."

[60] Locke, *Of the Conduct of the Understanding*, p. 174.

[61] See also Spellman, *John Locke and the Problem of Depravity*, pp. 108 ff.

[62] Locke, *Of the Conduct of the Understanding*, p. 168.

have developed or at their natural abilities, we don't seem to have any cut-off point at which we could say *this* intellectual apparatus or *this* degree of rational ability marks a being as entitled to equality with all other embodied creatures that rise above the threshold.

x

Locke needs to specify a threshold.[63] Here's how I think he does it. In Book II of the *Essay*, he argued that what distinguishes humans from other animals is not their capacity to reason *per se* – for brute animals have some sort of reason – but rather the "power of *Abstracting*," the capacity to reason on the basis of general ideas. Animals have and act on ideas, and therefore have some reason: "but it is only in particular *Ideas*, just as they receiv'd them from their Senses" – they don't have "the faculty to enlarge by any kind of *Abstraction*" (E: 2.11.11). It is "the having of general ideas," a faculty connected of course with the use of language, which puts "a perfect distinction betwixt man and brutes," if not in the sense of biological taxonomy, then at least in the sense required for the moral application of the idea of corporeal rationality. And there is a similar reference to the capacity to entertain general ideas in that passage I mentioned at the end of section VII where Locke inquires about the moral application of his skepticism about species (E: 3.11.16). So, maybe *this* is Locke's equality-threshold. Can we say that he regards possession of the power of abstraction as the basis of a bright line on the rationality scale, for the purposes of his moral definition of humanity and his belief in basic equality?

It won't do as a species distinction of course. True, Locke's claim in Book II of the *Essay* is that it is "in this, that the Species of Brutes are discriminated from Man" (E: 2.11.11). But he quickly indicates that many who bear the nominal essence of man lack the ability to abstract. Many of those we call idiots or naturals "cannot distinguish, compare, and abstract" (E: 2.11.12). And if there were an animal "that had Language and Reason, but partaked not of the usual shape of a Man, I believe it would hardly pass for a man," in the taxonomic sense. So Locke is not offering this capacity to abstract as the real essence of the species *human*.

---

[63] Cf. the solution proposed in Grant, *John Locke's Liberalism*, pp. 31–3, which does not involve any bright-line threshold. Instead, Grant talks about "'gray areas' at the boundaries in considering species" and suggests that this sort of "open texture" is unavoidable in legal contexts. She is right in that last point (cf. Hart, *Concept of Law*, pp. 128–36) but I do not find her approach satisfactory: open texture at this level would indicate a fundamental indeterminacy in what one is trying to say about equality.

He is offering it as an interesting resemblance among all the beings we are disposed to call "rational" for moral purposes, distinguishing them from all the beings (human-shaped or not) that we are disposed to call "brutes."

XI

I think this is a promising lead. But of course it is not enough, in an area fraught with this much difficulty, simply to point to a similarity. It must be an interesting or relevant similarity for the purposes of the weight that is going to be placed upon it. And in the realm of basic equality, that weight is very heavy indeed. To put it another way, it is not enough just to *announce* a bright line. It is not enough to *stipulate* a threshold. The threshold in question has to be explained and it has to be defended. Locke has to show that even when there are differences in people's capacities above this line – differences that he acknowledges may be important for various practical purposes (2nd T: 54) – still the fact that an entity is above rather than below the threshold is of overwhelming significance so far as the basics of social and political organization are concerned. And he has to explain *why* that is so, why differences above the line should matter much less than the difference indicated by the line itself.

One way of putting this is to say that for Locke the real resemblance on which basic equality rests – the ability to form and work with abstract ideas – must work rather like what modern political philosophers call a *range property*. The idea of a "range property" was introduced into the modern discussion of equality by John Rawls in *A Theory of Justice*,[64] though it has not, I'm afraid, been very widely discussed in that context.[65] A range property may be understood in terms of a region on a scale. The idea is that although there is a scale on which one could observe differences of degree, still once a range has been specified, we may use

[64] Rawls, *Theory of Justice*, p. 508: "[I]t is not the case that founding equality on natural capacities is incompatible with an egalitarian view. All we have to do is to select a range property (as I shall say) and to give equal justice to those meeting its conditions. For example, the property of being in the interior of the unit circle is a range property of points in the plane. All points inside this circle have this property although their coordinates vary within a certain range. And they equally have this property, since no point interior to a circle is more or less interior to it than any other interior point."

[65] There is some discussion of Rawls's own use of the idea in the following books and articles: Lloyd Thomas, "Equality Within the Limits of Reason Alone," p. 549; Wikler, "Paternalism and the Mildly Retarded," p. 384; Gorr, "Rawls on Natural Inequality," pp. 11–16; and Coons and Brennan, *By Nature Equal*, pp. 32–3. But I have not been able to find any general discussion of the idea of a range property in relation to equality.

the binary property of *being within the range*, a property which is shared by something which is in the center of the range and also by something which is just above its lower threshold.

A juridical example may help. Consider the legal or administrative characteristic which a town might have of *being in New Jersey* (e.g. as opposed to being in New York or being in Pennsylvania). Though the city of Princeton is in the heart of New Jersey, well away from the state line, and Hoboken is just over the river from New York, right on the boundary, still Princeton and Hoboken are both *in New Jersey*, and they are both in New Jersey *to the same extent*, so far as the law is concerned. One could point to the scalar geographical difference between them and for various reasons that might be important; but jurisdictionally it is irrelevant. *Being in New Jersey*, then, is a range property, ranging over all the points within the boundaries of the state.

In John Rawls's own use of the idea, the relevant range property is *the capacity for moral personality*. That's what he takes as the basis of equality, the basis on which an individual is entitled to the benefit of the Rawlsian theory of justice.[66] Like *being in New Jersey*, Rawls's *capacity for moral personality* ranges over a class of cases which *might* be classified on a scale (variation in capacity for a sense of justice, and geographical position, respectively); but in fact it classifies them in a non-scalar way. Another example of a range property might be found in Thomas Hobbes's account of equality of bodily strength. Remember how Hobbes argued in *Leviathan*:

Nature hath made men so equall . . . that, though there be found one man sometimes manifestly stronger in body . . . than another, yet when all is reckoned together the difference between man and man is not so considerable . . . For as to the strength of body, the weakest has strength enough to kill the strongest.[67]

Though there *is* an important scalar property here – namely, strength of body – the relevant *range property* is the property of being a non-dismissible mortal threat. When I look at all the animals around me, I might rank them on a scale of bodily strength. But what should particularly interest me about that scale (according to Hobbes) is the threshold at which some

---

[66] Rawls, *Theory of Justice*, p. 506: "It should be stressed that the sufficient condition for equal justice, the capacity for moral personality, is not at all stringent . . . Furthermore, while individuals presumably have varying capacities for a sense of justice, this fact is not a reason for depriving those with a lesser capacity of the full protection of justice. Once a certain minimum is met, a person is entitled to equal liberty on a par with everyone else."

[67] Hobbes, *Leviathan*, Ch. 13, pp. 86–7.

animal becomes a non-dismissible threat. In Hobbes's view all humans are above that threshold; and particular theories of human inequality – such as the suggestion that women are not men's equals – are refuted by showing that all of the putative unequals are above that threshold too.[68]

Notice the way that, in the Hobbesian example, a particular interest – the interest in survival – drives us away from the scalar differentiations, and drives us to concentrate on the mere fact that something is a mortal threat. And there is an interest doing this work too in the New Jersey example – a constitutional and administrative interest. Relative to the interest driving the specification of the range property, the precise location of an entity on the scale is uninteresting. That it is *within the range* is all we need to know. Without such an interest, of course a range property seems merely arbitrary. One might stipulate it. But it would be hard to see the point. To return to some terminology we introduced at the beginning of this chapter, the interest shapes the range property and makes it intelligible.[69]

Is there anything which can do this work for Locke? Is there anything which can give the Lockean basis of equality – the power of abstraction – its appropriate sense and shape as a range property? Is there anything which can motivate our attention to this as a threshold and our refusal to be distracted by intellectual differences above it?

This, at last, is where the religious argument comes in, on my interpretation. To motivate and explicate the power of abstraction as the relevant equality-threshold, we must consider the moral and theological pragmatics which lie at the back of Locke's account of the human intellect. We must look at what he says about the fundamental *adequacy* of our mental powers and the reasons he has for saying that in the case of all standard-model humans, each of them has *intellect enough*, for some fundamental purpose, whatever the intellectual differences between them. In this discussion, Locke insists (in terms not dissimilar to Hobbes on mental equality)[70] that humans have reason to be satisfied with their mental capacities:

---

[68] Hobbes, *Leviathan*, Ch. 20, p. 139: "And whereas some have attributed the Dominion to the Man only, as being of the more excellent Sex, they misreckon in it. For there is not always that difference of strength or prudence between the man and the woman as that the right can be determined without War."

[69] Above, pp. 47–8. I am grateful to Jules Coleman for this point.

[70] There is, in Hobbes (*Leviathan*, Ch. 13, p. 87), a nice joke about intellectual equality: "And as to the faculties of the mind . . . I find yet a greater equality amongst men than that of strength . . . For such is the nature of men that howsoever they may acknowledge many others to be more witty, or more eloquent or more learned, yet they will hardly believe there be many so wise as themselves;

For though the *Comprehension* of our Understandings, comes exceeding short of the vast Extent of Things; yet . . . Men have Reason to be well satisfied with what God hath thought fit for them, since he hath given them . . . Whatsoever is necessary for the Conveniences of Life and Information of Vertue; and has put within the reach of their Discovery the comfortable provision for this life, and the way that leads to a better.[71]

No matter how inadequate the average human intellect is for a "universal, or perfect Comprehension,"

it yet secures their great Concernments, that they have Light enough to lead them to the Knowledge of their Maker, and the sight of their own Duties . . . It will be no Excuse to an idle and untoward Servant, who would not attend his Business by Candle-light, to plead that he had not broad Sun-shine. The Candle that is set up in us, shines bright enough for all our Purposes.[72]

"[T]hey have Light enough to lead them to the Knowledge of their Maker." The implicit reference here is Locke's argument for the existence of God. The existence of God, Locke believes, is something that can be established by the unaided human intellect, whatever that intellect's other limitations. It is not an idea that is innate in us (E: 1.4.8 ff.) but it is readily attainable. All that is needed is some power of abstraction applied to what we see in the world around us: "For the visible marks of extraordinary Wisdom and Power appear so plainly in all the Works of the Creation, that a rational Creature, who will but seriously reflect on them, cannot miss the discovery of a *Deity*" (E: 1.3.9). Some argue, says Locke, that it is "*suitable to the goodness of God*" (E: 1.4.12) to imprint an idea of His being directly on our minds. But God has used a different strategy. He has conferred on those whom He intends to serve Him the rational power that is required for easy recognition of His existence. Thus we can identify the class of those whom God intends to serve Him by discerning which beings have and which beings do not have these powers.

So Locke's position seems to be this. Anyone with the capacity for abstraction can reason to the existence of God, and he can relate the idea of God to there being a law that applies to him both in his conduct in this world and as to his prospects for the next. The content of that law may not be available to everyone's reason, but anyone above the threshold

---

for they see their own wit at hand, and other men's at a distance. But this proveth rather that men are in that point equal, than unequal. For there is not ordinarily a greater sign of the equal distribution of anything than that every man is contented with his share."

[71] Locke, *Essay*, Introduction, p. 45.   [72] Ibid.

has the power to relate the idea of such law to what is known by faith and revelation about God's commandments, and is in a position therefore to use such intellect as he has to follow and obey those commandments. Moreover, he can think of himself, abstractly, as a being that endures from moment to moment, and as the same being that may commit a sin today and have to account to the Almighty for it tomorrow: in short he has the minimal capacity to think of himself as a *person*. No doubt there are all sorts of differences in the ways in which people figure all this through – some attempt the precarious path of reason, some wander through the minefield of revelation. (I'll talk more about this in the next chapter.) But the fact that one is dealing with an animal that has the capacity to approach the task one way or another is all-important, and it makes a huge difference to how such a being may be treated in comparison to animals whose capacities are such that this whole business of knowing God and figuring out his commandments is simply out of the question.

The fact that a being can get this far, intellectually, by whatever route, shows that he is a creature with a special *moral* relation to God. As a creature who knows about the existence of God and who is therefore in a position to answer responsibly to His commandments, this is someone whose existence has a special significance. Now, that specialness is a matter of intense interest first and foremost, of course, to the person who has the ability. Knowing that he has been sent into the world by God, "by his order, and about his business," the individual person has an interest in finding out pretty damned quick what he is supposed to do.[73] But Locke believes this also affects fundamentally the way we ought to deal with one another. When I catch a rabbit, I know that I am *not* dealing with a creature that has the capacity to abstract, and so I know that there is no question of this being one of God's special servants, sent into the world about his business. But if I catch a human in full possession of his faculties, I know I should be careful how I deal with him. Because creatures capable of abstraction can be conceived as "all the servants of one Sovereign Master, sent into the World by his order, and about his business," we must treat them as "his Property, whose Workmanship

---

[73] Cf. Locke, *Letter Concerning Toleration*, p. 46: "Every man has an immortal soul, capable of eternal happiness or misery; whose happiness depending upon his believing and doing those things in this life which are necessary to the obtaining of God's favour, and are prescribed by God to that end. It follows from thence ... that the observance of these things is the highest obligation that lies upon mankind and that our utmost care, application, and diligence ought to be exercised in the search and performance of them; because there is nothing in this world that is of any consideration in comparison with eternity."

they are, made to last during his, not one anothers Pleasure" and refrain from destroying or harming or exploiting them.[74] *That*, it seems to me, is the interest that is driving and shaping Locke's moral conception of "man," and motivating the interest in the particular range of capacities that forms the basis for Lockean equality.

XII

If all this is accepted, then it is pretty clear that the *bracketing* strategy we spoke about at the beginning of this chapter – bracketing off the God stuff from the equality stuff – is simply not going to work. The two parts of the Lockean doctrine are intricately related. Once we see Locke acknowledging that he is not entitled to help himself to any ready-made notion of the human species, then it is clear that he has no choice but to shape his theory of equality on the basis of certain resemblances among created beings. And the significance of those resemblances – their relevance *qua* resemblances at this level of moral theory – can be established only in the light of certain theological truths.

Someone in denial of or indifferent to the existence of God is not going to be able to come up with anything like the sort of basis for equality that Locke came up with. An atheist may pretend to talk about the equality of all members of the human species, but his conception of the human species is likely to be as chaotic and indeterminate as Locke's was in Book III of the *Essay*. The atheist may pretend to ground our equality in our rationality, but he will be at a loss to explain why we should ignore the evident differences in people's rationality. He will be at a loss to defend any particular line or threshold, in a non-question-begging way. (At best, he will have to stake his rationality threshold on an already accepted principle of human equality rather than the other way round, leaving the principle itself bare of any rationalization.) Locke emphasized possession of a degree of rationality that consisted in the power of abstraction and the power to relate an abstraction like God to the idea of one's own actions and one's own person. There is no reason for an atheist to recognize such a threshold, and there is no reason to believe that he could defend it if he did. The atheist has no basis in his philosophy for thinking that beings endowed with the capacity that

---

[74] Hence the fearful dissent of Supreme Court Justice McLean in *Dred Scott* v. *Sandford*, 60 US 393 (1856), at 550: "A slave is not a mere chattel. He bears the impress of his Maker, and is amenable to the laws of God and man; and he is destined to an endless existence."

Locke emphasizes are for that reason to be treated as special and sacred in the way Locke thought.

If this account of Locke's philosophical strategy is anything like correct, then Alasdair Macintyre is right and the Waldron of 1982 is wrong. Locke's equality claims are not separable from the theological content that shapes and organizes them. The theological content cannot simply be bracketed off as a curiosity. It shapes and informs the account through and through; the range property on which Locke relies is simply unintelligible apart from these religious concerns. And so there is no way round it – Lockean equality is not fit to be taught as a secular doctrine; it is a conception of equality that makes no sense except in the light of a particular account of the relation between man and God.

4

"The Democratic Intellect"

Locke's political theory has been associated so insistently with a correlation between class or status on the one hand, and differences in
rationality on the other,[1] that it may seem perverse of me to attribute to
him a *democratic* view of the human intellect. But that is what I now want
to argue.

The gist of my argument in Chapter 3 was that humans are one another's equals, in Locke's eyes, by virtue of their possession of a rather
modest intellectual capacity – the capacity to form and manipulate abstract ideas, which enables a person to reason to the existence of God and
to the necessity of finding out what if anything God requires of him. The
existence of this capacity in a very wide array of the beings we call human
is of course compatible with enormous variations in other aspects of their
intellect and rationality. And Locke never denies that. But his position
seems to be that the capacity to abstract trumps these other differences so
far as the establishment of our basic moral status is concerned. Consider
the greatest statesman and the most humble day-laborer. Even if they do
not differ in their "natural constitutions" (a possibility that Locke leaves
open),[2] the first has greater experience and has had more opportunity
to exercise his intellectual faculties, while the second "has commonly
but a small pittance of knowledge, because his ideas and notions have
been confined to the narrow bounds of a poor conversation and employment," and he is virtually incapable of following a train of argument of
any complexity.[3] That's a huge difference. Yet if both of them have the
capacity to reason to an understanding of the existence of God, then
they are one another's equals so far as any relations of authority are
concerned. This modicum of rationality is a mark of the fact that each
of them is the servant (not just a creature) of God, "sent into the World

---

[1] See especially Macpherson, *Political Theory of Possessive Individualism*, pp. 221 ff.
[2] Locke, *Of the Conduct of the Understanding*, p. 168.   [3] Ibid., pp. 171 and 178–9.

by his order, and about his business, . . . made to last during his, not one
another's pleasure" (2nd T: 6). It is to this that Locke refers when he says
that humans are "furnished with *like* Faculties" (2nd T: 4 – my emphasis),
not like in all respects or by all measures, but like in this fundamental
ability. And this is the basis from which he infers not only that we are
not authorized to destroy or exploit one another "as if we were made
for one anothers uses, as the inferior ranks of Creatures are for ours,"
but that we "should also be equal one amongst another without Subordination or Subjection" (2nd T: 4 and 6). Basic equality is predicated
on this very lowly intellectual capacity, so that no one who has that capacity, whether high or low, male or female, rich or poor, smart or dim,
"can be . . . subjected to the Political Power of another, without his own
Consent" (2nd T: 95).

I have entitled this chapter "The Democratic Intellect,"[4] but its topic
is not really democracy in the political sense. In the recent Locke literature, inspired in large part by Richard Ashcraft, there has been a lot of
discussion about Locke's attitude to democracy and his views about the
basis of the franchise – both what it was and what it ought to be – in late
seventeenth-century England. I don't really want to get into that here,
though for what it's worth, I am persuaded by Ashcraft's argument that
Locke's political views were more radical – rather closer to the Levellers –
than has sometimes been supposed.[5] I will say more about democracy
in the political sense in Chapter 5. In the present chapter, however, I am
going to use the term "democratic intellect" in a broader, perhaps more
Tocquevillian sense of "democratic" than just these matters of political
suffrage. My questions are the following. What was Locke's understanding of the relation between the low-level rationality of the poorest class
in society, and the extraordinary reason of (say) a philosopher like himself? Did he denigrate the former and privilege the latter? Did he regard
scientific reason as an ideal for moral, political and religious purposes,
and treat the ordinary reason of the common man as a sort of dim approximation – or worse, a social and political disqualification? We know
that Locke believed it was possible to improve the use that people made
of the intellectual capacities that God had given them: he devoted his
700-page *Essay* to the subject. But does this mean that he despaired of
the intellect in its most modest manifestations?

---

[4] I adapt this phrase from George Davie's study of Scottish universities, *The Democratic Intellect*.
[5] Ashcraft, *Revolutionary Politics*, pp. 164–5 and 580–5. Compare Schochet, "Radical Politics";
Wootton, "John Locke and Richard Ashcraft's *Revolutionary Politics*"; and Marshall, *Locke*,
pp. 205–91.

I think not. There are hints at times of a view that is almost exactly the opposite. It is in many ways the *educated* intellect that Locke regarded as a social danger. He often said that the capacities and dispositions of ordinary people were much more reliable morally and politically than the effete corrupt sensibility of "all-knowing Doctors" and "learned Disputants" (E: 3.10.9). When he cited those who had undermined the basis of trustworthy government in England, it was learned men – scholars, statesmen, bishops, "the Divinity of this last Age," and "Flatterers [who] talk to amuse Peoples Understandings" (2nd T: 94 and 112). There is no suggestion of any threat from masterless men or from halting attempts at political thinking by uppity laborers. On the contrary, when Locke considers lower-class malcontents, he is anxious to assure his readers that they are not a real threat at all, certainly not compared to those who are in a position to flatter and encourage the pretensions of absolute power (2nd T: 230). I don't think we should exaggerate the point: obviously someone in Locke's position is not going to say that the educated intellect is worthless. But what he does say on the matter we will find sufficient to acquit him of the charge of attaching political, social, or religious privilege to the sort of reasoning that he himself deployed in his political, social, and theological thought.

I

According to C. B. Macpherson, John Locke shared the view of most of his contemporaries "that the members of the laboring class do not and cannot live a fully rational life."[6] Macpherson acknowledges that Locke wasn't entirely consistent in this. He thinks the lack of consistency is a reflection of Locke's having adopted uncritically the view prevalent in his society: since he took the view for granted, he carried it into his premises without the need for argumentation, and it is only argumentation that would have revealed its inconsistency with some of the other things he argued.[7] But Macpherson is wrong. The position he attributes to Locke is certainly inconsistent with the premises of Locke's argument in social and political philosophy; but Macpherson is wrong to think that there is anything in Locke that warrants the attribution to him of this position, even acknowledging the inconsistency. We are not dealing here with anything like the situation we considered in Chapter 2 – a patent inconsistency between what Locke said about women's subjection to their

---

[6] Macpherson, *Political Theory of Possessive Individualism*, pp. 222 and 232.   [7] Ibid., pp. 229–30.

husbands and what he said about basic equality. In the case of the laboring class, Locke does not even stake out the inegalitarian position that Macpherson attributes to him, let alone hold it inconsistently with his foundational theory of equality.

I will not be able to do full justice to Macpherson's argument in this chapter: there are aspects of his case whose consideration I would like to postpone until later chapters. In Chapter 6, for example, we will consider the inferences about differential rationality that Macpherson wants to draw from what Locke says about property, specifically from his suggestion that "God gave the World to . . . the Use of the Industrious and Rational" (2nd T: 34).[8] Right now, though, I want to look at the most direct evidence that can be adduced for the Macpherson interpretation "that Locke assumed in his own society a class differential in rationality which left the labouring class incapable . . . of ordering their lives by the law of nature or reason."[9]

In Chapter 20 of Book IV of the *Essay*, Locke talks about the epistemic situation of those, "the greatest part of Mankind, who are given up to Labour, and enslaved to the Necessity of their mean Condition; whose Lives are worn out, only in the Provisions for Living" (E: 4.20.2).[10] Locke says that the "Opportunities of Knowledge and Enquiry" for such persons "are commonly as narrow as their Fortunes"; they have little energy for instruction or improvement "when all their whole Time and Pains are laid out, to still the Croaking of their own Bellies, or the Cries of their Children" (E: 4.20.2). Such people, Locke goes on, have no experience of "the variety of Things done in the World," they lack the resources of "Leisure, Books, and Languages, and the Opportunity of conversing with variety of Men," and they are in no position to collect or consider "those Testimonies and Observations, which are in Being, and are necessary to make out many, nay most of the Propositions, that, in the Societies of Men, are judged of the greatest Moment; or to find out Grounds of Assurance so great, as the Belief of the points he would build on them, is thought necessary" (E: 4.20.2). They simply lack the resources that are required for the scientific or philosophic use of the intellect.

What does Locke infer from this? Does he conclude, as Macpherson says he does, that people in this predicament are incapable of ordering their lives by reason? Well, the passage is complicated in two ways. First, although Macpherson thinks Locke is distinguishing here between those

[8] Ibid., pp. 231–8. See Chapter 6, pp. 173–7.
[9] Macpherson, *Political Theory of Possessive Individualism*, p. 232.
[10] Ibid., p. 225, where this passage is cited.

who have the ability to think for themselves and those who must submit to the intellectual leadership of others,[11] Locke is in fact very reluctant to infer from the predicament of the laboring classes any general doctrine of submission to authority. Far from saying that the laborers must defer to the intellects of their betters, he compares their position to "those who are *cooped in* close *by the Laws* of their countries" concerning political censorship and indoctrination (E:4.20.4), and he evinces considerable alarm on the laborers' behalf at the prospect of their having to take certain truths on faith from authority:

Are the current Opinions, and licensed Guides of every Country sufficient Evidence and Security to every Man to venture his great Concernments on … ? Or can those be the certain and infallible Oracles and Standards of Truth, which teach one Thing in *Christendom*, and another in *Turkey*? (E: 4.20.3)

Locke knows that those who actually have political authority are unlikely to be reliable guides, for they are mainly interested in tailoring their doctrines to accumulate as many followers as possible, rather than seeking followers for what they have reason to believe is the truth (E: 4.20.18). And anyway, as Locke emphasizes in the *Letter Concerning Toleration*, people have a responsibility to think for themselves. There are "things that every man ought sincerely to inquire into himself, and by meditation, study, search, and his own endeavours, attain the knowledge of" (LCT: 36). So far as those things are concerned there is just no option, according to Locke. Even the hard-pressed day-laborer must regard the honest workings of his own intellect, not the learning of others, as normative in the conduct of his life. Any other strategy is too much of a risk: "Or shall a poor Country-man be eternally happy, for having the Chance to be born in *Italy*; or a Day-Laborer be unavoidably lost, because he had the ill Luck to be born in England?" (E: 4.20.3).

Of course there is risk on both sides.[12] But – and this is my second point – the risk that Locke is urging the laborer to take is underwritten once again by his conception of the fundamental adequacy of even the meanest intellect.

God has furnished Men with Faculties sufficient to direct them in the Way they should take, if they will but seriously employ them that Way, when their ordinary Vocations allow them the Leisure. No Man is so wholly taken up with the Attendance on the Means of Living, as to have no spare Time at all to think of his Soul, and inform himself in Matters of Religion. Were men as intent upon

---

[11] Ibid., pp. 245–6.
[12] For a fine account, see Woltersdorff, *John Locke and the Ethics of Belief*, pp. 118–48.

this as they are on things of lower concernment, there are none so enslaved to the necessities of life who might not find many vacancies that might be husbanded to this advantage of their knowledge. (E: 4.20.3)

That – and not any Macpherson thesis about differential rationality – is Locke's position on the intellectual predicament of the laboring class. And it is, I think, striking that this re-endorsement of his position about the fundamental basis of equality – the capacity that almost everyone has to engage in abstract thought sufficient "to think of his Soul, and inform himself in Matters of Religion" – comes immediately upon the heels of the passage we have just been discussing, the passage most frequently cited to support the proposition that Locke did not believe day-laborers were our equals.

II

In fact, if one reads the *Essay* as a whole with an eye to the possibility of class differentials of rationality – but keeps that eye open in all directions, rather than alert only to his supposed denigration of the lower classes – one is likely to come up with a picture that is much more favorable to the ordinary laborer than Macpherson supposes and much less favorable to those whom we are accustomed to regard as the intellectual elite.[13] The point is intimated in the imagery Locke uses, most notably the constant references to intellectual activity as labor – "all that Industry and Labor of Thought" (E: 4.3.6). Now it is true that Macpherson associates Locke's celebration of the "Industrious and the Rational" (2nd T: 34) with his privileging entrepreneurial acquisitiveness.[14] And so comparing the business of serious thought to industry need not mean comparing it to the industriousness of the day-laborer. But that Macpherson's understanding is a distortion in the present context is indicated, remarkably, by Locke's own famous self-description at the beginning of the *Essay*. He is not one of the entrepreneurial "Master-Builders, whose mighty Designs, in advancing the Sciences, will leave lasting Monuments to the Admiration of Posterity."[15] In the industry of thought, it is "ambition enough to

---

[13] This resonates with Charles Taylor's hypothesis of the development of an ethic of everyday life, replacing the more flamboyant ethic of aristocratic display at this time. See Taylor, *Sources of the Self*, p. 240, where it is oberved that Locke's ethical outlook "was plainly an endorsement of the serious, productive, and pacific improver of any class, and against the aristocratic, caste-conscious pursuit of honour and glory through self-display and the warrior virtues. Locke continued and further developed the inversion of the old hierarchy of values which the ethic of ordinary life entailed."

[14] Macpherson, *Political Theory of Possessive Individualism*, p. 233.

[15] Locke, *Essay*, p. 9 ("Epistle to the Reader").

be employed as an Under-Laborer in clearing the Ground a little, and removing some of the Rubbish, that lies in the way to Knowledge."[16] The trained Lockean understanding is not classy or flamboyant in its operation: it proceeds by repetitive steps, and its method is "not without pains and attention" (E: 4.2.4). I know we mustn't read too much into this. The rhetoric of humility is a conventional device, particularly in introducing a work, and it might not be much more significant than Locke's comparison of himself in the "Epistle Dedicatory" with a poor man offering a basket of flowers or fruit to his rich neighbor. If it stood alone, this rhetoric would signify very little.[17]

In fact it stands with a wealth of explicit, non-figurative reflection on the correlation of pragmatic effectiveness with class-based intellectual pretensions. When Locke took the opportunity to stigmatize members of some classes for their intellectual laziness, his target was not the idle poor but rather those "[w]ho though they have Riches and Leisure enough, and want neither parts nor other helps, are yet never the better for them" (E: 4.20.6) in their intellectual life. He does mention drudgery as an obstacle to the improvement of the understanding, but it is not the drudgery of labor or quasi-enslavement (2nd T: 24), but rather "constant drudgery in business" (E: 4.20.6). In these comments, Locke's only reference to the laboring classes is a suggestion that the rich and leisured are often put to shame "by Men of lower Condition who surpass them in knowledge" (ibid.). Again, when he wrote, at the beginning of the *Essay*, about "the lazy and inconsiderate part of Men, making the far greater number, [who] took up their Notions by chance, from common Tradition and vulgar Conceptions, without much beating their Heads about them" (E: 1.4.15), it is clear from the context that this was supposed to apply much more to those who squandered the opportunities of reason than to those who had no choice but to take things on faith. Even today (especially today!) we are all familiar with people who claim to live the life of the intellect but who nevertheless and in the very activity they call reasoning, "[take] up their Notions . . . from common Tradition and vulgar Conceptions, without much beating their heads about them" (E: 1.4.15).[18]

---

[16] Ibid., p. 10.

[17] But for comment on another of Locke's rhetorical devices – the "conversational tone" of the *Essay*, which may be read as "a deliberate bid to engage lots of readers, to make it clear that science and philosophy . . . are open to any and all interested in them" – see Herzog, *Happy Slaves*, pp. 58–9.

[18] There is an accurate and provocative account of this tendency among modern scholars in Posner, *Problematics*, pp. 3–90.

Locke was certainly not beyond associating intellectual disability with social marginality. His comments about the difference between "*Westminister-hall*, or the *Exchange* on the one hand; [and] *Alms-Houses* and *Bedlam* on the other" (E: 4.20.5) are a sufficient indication of that. But the overall tenor of his account is that of an equal-opportunity condemnation of intellectual failings. "All Men are liable to Errour, and most Men are in many Points, by Passion or Interest, under Temptation to it" (E: 4.20.17).[19] In the *Essay*, his criticisms are directed at the "intelligent Romanist" who is prepared against all the odds to accept the doctrine of transubstantiation (E: 4.20.10), the "learned Professor" who is not willing to entertain the possibility that his scholarly energies may have been wrongly invested (E: 4.20.11), and "a Man, passionately in Love" who rejects all evidence of his lover's infidelity (E: 4.20.12). On the one hand, the "Mud-Walls" of intellectual obtuseness (E: 4.20.12) can be found anywhere, in any class; and yet on the other, Locke is prepared to conclude his discussion by saying "[t]here are not so many Men in Errours, and wrong Opinions, as it is commonly supposed" (E: 4.20.18). This is not explicitly presented as a vindication of the working-class intellect; but it is evidently a vindication of the ordinary intellect, the intellect possessed by a majority of persons, and it is maintained explicitly by Locke "notwithstanding the great Noise [that] is made in the World about Errours and Opinions" (E: 4.20.18).

I could continue in this vein for some time. When Locke talks darkly in the Introduction to the *Essay* of "Men, extending their Enquiries beyond their Capacities, and letting their Thoughts wander into those depths where they can find no sure Footing" (E: 1.1.6), it is not the impudence of the laboring classes that he has in mind. On the contrary, it is his peers in philosophy, who "raise questions and multiply disputes, which, never coming to any clear resolution, are proper only to continue and increase their doubts, and to confirm them at last in perfect scepticism" (ibid.). In the *First Treatise*, when he considers the tendency of "the busie mind of Man [to] carry him to a Brutality below the level of Beasts," it is not the poor or under-privileged he has in mind. It is the effect of imagination reinforced by fashion and custom and the desire for reputation[20] among those who are socially well-established and "in the know." And it is his disdain for *that* class of men that leads Locke to speculate that perhaps

---

[19] See also Ashcraft, *Locke's Two Treatises of Government*, pp. 247–8, for a similar account of where the normative edge of Locke's epistemology is directed.

[20] For the influence on ethics of the desire for reputation and esteem, see Locke, E: 2.28.12.

"the Woods and Forest . . . are fitter to give us Rules, than Cities and Palaces, where those that call themselves Civil and Rational, go out of their way, by the Authority of Examples" (1st T: 58). Notice that this almost Rousseauian vision of the noble savage is not a reversion to innatism; it is rather Locke's indication that sometimes even the most necessitous will do better using their own meager reason to figure things out than to follow the example or authority of those who are established as their betters.

In a similar vein, Locke shows a healthy awareness of the foibles of scholars, particularly their vanity and love of power. Scholars, he said, are besotted with "Glory and Esteem" (E: 3.10.8), and many of their professional virtues aim rather at flattery and admiration than at hard, sometimes unpalatable truth. He contrasts the straightforward intellect of the plain man with the "learned gibberish" of scholars, philosophers, and lawyers with their "multiplied curious Distinctions, and acute Niceties" (E: 3.10.12).

[T]he philosophers of old . . . and the Schoolmen since, aiming at Glory and Esteem, . . . found this a good Expedient to cover their Ignorance, with a curious and inexplicable Web of perplexed Words, and procure to themselves the admiration of others, by unintelligible Terms, the apter to produce wonder, because they could not be understood: whilst it appears in all History, that these profound Doctors were no wiser, nor more useful than their Neighbours; and brought but small advantage to humane life, or the Societies wherein they lived . . . For, notwithstanding these learned Disputants, these all-knowing Doctors, it was to the unscholastick Statesman, that the Governments of the World owed their Peace, Defence, and Liberties; and from the illiterate and contemned Mechanick (a Name of Disgrace) that they received the improvements of useful Arts. (E: 3.10.8–9)

The parenthesis here for the illiterate mechanic – "(a Name of Disgrace)" – indicates yet again that Locke regards himself as arguing against the conventional estimation of these matters. He thinks of himself as *more* sympathetic to the abilities and contributions of members of the working class than most of his contemporaries, and he would probably recoil in horror at the interpretive fashion that became popular in the twentieth century, whereby for the sake of *faux*-historical sophistication we read his contemporaries' views back into his own rather more radical writings.

I don't know if the unpleasant portrait of a vain and supercilious Locke painted by Ian Pears in his wonderful novel about 1660s

Oxford – *An Instance of the Fingerpost* – is accurate.[21] But Locke's contemporaries expressed a somewhat different view immediately after his death:

Many who knew him only by his Writings, or by the reputation he had gained, of being one of the greatest Philosophers of the age, having imagined to themselves that he was one of those Scholars, that being always full of themselves and their sublime speculations, are incapable of familiarizing themselves with the common sort of mankind, . . . were perfectly amazed to find him . . . much more desirous of informing himself in what they understood better than himself, than to make a show of his own Science.[22]

Locke, I think, did not succumb to the occupational hazard of philosophers, which is to infer – quite fallaciously – from the assumption that their own work is worth doing, that the qualities they use in doing it should be rated high in the pantheon of civic and political virtue. On the contrary, he often displayed a healthy disdain for the particular technical skills of the scholar. "He who shall employ all the force of his Reason only in brandishing of *syllogisms*, will discover very little of that Mass of Knowledge, which lies yet concealed in the secret recesses of Nature; and which I am apt to think, native rustic reason . . . is likelier to open a way to." (E: 4.17.6). One of the few places in his work where Locke disagrees with "the judicious" Richard Hooker[23] is in regard to the latter's suggestion (considered by Locke in the *Essay*) that there might be discovered such "right helps of true Art and Learning" as to establish "almost as much difference in Maturity of Judgment between men therewith inured, and that which Men now are, as between Men that are now, and Innocents."[24] Locke is quite wary of this suggestion, certainly of any implication these right aids are confined to the "Syllogism, and the Logick now in Use" (E: 4.17.7). He has little patience for the view that possession of the technical apparatus of philosophical argument marks an important distinction between types of reasoners, or that people have to be taught rational thought by a specialist – as though God had been "so sparing to men to make them barely two-legged Creatures, and left it to Aristotle to make them rational" (E: 4.17.4).[25] In fact he thinks the

---

[21] Pears, *Instance of the Fingerpost*, Ch. 12, p. 96.   [22] Coste, "The Character of Mr. Locke," p. 338.

[23] For the epithet "Judicious" as applied to Richard Hooker, see Locke, 2nd T: 5.

[24] Hooker, *Laws of Ecclesiastical Polity*, cited in Locke, E: 4.17.7.

[25] In fairness to Aristotle he adds: "I say not this any way to lessen Aristotle, whom I look on as one of the greatest men amongst the ancients; whose large views, acuteness, and penetration of thought and strength of judgment, few have equalled; and who, in this very invention of forms of argumentation, wherein the conclusion may be shown to be rightly inferred, did great service against those who were not ashamed to deny anything" (E: 4.17.4).

technical logic of a philosopher is as often an obstruction as an aid to sound and useful reasoning: "He that in the ordinary Affairs of Life, would admit of nothing but direct plain Demonstration, would be sure of nothing, in this World, but of perishing quickly" (E: 4.11.10).

> Tell a Country Gentlewoman, that the Wind is South-West, and the Weather louring, and like to rain, and she will easily understand, 'tis not safe for her to go abroad thin clad, in such a day, after a Fever: she clearly sees the probable Connexion of all these, *viz.* South-West-Wind, and Clouds, Rain, wetting, taking Cold, Relapse, and danger of Death, without tying them together in those artificial and cumbersome Fetters of several Syllogisms, that clog and hinder the Mind . . . and the Probability which she easily perceives in Things thus in their native State, would be quite lost, if this Argument were managed learnedly, and proposed in Mode and Figure. (E: 4.17.4)

I don't mean to exaggerate this. Locke is not an opponent of reason. He thinks technical logic has a particular job to do. But its function is not to browbeat or bamboozle the unschooled, but to discipline and correct the errors "that are often concealed in florid, witty, or involved Discourses" (E: 4.17.4). Some people – people of all classes – need this sort of correction. But that doesn't show its general indispensability: "Some Eyes want Spectacles to see things clearly and distinctly; but let not those that use them therefore say, no body can see clearly without them" (E: 4.17.4).

More generally, Locke accepts that those who have the skill to undertake philosophical inquiry ought to use it to the best of their ability. It becomes us, "as rational Creatures, to employ those Faculties we have about what they are most adapted to" (E: 4.12.11). If reason *can* practicably establish a truth, then that's the best way.[26] Locke's pessimism about scholarly reason, then, is not intellectual nihilism. He accepted the premise of what I am calling the philosophers' fallacy: philosophical reason has important work to do. He just didn't draw the conclusion – that therefore the possession of philosophical reason is an important credential or the basis of any important entitlement in social and political life.

---

[26] "God might, by Revelation, discover the Truth of any Proposition in *Euclid* . . . [But] [i]n all Things of this Kind there is little need or use of *Revelation,* God having furnished us with natural, and surer means to arrive at the Knowledge of them. For whatsoever Truth we come to the clear discovery of, from the Knowledge and Contemplation of our own *Ideas,* will always be certainer to us, than those which are conveyed to us by *Traditional Revelation.* For the Knowledge, we have, that this *Revelation* came at first from God, can never be so sure, as the Knowledge we have from the clear and distinct Perception of the Agreement, or Disagreement of our own *Ideas.*" (E: 4.18.4).

I now want to focus the discussion more narrowly on the nature of moral inquiry, and in particular on the contrast that Locke was eventually led to concede between his own activity as a philosopher seeking to establish rational foundations for morality and the means by which moral truth could in fact be made available to most members of a political community. It is tempting to say that of these two routes to moral understanding, someone like John Locke would of course privilege the former, and that to the extent that moral understanding is a large part of civic virtue, this would correspond to a social and political denigration of those who had no option but to take the second, non-philosophical route. However, the trajectory of Locke's own intellectual enterprise refutes any such correlation. Certainly Locke himself was led by the prospect of a rational grounding for morality to undertake and complete his most substantial philosophical work. But he always had doubts about this as a normal or normative route to moral understanding (as opposed to viewing it as a philosophical exercise that might validate and underwrite the normal or normative route). And he eventually became aware that this mode of establishing moral truth might not even succeed on its own terms. Far from offering a basis of moral understanding that could serve as a mark of social and political superiority, it turns out that the path of reason threatens to lead those who take it into a realm of greater perplexity and vulnerability to moral danger.

Let's begin, though, with the optimism and the rationalist aspiration. We know that the *Essay Concerning Human Understanding* was undertaken not as a pure exercise in epistemology, but with a view to the necessity of establishing secure rational foundations for morality.[27] We have to be quite careful, however, about what it was that Locke set out to do in this regard. In the *Essay*, he commits himself to the claim that "*moral Knowledge is as capable of real Certainty* as mathematics" (E: 4.4.7). But "*capable*" is a slippery word. "*[C]apable of Demonstration*"[28] might be taken to mean that we can reasonably expect a mathematical demonstration of morality in the near future – perhaps from John Locke himself. That is certainly how some of Locke's critics affected to take it. There is a very testy response by

---

[27] See Dunn, *Political Thought of John Locke*, pp. 187 ff.

[28] Locke writes (E: 4.3.18): "The *idea* of a supreme Being, infinite in Power, Goodness, and Wisdom, whose Workmanship we are, and on whom we depend; and the *idea* of our selves, as understanding, rational Beings . . . would, I suppose, if duly considered, and pursued, afford such foundations of Our Duty and Rules of Action as might place Morality *amongst the Sciences capable of Demonstration.*"

Locke to a criticism along these lines by one Thomas Burnet. Locke says things like: "I have said indeed in my book that I thought morality capable of demonstration as well as mathematics. But I do not remember where I promised this gentleman to demonstrate it to him."[29] Now actually this is more than a little disingenuous, for in the *Second Treatise* Locke insists several times that the law of nature is "plain and intelligible to all rational Creatures,"[30] while in the *Essay*, he actually spoke of his "confidence" that "if Men would in the same method, and with the same indifferency, search after moral, as they do mathematical Truths, they would . . . come nearer perfect Demonstration, than is commonly imagined" (E: 4.3.20).

Even so, I think we are unfair to Locke when we say, with John Dunn and others, that he never actually got round to providing any of the particulars of the law of nature or that he never got round to setting out the rational arguments that he claimed were capable of being produced.[31] An awful lot of the *Second Treatise* just *is* a presentation of natural law; it adds up to a natural law argument, roughly demonstrative in form, on issues such as property, punishment, and politics. Locke *shows* us what a natural law argument would be, even if he doesn't describe very explicitly the process he is using. The argument about equality, which we reconstructed in Chapter 3 for example, is in the form of a rational argument, albeit a rational argument imbued with religious content.[32] There Locke is arguing that a being with the power of abstraction can recognize that it has an obligation to act in accordance with God's purposes; and when it sees the same power of abstraction manifested by others, it can recognize that they too have been sent into the world about God's business, and so they must be respected – equally with oneself – as beings commissioned by the purposes of God. That is a natural law argument. Also, the *Second Treatise* chapter on property – which I will talk about in Chapter 6 – is a sustained piece of natural law reasoning, presented by Locke, in his own voice as a long, demonstrative body of argument. It may not be a perfect or completely persuasive argument. But it surely furnishes an impressive sample of the sort of thing Locke thought could in fact be provided. What I am saying, then, is that sometimes it is less important to see what Locke *says* about argumentation in morals, and more important to see what he *does*, what he *produces* in the way of such argumentation. That's

---

[29] See Burnet, *Remarks on John Locke*, p. 34.   [30] See 2nd T: 12 and 124.

[31] Dunn, *Political Thought of John Locke*, p. 187; Laslett, "Introduction," p. 81.

[32] And just to avoid any misunderstanding: the idea of a rational demonstration of morality does not mean a *secular* demonstration. It means that we reason from the rational – and, in Locke's view, rationally demonstrable – idea of God, rather than from any particular revelation.

what provides our clearest indication of what natural law argumentation is supposed to be like.

In another regard, too, Locke's irritation with Burnet's complaint is not entirely unreasonable. For "capable of Demonstration" might also mean that there is *in principle* no *obstacle* to demonstration – that we have no reason to believe there is anything in morality which (so to speak) inherently defies rationality, or obstructs demonstration – without it being the case that the demonstration is actually within our power (as things stand). For us, the toughest part of the case to make in this regard would be to establish the existence of a personal deity, who takes an interest in human affairs, who "has a superiority and right to ordain, and also a power to reward and punish according to the tenor of the law established by him."[33] But Locke did not see this as a particular problem: "This sovereign lawmaker . . . is God . . . whose existence we have already proved."[34] If showing that had required an irrational *leap* of faith, then morality would not in principle be capable of demonstration. Beyond that, it is a matter of figuring out first, whether God, whose existence we have demonstrated, requires anything of us. Thus in the 1686 manuscript fragment, "Of Ethic in General" (where he is setting out his agenda in moral philosophy), Locke says: "The next thing then to show is, that there are certain rules . . . which it is his will all men should conform their actions to, and that this will of his is sufficiently promulgated and made known to all mankind."[35] Now I read that quite pedantically. What the philosopher undertakes to show is "*that there are* certain rules," which is not at all the same as undertaking to establish their contents. The point is that Locke thinks reason refutes the deist's claim that God might have no concern with human affairs. And near the beginning of *The Reasonableness of Christianity*, there is a quite convincing argument that reason must be normative for beings like us, even if we are bound to fall short of its demands. The argument is more or less *a priori*, at least once it is granted that we are created beings endowed with reason. Reason, Locke says, must be normative for man,

> unless God would have made him a rational creature, and not required him to live by the law of reason; but would have countenanced in him irregularity and disobedience to that light which he had, and that rule which was suitable to his nature . . . if rational creatures will not live up to the rule of their reason, who shall excuse them? If you will admit them to forsake reason in one point, why not in another? Where will you stop? (RC: 11).

---

[33] From manuscript fragment: Locke, "Of Ethic in General," p. 304.   [34] Ibid.   [35] Ibid.

As for the content of natural law, Locke insists that God's commands are necessarily reasonable: God gave man reason, "and with it a law: that could not be otherwise than what reason should dictate; unless we should think, that a reasonable creature should have an unreasonable law" (RC: 157). The final thing that reason undertakes to show is that God's will "is sufficiently made known to all mankind,"[36] which again is not the same as establishing the content of what has been made known. Locke's philosophical agenda would be satisfied if reason pointed us reliably in the direction of moral revelation, and if reason also provided resources for establishing the veracity of revelation and for figuring out its (complex) relation to reason. And again Locke thinks that work *is* done, in Book IV of the *Essay*. So it is a little insensitive to the complexity involved to say that Locke simply balked at the task of establishing a rational foundation for morality. The task has many parts, and many parts of it were in fact completed, in Locke's work, more or less to his satisfaction, if not to that of all his readers.

Once the groundwork had been laid, once the in-principle possibility of a rational demonstration of morality had been established, Locke could afford to acknowledge the practical and real-life difficulties of actually accomplishing the demonstration. The practical difficulties might well be formidable. "*Moral Ideas*," says Locke, "are commonly more complex than those of the Figures ordinarily considered in Mathematics" (E: 4.3.19). Even in mathematics, things are not always straightforward. As he observes in the *Third Letter for Toleration*, "It is demonstration that 31876 is the product of 9467172 divided by 297, and yet I challenge you to find one man of a thousand, to whom you can tender this proposition with demonstrative or sufficient evidence to convince him of the truth of it in a dark room."[37] Though ultimately deductive reasoning is just perception of the agreement and disagreement of ideas, yet "it is not without pains and attention" (E: 4.2.4). It proceeds "by single and slow Steps, and long poring in the dark" (E: 4.3.6), and it requires "steddy application and pursuit," and "a Progression by steps and degrees, before the Mind can in this way arrive at Certainty" (E: 4.2.4).

Thomas Hobbes once remarked that the success of any intellectual enterprise is often adversely affected by conflicts of interest. We may not expect this in science or mathematics, though even there, he said,

I doubt not, but if it had been a thing contrary to any man's right of dominion, or to the interest of men that have dominion, that the three Angles of a Triangle

---

[36] Ibid.   [37] Locke, *Third Letter for Toleration*, p. 297.

should be equal to two Angles of a Square, that doctrine should have been, if not disputed, yet by the burning of all books of Geometry suppressed, as far as he whom it concerned was able.[38]

In ethics and in natural law reasoning, by contrast, interest and ambition are pervasively present, and they present a constant threat to the integrity of our thinking. I have already mentioned the passage in which Locke notices how "the busie mind of Man" is as capable of carrying us to absurdity and monstrosity, as to truth, reason, and light: "nor can it be otherwise in a Creature, whose thoughts are more than the Sands, and wider than the Ocean" (1st T: 58). There is, in Locke as there is in Hobbes, something like a radical version of what John Rawls calls "the burdens of judgment" – the many obstacles and pitfalls that beset our reasoning and, in a practical sense, obstruct any arrival at consensus or agreement.[39] "Our Reason is often puzzled, and at a loss, *because of the obscurity, Confusion, or Imperfection of the* Ideas *it is employed about*; and there we are involved in Difficulties and Contradictions" (E: 4.17.10). And again:

> The Mind, *by proceeding upon false principles* is often engaged in Absurdities and Difficulties, brought into Straits and Contradictions, without knowing how to free it self: And in that case it is in vain to implore the help of Reason, unless it be to discover the falsehood, and reject the influence of those wrong Principles. Reason is so far from clearing the Difficulties which the building upon false foundations brings a Man into, that if he will pursue it, it entangles him the more, and engages him deeper in Perplexities. (E: 4.17.12)

The burdens of judgement are particularly heavy in moral reasoning, for in addition to the inherent difficulty of the subject, and almost inevitable distortions introduced by self-interest, we have to contend also with the influence of "depraved Custom and ill Education" (E: 1.3.20). Custom, Locke says, is "a greater power than Nature" and often makes people "worship for Divine, what she hath inured them to bow their Minds, and submit their Understandings to" (E: 1.3.25). This is true of children and the illiterate and it is, Locke thinks, scarcely less true of those who have the "leisure, parts, and will" to engage in abstract moral inquiry. Even among this class,

> [w]ho is there almost that dare shake the foundations of all his past Thoughts and Actions, and endure to bring upon himself the shame of having been a long time wholly in mistake and error? Who is there hardy enough to contend with the reproach which is everywhere prepared for those who dare venture

---

[38] Hobbes, *Leviathan*, Ch. 11, p. 74.   [39] Rawls, *Political Liberalism*, pp. 54–8.

to dissent from the received Opinions of their Country or Party? And where is the man to be found that can patiently prepare himself to bear the name of Whimsical, Sceptical, or Atheist; which he is sure to meet with, who does in the least scruple any of the common Opinions? (E: 1.3.25)

We all feel the influence of fashion and custom to some extent. But those of higher social status are particularly vulnerable to it, and so there is no question but that Locke recognized the special danger they were in, in their reasoning on moral and political matters.

All this leads our author towards what is in the end a quite pessimistic view of what reason and scholarly intellect can accomplish in the way of a socially useful demonstration of morality. Such pessimism finds its culmination in *The Reasonableness of Christianity*, where Locke's conclusion is stark:

Experience shows, that the knowledge of morality, by mere natural light . . . makes but a slow progress, and little advance in the world. And the reason of it is not hard to be found in men's necessities, passions, vices and mistaken interests . . . or whatever else was the cause, it is plain, in fact, that human reason unassisted failed men in its great and proper business of morality. It never from unquestionable principles, by clear deductions, made out an entire body of the law of nature. (RC: 140)

I know we are supposed to be very careful about the continuity between the *Essay* and the *Two Treatises*, on the one hand, and the sober picture that is painted of "human reason unassisted" in the *Reasonableness of Christianity*, on the other. John Dunn says it is "historically inept to see the *Essay* as implying the *Reasonableness of Christianity* or indeed the *Reasonableness* implying the *Essay*."[40] The *Essay* was launched with an aspiration that, by the time the *Reasonableness* was written, Locke had come to see as impossible of fulfillment, so there is in some sense a dynamic rather than a static relation between them.[41] Still, as Dunn also points out, Locke published editions of the *Essay* after as well as before writing the *Reasonableness*.[42] We have seen that many of the doubts that surface finally in the *Reasonableness* are adumbrated in the *Essay*. Certainly the critique of the contribution of professional philosophy is there. It is, after all, in the *Essay* that Locke observes that "the increase brought into the

---

[40] Dunn, *Political Thought of John Locke*, p. 192.

[41] See also Kato, "The *Reasonableness* in the Historical Light of the *Essay*," pp. 53–7.

[42] "[S]ince Locke wrote the *Reasonableness* at least in part after two editions of the *Essay* had been published and proceeded to complete two further editions of the *Essay* in his own lifetime, he must have regarded the implications of the two works as compatible." (Dunn, *Political Thought of John Locke*.)

Stock of real Knowledge, has been very little, in proportion to the Schools, Disputes, and Writings, the World has been filled with" (E: 4.3.30). All that the *Reasonableness* does is apply that to the particular topic of morality: "[H]e that shall collect all the moral rules of the philosophers ... will find them to come short of the morality delivered by our Savior, and taught by his apostles; a college made up, for the most part of ignorant, but inspired fishermen." (RC: 140). I know also that we are supposed to pay attention to the particular theological disputes in which Locke was embroiled at the time of writing the *Reasonableness*. He was responding to the accusation – perhaps not entirely unjustified – of Socinianism, and searching for a way to express his own hesitations about Protestant Trinitarianism.[43] Certainly these were the themes to which the first generation of readers of the *Reasonableness* responded; they seem to have been more or less completely uninterested in Locke's comments, towards the end of the work, about the moral failings of "human reason unassisted."[44] But that doesn't make the latter comments any less part of Locke's position, particularly when they tend to put on display – as I think they do – Locke's refusal to accord greater credit or privilege to the reasoning of the moral philosopher than to the moral thinking of the poor and the illiterate to whom the Christian message was in the first instance entrusted.

The verdict of the *Reasonableness* on the failure of moral philosophy is really quite remarkable: "it is too hard a task for unassisted reason to establish morality in all its parts, upon its true foundation" (RC: 139). The Greeks were as smart as can be, says Locke (RC: 136), but we know how unsuccessful the attempts of Socrates, Plato, Aristotle, and Solon were in this regard before the Christian era. "Philosophy seemed to have spent its strength, and done its utmost" (RC: 145–6), to little avail. He poses a hypothetical question from the ancient world: if Brutus or Cassius had asked a contemporary philosopher for natural law guidance on their rights and duties against Caesar, where would the philosopher have turned for advice?

Where might they find the law they were to live by, and by which they should be charged or acquitted, as guilty, or innocent? If to the sayings of the wise, and the declarations of philosophers, he sends them into a wild wood of uncertainty, to an endless maze, from which they should never get out. (RC: 143)

---

[43] There is an excellent account in Marshall, *John Locke*, pp. 398–413. We are also supposed to attend to the fact that the *Reasonableness* was addressed to deists who thought that morality could survive perfectly well without Christianity (see Woltersdorff, *John Locke and the Ethics of Belief*, p. 128), which is closer to the dimension of Locke's project that I am going to emphasize.

[44] See the extracts collected in Nuovo (ed.) *John Locke and Christianity*.

And the ability of "christian philosophers," i.e. those who study moral philosophy in the era since the ministry of Jesus Christ, to do any better is not due to the quality of their philosophizing but to their having been given by revelation certain basic truths to work with (RC: 140). They may credit their reason with these truths, and that is an understandable artifact of the vanity that is everywhere associated with philosophical skills. But the credit is mis-assigned:

A great many things which we have been bred up in the belief of, from our cradles . . . we take for unquestionable obvious truths, and easily demonstrable; without considering how long we might have been in doubt or ignorance of them, had revelation been silent. And many are beholden to revelation, who do not acknowledge it. It is no diminishing to revelation, that reason gives its suffrage too, to the truths revelation has discovered. But it is our mistake to think, that because reason confirms them to us, we had the first certain knowledge of them from thence; and in that clear evidence we now possess them. (RC: 145)

I will return to this theme at the end of Chapter 8, as part of Locke's answer to the secular egalitarian, who disdains the benefit of a religious argument for equality.[45]

What exactly is it that Locke says has been lacking in the autonomous efforts of moral philosophy? Ian Harris says that Locke's view in the *Reasonableness* was that "[i]t was the obligation rather than the content of natural law that was lacking."[46] After all, it is not as though the New Testament adds very much to our moral and political philosophy. It gives us the Golden Rule, certainly, and Locke seems to have subscribed to the conventional view that the Golden Rule epitomized the rest of natural law. It is certainly crucial to our understanding of equality.[47] Even so, if the problem with moral philosophy was that it failed to set out all the parts and details of the natural law (RC: 142), the Gospels don't seem to have done much better. They certainly do not yield up a complete moral and political philosophy; if anything they seek deliberately to avoid the topic as much as possible.[48] On Harris's view, then, Locke's position in the *Reasonableness* was that the philosophers may have succeeded in setting out the content of the natural law, but they failed to provide an adequate account of its normativity.

---

[45] See Chapter 8, pp. 241–3.   [46] Harris, *Mind of John Locke*, p. 309.
[47] See particularly the argument, drawn partly from Hooker, connecting basic equality with the Golden Rule in 2nd T: 5. I discuss this in Chapter 6 at pp. 155–8.
[48] See Chapter 7 for a full account of the problem of the relation between New Testament teaching and the *Two Treatises of Government*.

The issue of normativity that Harris mentions is certainly a prominent theme in Locke's critique of moral philosophy. Even if we grant that the philosophers knew the content of morality before the ministry of Jesus, "[w]hat will all this do, to give the world a complete morality, that may be to mankind the unquestionable rule of life and manners?" (RC 141).

> Did the saying of Aristippus, or Confucius, give it an authority? Was Zeno a law-giver to mankind? If not, what he or any other philosopher delivered, was but a saying of his. Mankind might hearken to it, or reject it, as they pleased; or as it suited their interest, passions, principles or humors. They were under no obligation: the opinion of this or that philosopher was of no authority . . . [T]hese incoherent apophthegms of philosophers, and wise men, however excellent in themselves, and well intended by them . . . could never rise to the force of a law, that mankind could with certainty depend on. (RC: 141–2)

The same applies if we think of a systematic deduction of morality along broadly utilitarian lines. "The law of nature, is the law of convenience too" (RC: 142), and as such its principles have been understood "as bonds of society, and conveniences of common life, and laudable practices" (RC: 144). But still that's not morality.[49] Locke's complaint raises something like the issue that was raised in the middle of the twentieth century by students of Hobbes's thought: it is one thing to present the laws of nature as theorems conducive to survival; it is quite another to present them deontologically as *laws*.[50]

But Locke's assumption here – granting that the philosophers knew the content of morality before the ministry of Jesus – is made in the *Reasonableness* purely for the sake of argument. What he actually says is: "let it be granted (*though not true*) that all the moral precepts of the gospel were known by somebody or other, amongst mankind before" (RC: 141, my emphasis). Now, the point is not that nothing but revelation can provide moral *certainty*. Locke denies that outright in the *Essay* (E: 4.18.5), and there is no reason to suppose he went back on that denial. But in the end it *is* a matter of content. Locke believed that there were certain elements of morality which are just not accessible to reason in the ordinary way. The philosophers "depended on reason and her oracles, which contain nothing but truth: but yet some parts of that truth lie too deep for our natural powers easily to reach, and make plain and visible to mankind; without some light from above to direct them" (RC: 144).

---

[49] See also Wolterstorff, *John Locke and the Ethics of Belief*, pp. 138–9.
[50] Hobbes, *Leviathan*, Ch. 15, p. 111. See also Taylor, "The Ethical Doctrine of Hobbes"; and Brown, "Hobbes: The Taylor Thesis."

"[T]oo deep for our natural powers": in the light of this sort of claim, it is starting to be clear, by the time of writing the *Reasonableness*, that Locke no longer believed that reason and revelation were two alternative ways – two complete alternative ways – of apprehending the content of the law of nature. One might lead us so far; but it could not lead us further. Its perplexities and inconclusiveness were therefore bound to cast doubt on any claim to social or political privilege based on one's ability to set off down this route. Even those with the leisure and resources to begin that journey would find eventually that they had to turn around and take the lower, safer route.

It will not, then, seem remarkable that Locke's prescription for the impasse which reason seemed to have reached in regard to morality was not a prescription for more and better philosophy. It is not a question of the philosophers having failed and being sent away to do better: "If any one shall think to excuse human nature, by laying blame on men's negligence, that did not carry morality to an higher pitch; and make it out entire in every part, with that clearness of demonstration which some think it capable of; he helps not the matter" (RC: 143–4). What was needed was not more expert philosophy, or more studious attention to the deliverances of good philosophy by those who were capable only of bad. What was needed was something different altogether: that people should be told their duties by "one manifestly sent from God, and coming with visible authority from him" (RC: 139). The specific resource which, according to Locke, affords the clearest basis for our knowledge of and obedience to natural law and morality, is the Christian religion, the teachings of Jesus Christ,[51] underwritten by the miracles that demonstrate His credentials, inspired by the example of His life and ministry, and taught as by "one having authority" (RC: 143 and 148).[52] This prescription turns out to be crucial in underwriting the claims Locke is making on behalf of the ordinary intellect. Locke's Christianity, I am going to argue, is intimately connected with his faith in the democratic intellect. It is, he says, "a religion suited to vulgar capacities" (RC: 157). It was preached, in the first instance, to "poor, ignorant, illiterate men" (RC: 83), "a college made up, for the most part,

---

[51] So far as the revelation to ancient Israel was concerned, Locke says that "that revelation was shut up in a little corner of the world, amongst a people, by that very law, which they received with it, excluded from a commerce and communication with the rest of mankind" (RC: 137), whereas "our Savior, when he came, threw down this wall of partition" between Jews and Gentiles (RC: 138).

[52] Matthew 7:29.

of ignorant, but inspired fishermen" (RC, 140),[53] and it contains a message as well as a method that privileges the humbler human intellects of the world:

> Had God intended that none but the learned scribe, the disputer, or wise of this world, should be Christians . . . thus religion should have been prepared for them, filled with speculations and niceties, obscure terms, and abstract notions. *But men of that expectation, men furnished with such acquisitions, the apostle tells us I Cor. i. are rather shut out from the simplicity of the gospel* . . . That the poor had the gospel preached to them; Christ makes a mark, as well as business of his mission, Matt. xi. 5 And if the poor had the gospel preached to them, it was, without doubt, such a gospel as the poor could understand; plain and intelligible. (RC: 158, my emphasis)

In other words, not only did Locke define the threshold of equality (as we saw in Chapter 3) around very ordinary capacities; he also understood that in the end these were the capacities on which the appeal of natural law, morality, and religion were going to have to be based, specialist philosophy having "spent its strength, and done its utmost" (RC: 146).

C. B. Macpherson reads the passages I have been considering as having a different tendency.[54] He says that Locke's argument in *The Reasonableness of Christianity* is further evidence of his "assumption that the members of the labouring class are in too low a position to be capable of a rational life – that is, capable of regulating their lives by those moral principles Locke supposed were given by reason."[55] He

---

[53] Locke connects this point to Jesus Christ's modesty about his mission:

> Men, great or wise in knowledge, of the ways of the world, would hardly have been kept from prying more narrowly into his design or conduct; or from questioning him about the ways or measures he would take . . . Abler men, of higher births or thoughts, would hardly have been hindered from whispering . . . that their master was the Messiah . . . Whether twelve other men, of quicker parts, and of a station or breeding, which might have given them any opinion of themselves, or their own abilities, would have been so easily kept from meddling, beyond just what was prescribed them . . . I leave to be considered. (RC: 83–4)

> For a somewhat overwrought gloss on the element of concealment in this, see Strauss, *Natural Right and History*, pp. 207–9 and Rabieh, "The Reasonableness of Locke," pp. 934–5.

[54] I am going to criticize Macpherson's account, but I should note at once that he is quite right to say that the *Reasonableness* "is not, as might be thought, a plea for a simple rationalist ethical religion to replace the disputations of the theologians" (Macpherson, *Political Theory of Possessive Individualism*, p. 225). It is not like Kant's *Religion within the Limits of Reason Alone*. On the contrary, what Locke extols about Christianity in the *Reasonableness* is the firmness and authority of Jesus' teaching, and even some of the threats associated with it, not its intellectualism; it is in these respects that he compares it favorably with moral philosophy.

[55] Macpherson, *Political Theory of Possessive Individualism*, p. 224. Again, I am pleased to find that my discussion is very close to that of Ashcraft, *Locke's Two Treatises of Government*, pp. 253–8.

takes particular note of Locke's argument to the effect that a successful philosophical explication of the natural law would not provide a basis for teaching morality to members of the working class:

The greatest part of mankind want leisure or capacity for demonstration; nor can carry a train of proofs, which in that way they must always depend upon for conviction, and cannot be required to assent to, until they see the demonstration. Wherever they stick, the teachers are always put upon proof, and must clear the doubt by a thread of coherent deductions from the first principle, how long, or how intricate soever they be. And you may as soon hope to have all the day-labourers and tradesmen, the spinsters and dairy-maids, perfect mathematicians, as to have them perfect in ethics this way. (RC: 146)

It is undeniable that Locke says a lot along these lines:[56] "The greatest part cannot know and therefore they must believe" (RC: 146). But we also need to emphasize the proposition that Locke conjoins with this: that there is no philosophical demonstration of morality; there is no other way than this to uncover and teach the basics of morality. It is not a case of Locke thinking that there is Gospel teaching available for the poor and illiterate, and moral philosophy equally available for the rich and educated. Locke doesn't think that anyone – philosopher, bourgeois or dairy-maid – can "be satisfied in the rules and obligations of all parts of their duties" (RC: 143) except through teaching drawn from or inspired by elementary Christian doctrine. Towards the end of his discussion, Macpherson provides a rather shamefaced recognition of this when he concedes that "Locke was, of course, recommending this simplified Christianity for all classes."[57] And then he scrambles to save his interpretation by making it a matter of emphasis:

But the ability of his fundamental Christian doctrine to satisfy men of higher capacities Locke regards as only a secondary advantage. His repeated emphasis on the necessity of the labouring class being brought to obedience by believing

---

I refer readers particularly to his account of the "ludicrous" character of Macpherson's claim that the *Reasonableness of Christianity* credits the intellectual credentials of "members of the propertied classes in seventeenth-century England" (ibid., p. 255).

[56] Locke also says: "The greatest part of mankind have not leisure for learning and logic, and superfine distinctions of the schools. When the hand is used to the plough and the spade, the head is seldom . . . exercised in mysterious reasoning. It is well if men of that rank (to say nothing of the other sex) can comprehend plain propositions, and a short reasoning about things familiar to their minds, and nearly allied to their daily experience. Go beyond this, and you . . . may as well talk Arabic to a poor day-laborer." (RC: 157)

[57] Macpherson, *Political Theory of Possessive Individualism*, p. 225.

in divine rewards and punishments leaves no doubt about his main concern. The implication is plain: the labouring class, beyond all others, is incapable of leading a rational life.[58]

But this really will not do. The emphasis in the *Reasonableness* and in the *Essay* is all the other way. The mode of access that the laboring classes have to what has become, on account of the Christian revelation, widely dispersed moral common sense is the only reliable mode of access: it involves reasoning to the existence of God using the basic capacities of human rationality and to the idea of oneself as a person required to obey Him; and then it requires attention to what God has taught and revealed, and the integration of all that into a roughly reasoned compendium of duty. "The writers and wranglers" (RC: 157) might spurn the specifically Christian element and try their hand at a more elaborate intellectual approach; but they are taking a very grave risk.[59] And Locke does not believe that that risk is mitigated by the social distance set between them and "the illiterate and contemned Mechanick" (E: 3.10.9). If anything it is compounded, for high social status makes one's "unassisted reason" all the more vulnerable to the assistance of established fashion, craft, and folly.

IV

My theme in this chapter has been the democratic intellect. I hope it is clear from the excursus we made into *The Reasonableness of Christianity* that we cannot take any of *this* seriously – we cannot take seriously Locke's insistence on the role of Jesus Christ's teaching in clarifying natural law, and the nature of the audience for whom His message was intended and by whom His message was received, and the contrast that he draws between this and the confused state of philosophical intellect on moral matters – without seeing, in Locke's account of the connection between the theological and epistemic basis of morality, a profound validation of the claims of the ordinary intellect. That validation, I submit, lies at the heart of Locke's commitment to equality, and in that capacity it pervades every page of his politics. In Chapter 3 we saw that his theory of equality was predicated upon a quite modest estimation of the intellectual capacities that established the special place of human beings

---

[58] Ibid., p. 226.

[59] See Moore, "Locke on the Moral Need for Christianity," p. 66, for Locke's analogy between this risk and the risk undertaken by those who hope for salvation from their own good works alone.

in the moral structure of the universe. Now in this chapter we have seen that, despite Locke's own vocational respect for intellectual excellence, he does not fall into the trap of differentiating humans in their merit or moral or political standing by the sophistication of their intellects. The properties on which his theory of equality is grounded are matched by the properties that he respects, and which he regards as socially and politically sufficient for a practical grasp of morality.

5

Kings, Fathers, Voters, Subjects, and Crooks

It is important to remind ourselves – in the midst of our otherwise abstruse discussion of nominal essences, real resemblances, and range properties – that we are still proceeding with an eye to a *practical* principle of basic equality. John Locke has set basic equality some important political work to do, and that work has to be done among the variety of beings we call ordinary humans. Equality is supposed to tell us something fundamental about political life. One preliminary way of drawing it out is as follows. Between any *de facto* ruler and any *de facto* subject intent upon challenging that ruler, defending himself against that ruler, or even just calling that ruler to account, the egalitarian claim is that we will not see such a difference in faculties as to entitle us to say that the one is a natural superior to the other. A morally astute observer will see that on both sides of the comparison, the individuals in question have faculties *sufficiently similar* to put them on a par, so far as moral status is concerned. This fundamental equality means that the subject's demand or grievance cannot be dismissed as simple impudence or insubordination. The subject who challenges his ruler is owed an answer because, from a God's-eye point of view, he is as much a king as his ruler, his interests count for as much in politics as his ruler's interests, and his will is as much a source of authority. The moral status of the lowliest subject is the same as that of any noble or scholar or statesman or king: "all the Servants of one Sovereign Master, sent into the World by his order, and about his business, ... made to last during his, not one another's Pleasure" (2nd T: 6). Even if the beings that Locke called human oysters (E: 2.9.14), i.e. lunatics, idiots, and dotards, do not figure in these comparisons (except perhaps as kings in degenerate hereditary monarchies), still the argument is radical enough to give the benefit of this foundational equality to more or less anyone who has the wit to claim it.

The *Second Treatise* is the place where Locke gives the clearest account of the implications of this position for politics. It may not be the best guide to Locke's own political opinions on the particular issues that occupied Englishmen in the late 1670s and 1680s.[1] But it provides the clearest indication from Locke of what a well-thought-through set of political opinions ought to be based on. This chapter will focus rather more closely on the *Second Treatise* than the previous chapters have done. For I now want to consider what Locke's underlying egalitarianism implies so far as equality and inequality of power and authority are concerned.

I

That the starting point of the *Second Treatise* is egalitarian is beyond denial. It is there on the page (2nd T: 4–6). But the way in which Locke develops his theory of politics beyond its premises in this work does not seem particularly radical at first glance. He may begin with the claim that all men are equal, and "born with a Title to perfect Freedom . . . equally with any other Man, or Number of Men in the World" (2nd T: 87). But we are very quickly introduced in the pages of the *Second Treatise* to a cast of characters that is depressingly familiar from the sordid reality of ordinary inegalitarian politics. At the very beginning of the *Two Treatises*, we are told that they were written to vindicate the title of a king – "*to establish the Throne of our Great Restorer, Our present King* William"[2] – and in the midst of what purports to be a theory of radical resistance and revolution we are supposed to be reassured when Locke says, at the end of the work, that political turmoil always brings the English "back again to our old Legislative of King, Lords, and Commons" (2nd T: 223). In the context of this sort of reassurance, the prospects for a general characterization of Locke's theory as pervasively egalitarian do not look promising. Far from the single-status political community that one might expect, the social and political roles that Locke countenances in the book seem quite unequal. Think of some of the asymmetries Locke envisages in a well-ordered civil society. Besides the difference between husbands and wives that troubled us in Chapter 2, he seems to envisage unequal relations of power between parents and children, tutors and students, masters and servants, guardians and madmen, ministers and congregation, owners and paupers, farmers and laborers, residents and foreigners, representatives and constituents, majorities and out-voted minorities, nobles and

---

[1] See Wootton, "John Locke and Richard Ashcraft's *Revolutionary Politics*," p. 96, distinguishing between a radical text and a more compromised author.

[2] Locke, *Two Treatises*, Preface, p. 137. For some observations on Locke's enthusiasm for William's title, see Wootton, "John Locke and Richard Ashcraft's *Revolutionary Politics*," p. 92.

commoners, subjects and magistrates, law-abiding citizens and criminals, and conquerors and vanquished aggressors in a just war.

True, from time to time, Locke imagines forms of human society that
might be characterized by rough equality of status and outcome. But he
associates that possibility with the primitive and the impoverished: "The
equality of a simple poor way of liveing confineing their desires within
the narrow bounds of each mans smal propertie made few controversies
and so no need of many laws to decide them." (2nd T: 107). The more
people there are, it seems, the more complex their interactions in an
advanced society; and the more prosperous the economy and the greater
the proliferation of science and technology, the more variegated and
unequal the society will be in wealth, status, and power.

So, if we are going to argue that a Lockean political theory appropriate
for an advanced society is still fundamentally an *egalitarian* theory, everything will depend on our ability to show that a variety of outcomes which
are not themselves equal are traceable nevertheless to a premise of equality, and justifiable in a way that respects the importance of that equality
even in an argument for difference and distinction. Now, we know from
modern discussions of equality in political philosophy that this is not
out of the question. It is not permissible to infer unequal moral status
from a prescription of unequal shares or unequal outcomes.[3] Still, even
when that inference is avoided, there is hard work to be done. Can we
show that an array of apparently unequal roles and outcomes (including
inequalities of political authority) can be derived from a premise of basic
equality, and derived in a way that still entitles the theory as a whole to
be called egalitarian?

II

One issue that an egalitarian social theory has to confront is the issue
of children. What are we to say about the place of babies, infants, and
young children in what purports to be, at base, a single-status political
community?

Consider a young child, aged (say) one or two. The child has some
intellectual capacities that are recognizably human: he is beginning to
speak, to connect ideas, to generalize to some elementary abstractions,
and even – as every parent knows – to hold his own in argument, albeit

---

[3] See, for example, Dworkin, *Taking Rights Seriously*, p. 227, distinguishing between the right to equal
treatment and the deeper right to treatment as an equal. See also Chapter 1, above, pp. 3 and 6.

in a way that is often uncontaminated by logic. Still the child's reasoning is unlike that of most adults. Locke characterizes the difference in an interesting way. Some of what he says implies that the child has fewer ideas and less to work with, intellectually, because the child is less experienced. And sheer lack of experience might be important in the moral realm: John Marshall notes that in an amendment to a late edition of *Some Thoughts Concerning Education*, Locke had observed that it is difficult to explain the idea of justice to a child, because the idea of justice includes the idea of acquiring property by labor, and children often don't know what it is like to labor.[4] But it's not just a matter of experience and input; it is also a matter of the development of appropriate mental structures. The ability to form and manipulate abstract ideas – which, as we have seen, is key to moral status, for it is the basis of one's reasoning to and from the existence of God – is an ability that grows. It is not given to humans at birth: there are "few signs of a soul accustomed to much thinking in a new-born child" (E: 2.1.21). Adults have it; children don't. And without this ability, there is no question of the child's being able to figure out the natural law. Moreover, in the case of a young child, there is also the question of an appropriate linkage being established between his intellectual capacities (such as they are) and his agency or will. Whatever understanding of natural law the child has needs to be connected to his will "that so he might keep his actions within the bounds of it" (2nd T: 59). Of course, nobody's will is connected perfectly to his reason – that, I think, was part of the point about *corporeal* rationality, which we developed in Chapter 3.[5] Locke may have had doubts about original sin, but only in its literal form of inherited fault, not in the looser sense of our nature being inapt for perfectly rational control of our actions.[6] He did think that the linkage between understanding and will had to grow and that it required nurture and education. In young children, it was pretty much non-existent: the infrastructure was still being laid down. So in this respect too, there was a radical difference between the child's situation and that of an adult, even an adult possessed only of the quite modest capabilities we discussed in the previous chapter.

Now, think back to the idea that I defined in Chapter 3 – the idea of a scale of intellectual abilities, and the idea of a range property marking

---

[4] Marshall, *John Locke*, pp. 446–7. (Marshall wonders why Locke didn't recall that most children of the poor did labor, and most children of the rich did not experience laboring-for-a-living even when they grew up.)

[5] See above, p. 71.

[6] Harris, *The Mind of John Locke*, pp. 298–9. But see also Marshall, *John Locke*, p. 344, for the possibility that Locke envisaged human perfectibility.

out and privileging an area on that scale. There is clearly a gap between the reasoning power of a normal human adult and that of an infant. But we know that the idea of a range property is capable of accommodating large scalar gaps. So the question we must now ask is this: is the gap between the reasoning power of a normal human adult and that of an infant to be regarded as an interval within the range, or as an interval between points within the range and points outside it. (In terms of the analogy we used: is it like the distance between Princeton and Hoboken, so far as the range property *being in New Jersey* is concerned, or is it like the distance between Hoboken and Manhattan? I use this example, as always, to emphasize that it is not the sheer size of the gap that matters; it is its character relative to the interest that defines the range property.)

Egalitarians may take one of two approaches to questions like this. One approach starts from the premise that *of course the child is human*, and proceeds to define the relevant range accordingly. If we know that we want to include infants (and perhaps also people who are profoundly disabled mentally), then we will have to define the range of the human sufficiently broadly so that it includes both the child and the adult (and the disabled human as well). And then we announce: "Anything within this broad range gets the benefit of the principle of basic human equality." (Of course it wouldn't follow that children and the disabled are to be treated the same as adults – as we have seen, a principle of basic equality is not the same as a principle of equal treatment – but it lays the foundation for moral thinking about appropriate treatment.) But there are two further challenges we face. (a) We have to accept the consequences of defining the range so widely – namely, that if the range is broad enough to accommodate human babes in arms and profoundly disabled humans, it will almost certainly accommodate many non-human animals as well, such as adult chimpanzees and dolphins. (b) We also have to be able to *defend* the range, so defined; that is, we have to be able to show that its generous scope and shape make sense in terms of some underlying interest or value – some interest or value important enough to be the foundation of basic equality.

Animal rights theorists sometimes embrace (a), but forget about (b). They have in mind an outcome they want to reach – that certain higher primates are our equals – and certain assumptions they think we have embraced already – that not just human adults, but children and the profoundly disabled are persons with rights too. And they think nothing more than that is necessary to sustain the very generous range of equality that they are aiming at. But unless the delineation of that range is independently supported, the strength of this argument is no greater than the strength of the intuitions on which it builds. And if someone proposes a different account of appropriate moral treatment for the children and the profoundly disabled, there will be nothing left to motivate the drawing of the circle wide enough to include chimpanzees and dolphins as our equals.

The alternative approach, which is John Locke's approach, is to draw the range of normal human reason more narrowly, but then define a *special* relation of the human infant to that range.[7] What Locke does is to say, first, that infants are not at the moment within the relevant range, but, secondly, that human children are destined to grow up into the adult range: in the felicitous phrasing of the *Second Treatise*, children are born *to* this basic equality, even though they are not born *in* it (2nd T: 55). Parents therefore may not treat their children as simple unequals, and neglect or exploit them as such, as though they were animals. They have a responsibility to treat them as *potential* equals and to educate them, lead them out to the adult equality which is their natural destiny.

Of course, this approach makes no sense so long as the range of human equality is defined generously enough to include infants already. Then there is nothing to lead them on to; and basic equality will lack this teleological dimension. Paradoxically, then, the narrower way of defining the range makes better sense of parents' specifically equality-oriented duties in respect to their children. It is, I think, important to take the point this way, because it helps us understand that the principle of basic equality is not just a matter of recognizing those who currently are our equals; it is also a matter of an affirmative duty to nurture the basis of equality in those who may become, and are evidently intended by God to become, our equals. Equality works here as a principle of responsibility not just rights. We have dwelt a lot on the passage from the beginning of the *Second Treatise* where Locke talks about persons as God's property, "whose Workmanship they are, made to last during his, not one anothers Pleasure" (2nd T: 6). In the *First Treatise*, he makes fun of

---

[7] This is also John Rawls's approach to the problem of the profoundly disabled. Rawls insists that the idea of a range property is not supposed to solve problems posed by marginal cases such as humans who are so severely intellectually disabled as to be incapable of many of the forms of functioning we regard as "human" (see Rawls, *Theory of Justice*, p. 506). The idea is that once a range property is specified, cases of disability may be dealt with as tragedies in relation to the broad human range, rather than being treated as extensions of the range's outer limits. (However, see Wikler, "Paternalism and the Mildly Retarded," for cases where it is unclear which of these approaches to take.)

the idea that children are really their fathers' workmanship (1st T: 52–4). There Locke's case is a rebuttal of an affirmative claim of Filmer's, but in the *Second Treatise*, he develops the workmanship point as a principle of obligation: "[A]ll parents were, by the Law of Nature, *under an obligation to preserve, nourish, and educate the Children* they had begotten; not as their own Workmanship, but the Workmanship of their own Maker, the Almighty, to whom they were to be accountable for them" (2nd T: 56). They have a role to play in their children's formation, but it is a role governed by the equality that is grounded on God's vision for their offspring.

It also puts into perspective the parent's authority, the power that the parent currently has over the child. As we consider whether Locke's allocation of authority is really egalitarian or inegalitarian, it is tempting to focus simply on the point I noticed earlier about the will – Locke's point about the necessity of the parent's will acting as a substitute for the undeveloped will of the child: "[W]hilst he is in an Estate, wherein he has not *Understanding* of his own to direct his *Will*, he is not to have any Will of his own to follow: He that *understands* for him, must *will* for him too; he must prescribe to his Will, and regulate his Actions" (2nd T: 58). But the parent's role is not just to *be* the child's will; it is also to nurture and bring on a will in the child (related in the appropriate way to the child's developing understanding), a will that will eventually make the substitution of the parent's will for the child's will unnecessary. So, as I said, the child is to be brought up and educated to a state of equality with adults. In addition, Locke emphasizes the importance of educating the child *for* equality, so that he can take his place in a community of equals. Children, Locke thought, have a natural love of power and dominion, that reveals itself in greed for possessions, a need to boss others about, and peevishness when their desires are frustrated.[8] These inclinations must be replaced, through education, with more moderate desires and a more respectful attitude towards others if the child is going to be able to take his place in the natural community of equals, and in any set of plausible social and political arrangements built up on that basis.

III

Let us turn now to relations of political equality and inequality, superiority and inferiority, among adults in a Lockean commonwealth. I said at

---

[8] Locke, *Some Thoughts Concerning Education*, pp. 26 ff.

the beginning of Chapter 4 that I would not talk about Locke's views on the suffrage, nor would I take this occasion to enter the lists in support of Richard Ashcraft's suggestion that Locke's political radicalism led him in the direction of arguing in favor of manhood suffrage.[9] I am pretty much persuaded by Ashcraft's arguments, but nothing much turns on that here, because the question I want to explore is not John Locke's own political opinions on the suffrage, but the egalitarian basis he laid in his political philosophy for thinking about issues like this. Even some of those who reject Ashcraft's account acknowledge that the theory set out in the *Two Treatises* is about as radical as Ashcraft claims Locke's opinions were: they just don't think that Locke's opinions or his political practice are best understood through the prism of his most abstract political theorizing.[10]

I don't myself understand why our interest should be diverted away from the argument of the *Two Treatises* to the opinions and practices of Locke the political agitator (assuming that Ashcraft's critics are correct and the two diverge). It is the *Treatises* that have stood the test of time and excited our thinking, not John Locke as an archetype of political activism. We read Locke because we are interested in the question of how to argue in politics, not because we want to do as Locke did so far as various forms of conspiracy or political compromise are concerned. I guess the assumption is that if we pay attention to what Locke did in real-world contexts, we will be in a better position to understand what he said in the way of abstract political theory. But I have my doubts about this as a matter of hermeneutics. First, few theorists have managed successfully to establish a perfect unity between theory and practice, and when they have it has usually been in the context of institutional opportunities (academic tenure in a political environment already made safe for dissent) that are quite different from the environment in which Locke wrote. (I will develop this point further in Chapter 7, when we consider Locke's views on slavery.) And even apart from the question of environment, most of us wrestle with inconsistencies and hypocrisies of one sort or another: I wouldn't want my writings to be read through the prism of my mostly half-hearted and poorly thought-through political interventions. Secondly – and this will be one of my themes in the sections that follow – often Locke's political practice or the assumptions that may plausibly be attributed to all of Locke's contemporaries (such as "Of course women will be excluded from politics," or "Of course,

---

[9] Ashcraft, *Revolutionary Politics*, pp. 556 ff.
[10] See Wootton, "John Locke and Richard Ashcraft's *Revolutionary Politics*," p. 96.

there is no question of day-laborers having the vote") are cited not so
much to clarify arguments in the *Two Treatises* that would otherwise be
obscure or ambiguous, but to call in doubt the most obvious reading of
passages which – apart from the citation of these assumptions – would be
perfectly clear in their radicalism. Locke says, for example, no one can
be subjected to the political power of another without his own consent
and that therefore everyone who lives under the rule of a political community is entitled to participate in choosing the form of government for
that community. That seems pretty clear, and one has to work very hard
to make it difficult to an extent that the difficulty is thought tractable
only by imputing to Locke what we think is the opinion of his contemporaries, that "everyone" did not include day-laborers or women and
that "the people" means "the set of forty-shilling property holders." I'm
inclined to agree with Ashcraft that "[i]t is time ... to take the language
of the *Two Treatises* seriously,"[11] to read it as it stands and to follow it
where it leads, without any substantive assumptions about what Locke
"must have" meant. That may not be the best guide to John Locke's
practice; but it may be the best explanation of why people of all sorts,
in our day and his own, have found this work challenging, as well as
interesting.[12]

The best reason for not saying much in a work of this kind about
whether Locke was really in favor of giving all adults the vote was that
Locke made it perfectly clear, as a matter of abstract political theory,
that this was an open question: it was something for the members of
each political community to decide. The people, when they set up a
government, may organize its legislature, which Locke regarded as the
"supream Power" in any commonwealth (2nd T: 149), any way they
please. (It's a choice they make on the basis of majority-decision: I will
discuss this aspect later in the chapter, in section V.) They might organize
their legislative power as a direct democracy or they might "put the
power of making laws into the hands of a few select men" (ibid.), trusted

---

[11] Ashcraft, *Revolutionary Politics*, p. 578.
[12] In this regard, I find the following observation by Ashcraft in "Simple Objections and Complex
Reality," p. 108, very helpful, as a basis for thinking about the interpretation of Locke in the
context of late seventeenth-century England:

> We can easily discover Anglican clergy who clearly perceive the politically radical features of the
> Lockean argument, including the placing of electoral power in the hands of the "meaner" people.
> We can discover the endorsement of the Lockean argument by other radicals in the 1690s. What
> we cannot find is the aristocratic landlord proudly waving his copy of the Two Treatises to beat
> back the tide of radicalism ... Until such a context can be recovered from the 1680s rather than
> being arbitrarily foisted upon the text by contemporary interpreters, it simply does not have the
> evidential basis to make it a plausible reading of the text.

nobles or oligarchs, or representatives, or even into the hands of one
man, perhaps electively or on a hereditary basis (2nd T: 132). They
do this as they please, and Locke is adamant that the people's choice
in this regard – their "positive and voluntary Grant and Institution"
(2nd T: 141) – is to be accorded the utmost respect, and is not to be
trumped by any theorist's conclusion as to what the best or the wisest
choice would be. The legislature is the heart of the civil union:

> [It] is in their Legislative, that the Members of a Commonwealth are united,
> and combined together into one coherent living Body. This is the Soul that gives
> Form, Life, and Unity, to the Common-wealth: From hence the several Members
> have their mutual Influence, Sympathy, and Connexion. (2nd T: 213)[13]

And so the legislative power, Locke says, is "sacred and unalterable in
the hands here the Community have once placed it" (2nd T: 134), and
any attempt to alter it triggers the right to revolution immediately.

This does not mean that Locke had no views on the wisest choice
to be made in this regard. He had quite firm views but, like Thomas
Hobbes before him, he thought that his own views on the best form of
government were matters of prudence, not principle. Hobbes acknowledged that his argument for monarchy was "not demonstrated but put
with probability,"[14] and Locke, I think, would say the same about the
arguments he adduced in favor of the form of legislature he thought most
prudent – an assembly of part-time representatives, elected from among
the people. His arguments were partly arguments of convenience: "It is
not necessary, no, nor so much as convenient, that the *Legislative* should
be *always in being*…Constant *frequent meetings of the Legislative*, and long
Continuations of their Assemblies, without necessary occasion, could
not but be burdensome to the People" (2nd T: 156). But mostly it was a
familiar rule-of-law argument about the importance of having the legislators actually live among the people, and be bound as much as anyone
by the laws they had made. To ensure that there would be "one rule
for rich and poor, for the favourite at court, and the country man at
plough" (2nd T: 142), Locke argued for what he called "variable" legislative assemblies – "collective Bodies of Men" drawn for each session from
among the ordinary members of the community (2nd T: 94). You can
"call them Senate, Parliament, or what you please" (ibid.), but these assemblies ought to be legislatures "whose Members upon the Dissolution

---

[13] For further reflection on this passage, see Waldron, *The Dignity of Legislation*, pp. 65 and 91.
[14] Hobbes, *On the Citizen*, Preface, p. 14.

of the Assembly, are Subjects under the common Laws of their Country, equally with the rest" (2nd T: 138).

> By [this] means every single person became subject, equally with other the meanest Men, to Those Laws, which he himself, as part of the Legislative, had established: nor could any one, by his own Authority, avoid the force of the Law, when once made, nor by any pretence of Superiority, plead exemption, thereby to License his own, or the Miscarriages of any of his Dependents. (2nd T: 94)[15]

The argument, as I have said, is intended to be a prudential one and sensitive to the circumstances and culture of the society in question. Human frailty may be "apt to grasp at Power" in any circumstances (2nd T: 143), but in some societies it has been easier to trust to the civic virtue of leaders and representatives than in others. In the early ages of the world, "before Vain ambition, and . . . evil Concupiscence, had corrupted Men's minds" (2nd T: 111), it might have been possible to vest undifferentiated political authority in a father-king or a general-king, without much worry that it would be abused. In contemporary circumstances, however, that would be very unwise. I will say more about the distinctions of political virtue that this presupposes later in the chapter (section VII). For the moment, I raise it just to reinforce the point about the acknowledged contingency of the case that Locke is making for a representative legislative assembly.

One thing he is insistent upon, and this is not a prudential matter. Locke believed, as a matter of principle, that if his suggestions as to the general constitution of the legislature were not followed, it would be important to constitute a specific assembly of property-owners or taxpayers, to give (or withhold) consent to taxation. Governments "must not *raise Taxes* on the Property of the People, *without the Consent of the People*, given by themselves, or their Deputies" (2nd T: 142). It is tempting to read this as an argument for a property franchise. But that gets Locke's

---

[15] The argument is connected also with an early version of the constitutionalist argument for the separation of powers:

> And because it may be too great a temptation to human frailty, apt to grasp at Power, for the same Persons, who have the Power of making Laws, to have also in their hands the power to execute them, whereby they may exempt themselves from Obedience to the Laws they make, and suit the Law, both in its making, and execution, to their own private advantage, and thereby come to have a distinct interest from the rest of the Community, contrary to the end of Society and Government: Therefore in well order'd Commonwealths . . . the *Legislative* Power is put into the hands of divers Persons, who duly Assembled, have by themselves, or jointly with others, a Power to make Laws, which when they have done, being separated again, they are themselves subject to the Laws they have made; which is a new and near tie upon them, to take care, that they make them for the public good. (2nd T: 143)

point exactly the wrong way around. He is saying, and he says it several times, that a special convocation of property-holders or their deputies is necessary only if legislative power is vested in one man or a few with an interest evidently distinct from the people. Otherwise an ordinary representative legislature will take care of the matter (2nd T: 138).[16] Let me reiterate: I am not saying that Locke opposed a more robust property qualification – a forty shilling franchise or whatever. He leaves it open whether the people might think this prudent, and his remarks about the basis on which elections would be organized for the sort of representative assembly he favors are quite sketchy, and mostly concerned with issues of fairness and proportionality in the redistricting of rotten boroughs (2nd T: 157). The only principled case that he makes in the *Second Treatise* is that, one way or another, property-owners – the owners of any property liable to taxation – must be represented. He does not set out to make the case that a legislature must exclude everyone other than property-holders. There is no trace of any explicit argument for that proposition, not even a prudential argument.

IV

Locke said the people can constitute any form of legislative institution they like, and that once they do, the legislative power is "sacred and unalterable in the hands where the Community have once placed it" (2nd T: 134). But who are "the people," for the purposes of this proposition? Even if he did not argue specifically for a property franchise, might he not have restricted the meaning of "the people" so that it only included people with a certain amount of property? If the class of persons who are supposed to consent to government and who are supposed to agree to the institution of a legislature already excludes (say) paupers, laborers, and women, then we do not need to worry about the details of Locke's thoughts about the franchise. His theory of politics would already be founded on a platform of inequality and exclusion.

What we have seen so far is that you cannot run an argument in the other direction. From the fact that X is one of "the people," whose consent is required before he can be subject to political power, and who is entitled to participate along with the rest of "the people" in determining the constitution of the legislature, we cannot infer that he is entitled to

---

[16] Or, as Locke puts it in 2nd T: 142: "[T]his properly concerns only such governments where the legislative is always in being, or at least where the people have not reserved any part of the legislative to deputies, to be from time to time chosen by themselves."

vote in the election of legislative representatives. For X (and the rest
of "the people") might have chosen to institute a non-representative
legislature or a legislature elected on the basis of a restricted franchise
that excluded X. Ellen Meiksins Wood offers a further argument in this
direction.[17] Locke thought the basic consent that one might give to the
institution of political society could be given *tacitly* (2nd T: 119); it is not
necessary that it be given in the form of anything like a formal vote. In
Locke's day, it was common to run the two issues together – consent to be
governed and the basis of the franchise.[18] But Locke is evidently setting
his face against that conflation in his doctrine of tacit consent, making it
necessary (if one wants to make a case for universal suffrage) to make it
in two stages: first, an argument for the right of each person not to have
authority exercised over him without his own consent; and secondly, an
argument that each person who has the right to be ruled only by consent
also has a right to be ruled only by a representative assembly and a
right, too, to be included in the electorate for the purposes of choosing
representatives. As we have seen, Locke does not make any argument
of principle at the second stage. So let's focus our attention now on the
first.

Who are "the people"? Of whom is it true that political power may not
be exercised over them, except by their own consent? If we can answer
these questions, we can give an account of the primary constituents of a
Lockean polity, whether they are also voters (for representatives) or not.
The questions are fundamental in Locke's theory, for they ask about the
link between (1) the foundations of natural law and (2) Locke's specific
doctrine that government is based on the consent of the governed. Thus,
the *Second Treatise* begins with (1) an account of the "State all Men are
naturally in" (2nd T: 4), which is an elemental account of their relation
to their Creator and their relation to others in virtue of their relation
to their Creator, and it proceeds to (2) an account of what is required
before anyone can be subjected to the political power of another: "Men
being, as has been said, by nature, all free, equal, and independent, no
one can be put out of this estate, and subjected to the political power
of another, without his own consent" (2nd T: 95). Beyond (2), there is
also the possibility of (3) an account of individuals' rights to be represented in and to vote for representatives to the legislature. Now whatever
the relationship between (2) and (3) – and I have conceded already that

---

[17] Wood, "Locke Against Democracy," pp. 667–8.
[18] See, for example, the argument of the army radicals in the Putney Debates, in Sharp (ed.)
The English Levellers, p. 111.

that relation is problematic – it seems to me that the relation between (2) and (1) is very tight indeed. With a few exceptions, which I will say something about in a moment, any exclusion at the level of (2) – whose consent is required? – has to be represented as an exclusion at the level of (1) – to whom does natural law apply? And that is quite serious because (1) is the basis not only of a person's elementary rights, but also of his subjection to the duties of natural law. Unless a wedge can be driven between (2) and (1), it would seem to follow that if some individual X is not one of "the people" for the purposes of (2), he cannot plausibly be represented as obligated by the laws of nature, and so authority cannot legitimately be exercised over him on the basis that he is so obligated.

Locke's logic is very tight at this point. I don't think we are in a position to say, for example, that there is a person or group of persons in a given community who have a *natural duty* to defer to the rest of the community or its rulers without their own consent.[19] If they have a natural duty to obey, then they must be subject to natural law. And if they are subject to natural law, they are, in Locke's phrase, "free of [i.e. free under] that law" (2nd T: 59); they must have the status of naturally free individuals, of whom it is the case that they cannot be ruled without their own consent. If they have not given their consent, they may of course be punished by others for any violations of natural law: they are subject to the executive power of the law of nature. But they may also exercise that power, for it is a primal power possessed (on Locke's account) by anyone and everyone to whom the law of nature applies. So, as persons subject to the natural law, they have the power to enforce it and to make whatever contribution they think fit for the preservation of man under it, until such time as they themselves yield up those powers to the community (2nd T: 128).

The case of children fits this schema quite nicely. Though they are, in a loose sense, members of the political community to which their parents belong, they are not so by their own consent. They are basically under the parental authority of their fathers and mothers (2nd T: 118). Now, as we saw in section II of this chapter, that parental authority is regulated by the law of nature. But the child himself is not directly subject to the law of nature during this period of parental authority, "for no Body can be under a Law, which is not promulgated to him, and this Law being promulgated or made known by Reason only, he that is not come to the

---

[19] For the idea of natural duty as opposed to consent-based political obligation, see Rawls, *Theory of Justice*, pp. 114–17 and 333–42. See also Waldron, "Special Ties and Natural Duties," pp. 3 ff.

use of Reason, cannot be said to be under this law" (2nd T: 57). Thus the child is not actually – though he is potentially – covered by (1), and for that reason, as long as he is a child, he is not covered by (2) either: he is not one of those whose consent is required so far as the constitution of the community's political structure is concerned. But as soon as he is actually covered by (1) – as soon as he becomes subject to the law of nature in a direct sense – then *ipso facto* it becomes appropriate for his consent to be asked before political power is exercised over him or over any community to which he belongs. The one qualification brings the other with it.

Now let's try a more controversial case – women. Women seem to present a harder case, but I think the difficulty arises only on account of the inconsistency in Locke's discussion of the status of women, which we noticed in Chapter 2. I imagine that many of my readers will throw up their hands in despair when I say that I think "the people" in the *Second Treatise* should be read to include women as well as men. Even Ashcraft doesn't go this far: he seems to think "the people" includes only adult males (though it includes all of them).[20] After all, women weren't enfranchised in English public life for another 200 years, and do we really want to say that Locke was this far ahead of his time? Well, remember that we have already distinguished between (2) membership of "the people" and (3) possession of the franchise. The fact (if, as I shall argue, it is a fact) that Locke thought women were covered by (2) doesn't show that he thought they were covered by (3), though it would certainly follow that (3) was not out of the question so far as women were concerned. Basically, though, the application of (1) and (2) to women is a matter of what the arguments in the text will support, and the argumentative basis in Locke's text for the inclusion of women is really quite considerable.

First, Locke recognizes that women may be monarchs and he denies that their political power is affected by the fact of their marriage (1st T: 47).[21] When he talks of queens, he makes none of the disparaging

---

[20] Ashcraft, *Revolutionary Politics*, pp. 578–9.

[21] There is a complication here. It has to do with Locke's attitude to the joint monarchy of William and Mary. In the Preface to the *Two Treatises*, Locke writes as though only the throne of "King William" deserved his support (Locke, *Two Treatises*, p. 137). Laslett notes in his "Introduction," p. 53 n., that supporters of the Glorious Revolution were initially divided on the question of joint sovereignty, and that the faction that Locke belonged to initially supported sovereignty for William only. But I see no warrant for Laslett's suggestion (ibid., p. 174) that Locke would not have made the argument he made in 1st T: 47 after April 1689, when Mary Stuart was crowned joint sovereign with William. That event might have complicated his statement of the point, but

remarks he makes about other controversial cases – for example, fools and infants wearing the crown in actually existing monarchies (1st T: 123). Second, as we saw in Chapter 2, Locke insists often and stridently on the point that women share parental authority under natural law equally with the father of their children (1st T: 60–8 and 2nd T: 52–3). Parental authority may not be the same as political authority, but one would not expect that the rational qualifications for the exercise of the former would be less than the rational qualifications for participation in the latter. Third, women may be property-holders in their own right, and they are entitled to control their own property (2nd T: 183). Fourth, women's status in marriage is determined by a contract to which the woman is a full and equal partner: "Conjugal society is made by a voluntary Compact between man and Woman" (2nd T: 78). Even Locke's notorious comment about the husband having the final say in the marriage which gave us so much trouble in Chapter 2 (and I'll say a little more about it in a moment) is presented only as a weak and defeasible default condition for the contract, something that the parties may bargain around or something that may permissibly be displaced by a positive law stipulation of equality (2nd T: 82). Fifth, once the children are provided for (2nd T: 80), Locke is at pains to emphasize that women have a right to separate from their husbands, if they like, and resume a life as independent members of the community (2nd T: 81–2). All of this seems to indicate that women are regarded in the *Second Treatise* as ordinary functioning persons, with all the rights and protections of ordinary functioning persons, under natural law. Locke recognizes that as ordinary functioning persons, they are entitled to promote and protect their rights through contract, and the logic of contractarianism – "no rational Creature can be supposed to change his condition with an intention to be worse" (2nd T: 131) – applies to them too. This he applies explicitly to marriage, and it is impossible to see how its logic could fail to provide also for the process by which political authority is established over a woman. Her husband has no political authority over her (2nd T: 83), and it would seem that the only way such authority can be established over her, as over any member of "the people," is by her own consent.

Against this, those who think Locke excludes women from "the people" may cite two points. First, a verbal point. Locke's basic doctrine of consent is always and everywhere stated in terms of "man" and "men"

it would not have derogated from the point itself (viz. that political authority should not be at the mercy of obstetrics). See also Wootton, "John Locke and Richard Ashcraft's *Revolutionary Politics*," p. 92.

and using masculine pronouns (2nd T: 87, 95, 119, and 123). But this, I think, is inconclusive. It is true that Locke sometimes uses "man" in a significantly gendered sense, as for example in his discussion of marriage (2nd T: 78 and 82). But he makes it clear in his own account of the formation of the concept *man* in the *Essay Concerning Human Understanding* that its main use generalizes over males and females (E: 3.3.7).[22] Moreover, as we saw in Chapter 2, Locke rests an important argument in the *First Treatise* on the point that "Man" and "Mankind" have to be sufficiently capacious to accommodate Eve as well as Adam.[23] Attentive readers will remember that in this passage Locke also argues for an inclusive reading of pronouns; and more substantively, he argues too that women as well as men bear the intellectual nature, which is the likeness of God.

The other difficulty is Locke's espousal of the view that, unless their particular marriage contract provides otherwise, women are subject to the will of their husbands in "the Things of their common Interest and Property" (2nd T: 82). This, as we have seen, is inconsistent with most of the rest of what Locke says about women, and for that reason it is a weak foundation on which to base their exclusion from "the people." But even if it were not, it is hard to see how this doctrine could support any general or fundamental exclusion. It applies only to married women, not single women, widows or divorcees, who as we have seen may be property-owners in their own right. Locke himself is at pains to deny that it has anything to do with political authority. He emphasizes also that it may be displaced by the civil law of a particular community (2nd T: 83). Now this is an important point. If it is accepted, then I think it is logically impossible for the matrimonial subordination of women to be the basis of their exclusion from civil society. Civil society makes its decisions, first, and that frames the establishment of rights and duties within marriage (to the extent that they are not left to contract); not vice versa. This makes women's rights within marriage rather more like the suffrage on the account I have been giving. The people must decide whether to keep the right of election in themselves or vest it in some subset of the people; but even if it adopts the latter course, those who are not in the privileged subset are of course parties to the decision to vest the right of election in this subset. Similarly, unless there is some other reason for excluding women from "the people" (and Locke at any rate, as opposed to the custom of his day, provided none), women as well as men will be parties at some level directly or indirectly to the

---

[22] The passage is cited above, Chapter 2 (p. 37, note 37).   [23] See above, p. 25.

legislative decisions that are made about the structure of marriage: they will either be direct participants in that legislation about family law or at least members of the community that decided who should have the power to legislate on issues like this.

There is one class of individuals subject to natural law who may not be regarded as members of "the people" who constitute a particular political community. This is the class of aliens and foreigners, who spend time in a territory subject to the community in question, but belong to some other community that rules some other territory.[24] Locke offers two different accounts of the community's jurisdiction over aliens, but they are complementary rather than inconsistent. On the one hand, power may be exercised over them as a matter of basic natural law, the magistrates of the community in whose territory they reside having no less power over them "than what every Man naturally may have over another " (2nd T: 9). On the other hand, they may be thought to have given their consent for the time being to the authority of that community simply by virtue of living there (2nd T: 122).

Can the second of these accounts serve as a basis for the attribution to Locke of a more far-reaching exclusion of certain classes from "the people"? Some have thought so. They have discerned an analogy between foreigners, who "by living all their lives under another government, and enjoying the Privileges and Protection of it . . . are bound . . . to submit to its Administration, as far forth as any Denison; yet do not thereby come to be Subjects or Members of that Commonwealth" (2nd T: 122), and propertyless members of the laboring class whose political status also does not derive from their having a fixed stake in the community but simply from their "very being . . . within the Territories of that Government" (2nd T: 119). It has been suggested too that this distinction can be aligned with the distinction between express consent and tacit consent. Full members of civil society, with a tangible stake in the community give their consent to belong "by actual Agreement, and . . . express Declaration" (2nd T: 121), whereas in the case of mere sojourners (and laborers, if the analogy works) their consent, such as it is, is simply inferred from the fact that they inhabit the territory, lodge within it, and travel the highways (2nd T: 119).

---

[24] For a communitarian strand in Locke's thought, which suggests that in the case of foreigners the problem of political obligation may be overlaid with additional elements of distrust, see 2nd T: 107: "[T]hose, who like one another so well as to joyn into Society, cannot but be supposed to have some Acquaintance and Friendship together, and some Trust one in another; they could not but have greater Apprehensions of others, than of one another".

Now certainly this last alignment will not work, for Locke associates tacit consent primarily with the inheritance of landed property rather than with the situation of the propertyless (2nd T: 120). But the more general scheme *could* work to accommodate something like a class distinction of the sort that Macpherson and others have attributed to Locke. The only problem is that there is no evidence that Locke intended to use it in this way. He certainly made no explicit argument to this effect; and though this is not conclusive, it is telling, since Locke had little to lose politically or reputationally by arguing explicitly for the exclusion of the laboring classes if he intended to allow for such exclusion. Certainly, we cannot read any such argument into his frequent statements that the point of men's entering civil society is "the secure Enjoyment of their Properties" (2nd T: 95). Locke uses "property" in a wide sense and a narrow sense; in the narrow sense it means tangible possessions, particularly private ownership of land, whereas in the wider sense it includes life and liberty as well. Macpherson thinks that Locke always uses the narrower sense when he is talking about the people constituting a government to protect their property.[25] But this is not so. In the section which introduces his chapter "Of the Ends of Political Society and Government," we are told that the point of the enterprise is a willingness "to join in Society with others, who are already united, or have a mind to unite, for the mutual *Preservation* of their Lives, Liberties and Estates, which I call by the general name, *Property*" (2nd T: 123).[26] Locke's use of the wider meaning of "property" to describe the ends of government corresponds to a sense that everyone – rich and poor, owner and laborer – has proprietorial rights in his person and God-given liberty, which he may intelligibly enter society to protect and which he may legitimately defend himself, if need be, against despotical encroachment. And in his catalogue of the horrors of absolute government, Locke lists not just the monarch's power over the people "to alienate their Estates," but also his power "to sell, castrate, or use their Persons as he pleases, they being all his Slaves" (1st T: 9), and in general his ability arbitrarily and violently to restrict the liberty of the people (2nd T: 93, 137, and 210). But even if we were to concede that it is all about property in the narrow sense, it is certainly not true that it would comprise only large landed estates. The best example Locke gives of property's immunity from expropriation even by a legitimate power is, tellingly, the property of a common soldier:

[25] Macpherson, *Political Theory of Possessive Individualism*, pp. 247–50.
[26] See also 2nd T: 171: Political power "can have no other *end or measure*, when in the hands of the Magistrate, but to preserve the Members of that Society in their Lives, Liberties, and Possessions."

And to let us see, that even *absolute Power*, where it is necessary, is *not Arbitrary* by being absolute, but is still limited by that reason, and confined to those ends, which required it in some Cases to be absolute, we need look no farther than the common practice of Martial Discipline: for the Preservation of the Army . . . requires an *absolute Obedience* to the Command of every Superior Officer . . . but yet we see, that neither the Serjeant, that could command a Souldier to march up to the mouth of a Cannon, or stand in a Breach, where he is almost sure to perish, can command that Souldier to give him one penny of his Money; nor the *General*, that can condemn him to Death for deserting his Post, or for not obeying the most desperate Orders, can yet, with all his absolute Power of Life and Death, dispose of one Farthing of that Souldier's Estate, or seize one jot of his Goods. (2nd T: 139)

The significance of this example would not have been lost on Locke's audience, for they were well aware that it was from the army in the late 1640s that the most strident arguments had been made "that the poorest he that is in England has a life to live as the greatest he; and therefore . . . every man who is to live under a government ought first by his own consent to put himself under that government," and that the common soldiers "would fain know what we have fought for" in the Civil War if this claim were denied.[27]

Let me say finally that I am not convinced by David Wootton's argument that, since Locke approved of the Convention of 1689 which settled the English constitution after the flight and abdication of James II, a function corresponding to that assigned to "the people" at the end of the *Second Treatise* (2nd T: 243), he must have approved also of the definition of "the people" that the Convention enshrined, namely the ordinary property franchise.[28] One's actual political stances are always relative to a set of available options; and it seems absurd to infer from them any limitation on one's theory of the options that *ought* to be available. (For all I know, John Rawls voted Democrat in the 1992 Presidential election; but that doesn't mean that we should read the policies of Bill Clinton back into *A Theory of Justice!*) There is often a gap between what a theorist says and does as a political animal, and what he thinks he can justify theoretically. If someone wants to press the point, I'll say we should be interested in both. But I see no reason why one should dominate the other, nor do I see why our theoretical interest in his arguments should be held hostage to his political actions. I certainly don't think we should be in the business

---

[27] Colonel Rainborough at the Putney Debates (1647), in Sharp (ed.) *The English Levellers*, pp. 103 and 111.
[28] Wootton, "John Locke and Richard Ashcraft's *Revolutionary Politics*," pp. 94–7.

of rewriting the theorist's work to give it a spurious consistency with the principles that we think we can discern in his political activism.

v

Whoever they are, Locke thinks that the people must make their decisions by voting and majority-decision, which he regards as a natural rather than a conventional basis for decision-making. It can't be conventional, on his account, for any conventional decision-procedure must itself be the product of a prior decision by the people and that decision must be framed by a procedure. Locke argues moreover that majority-decision is the default decision-rule for any constituted body: "[I]n Assemblies impowered to act by positive Laws where no number is set by that positive Law which empowers them, the *act of the Majority* passes for the act of the whole, and of course determines, as having by the law of Nature and Reason, the power of the whole" (2nd T: 96).[29] Now it is worth noting that this too is a matter of equality. In its emphasis on assemblies, numbers, and majorities, this part of Locke's theory of politics embodies a respect for the average or ordinary participant, rather than those who exhibit extraordinary intellect or outstanding political virtue. We saw earlier (in section III) that legislation works best for Locke when the legislators are drawn from among the people, rather than being constituted as a separate and expert political caste. If anything, it is their lack of distinction – I mean distinction from the other ordinary men and women of the community – that counts for Locke, so far as the composition of a responsible legislature is concerned. And the same is true of the more primal decisions he attributes to the people. The status of each participant is that of one ordinary and equal person among others, and so majority-decision is a natural basis for their decision-making.

As I argued in *The Dignity of Legislation*, John Locke is in fact one of very few political philosophers who bother to pay much attention to the defense of majority-decision.[30] Most political philosophers either denigrate it or ignore it. The account Locke gives is not all that substantial; it comprises just a few paragraphs, at the beginning of Chapter 8 of the *Second Treatise*. The key to the argument is this passage:

---

[29] For a similar view about decisions on taxation, if there is a distinct assembly constituted for that purpose, see 2nd T: 140.

[30] See the discussion in Waldron, *Dignity of Legislation*, Ch. 7.

That which acts any Community, being only the consent of the individuals of it, and it being necessary to that which is one body to move one way; it is necessary the Body should move that way whither the greater force carries it, *which is the consent of the majority*: or else it is impossible it should act or continue one Body, *one Community*, which the consent of every individual that united into it, agreed that it should; and so every one is bound by that consent to be concluded by the *majority*. (2nd T: 96)

The first impression one gets from this is that Locke is trying to explicate majoritarianism on the basis of an analogy with physics or natural science. In nature, a body moves with the greater force: in politics, similarly, a political body moves at the behest of the majority, because *qua* majority it is stronger. We are asked to imagine a composite body, impelled internally by the various motions of its constituent parts or elements, to move in various directions. Some of the parts tend to move north, some of them south, and the body as a whole moves either north or south in accordance with the tendency of the greater number of its elements, as a result of their cumulative motion. (Or think of the body as a scrum in a rugby match; some players are pushing one way, the others in the opposite direction; and the scrum as a whole moves in accordance with the greater force. Now if one side has a full eight members in the scrum and the other side only six or seven, we would expect the weaker side to give way and the whole mass to move upfield, to the weaker side's disadvantage.)

Various commentators have criticized this argument for majority-decision.[31] Does a body always move in the direction of the greater number of its parts? No, they say, it depends how massive and powerful the parts are. An All Black pack comprising just seven players may push an eight-man English pack upfield, because they are heavier or stronger or because they bind and push with better technique. And similarly in politics, numbers are not everything: they are not necessarily the same as power to move the body politic. Different individuals strive politically with greater intensity and often they have unequal political resources at their disposal. So the analogy between the numerical majority and "the greater force" in Locke's argument does not work.

I think the critique is misconceived, and misconceived precisely in relation to the issues we have been discussing, about consent and equality. Though Locke uses the language of force and motion – "it is necessary the Body should move that way whither the greater force carries it" (2nd T: 96) – he does not intend this to be read in a physicalist way.

---

[31] See, for example, Kendall, *John Locke and the Doctrine of Majority-Rule*, p. 117.

John Dunn has suggested a more interesting reading which takes "force"
and "motion" as quite abstract conceptions, almost logical terms, which
may be imbued with various content, depending on whether we are dealing with material interactions or interactions of some different kind.[32]
And in fact Locke makes it clear that the physics he has in mind is
a physics of individual consent, not a physics of individual strength or
power. He prefaces the passage I quoted a little while ago by saying that
"that which acts any Community" – that which moves it – is nothing but
"the consent of the individuals of it" (idem). And it is on that basis that
he goes on to say that since it is "necessary to that which is one body to
move one way; it is necessary the Body should move that way whither
the greater force carries it, which is the *consent of the majority*" (2nd T: 96).
Consent does not carry physical force or even pure political force; rather,
it carries moral force with regard to the purposes for which consent is
required. So Locke is not making a factual claim, that the movement of
a political body depends on the force of individuals' participation. The
Lockean physics of consent is more in the nature of a normative theory.
The claim is that the only thing which *properly* moves a political body is
the consent of the individuals who compose it. For the purpose of that
normative proposition, consent is a matter of individual authorization.
People may vary in their political influence and know-how. But that is not
the same as a variation on the normative force of individual consent. In
that dimension we are equals, and the numerical account is the correct
one.

So Locke's insistence that, whatever the other variations among us,
we are each other's equals so far as authority is concerned (2nd T: 54)
turns out to be crucial to the case for majority-decision. Our natural
state, out of which the principle of majority-decision is to be conjured,
is a state "*of Equality*, wherein all Power and Jurisdiction is reciprocal, no
one having more than another" (2nd T: 4). The importance of consent
is based purely on this natural equality of legitimating authority, and
that carries through to make irrelevant any other differences in political
effectiveness among us, so far as the elements of political decision-making
are concerned. The premise of equality is therefore indispensable for
an understanding of how sheer numbers can do the work they do in
Locke's majoritarian argument. I am not saying that Locke anticipated
the modern demonstration in social choice theory that no other principle

---

[32] Dunn, *Political Thought of John Locke*, p. 129 n., suggests that it is "as plausible to see the concept
of force as moralized by the notion of consent as it is to see the notion of consent turned into a
term of social coercion."

respects equality of input more than majority-decision; no other principle gives greater weight to the views of any individual member except
by giving his views greater weight than that assigned to those of some
other individual member.[33] By giving each individual's view the greatest
weight possible compatible with an equal weight for the views of each of
the others, majority-decision presents itself as a *fair* method of decision-
making. Locke may not have known these proofs but he had an instinct
for their egalitarian foundation.

In our own constitutional philosophy, we are accustomed to think that
besides the majoritarian power in a community, there also ought to be
a *counter*-majoritarian power – some body that can check or limit the
legislative majority, particularly if the majority is abusing its authority by
encroaching on the rights of individuals or minorities. Locke was the first
to realize that legislative majorities are capable of abusing their power
in this way. He said that there are natural law limitations on legislative power: "The Law of Nature stands as an Eternal Rule to all Men,
Legislators as well as others" (2nd T: 135). The people have entrusted the
legislature with their natural rights, and if a legislative majority (or, for
that matter, a legislative monarchy) acts against that trust, if for example "the Legislators endeavour to take away, and destroy the Property
of the People, or to reduce them to Slavery under Arbitrary Power"
(2nd T: 222), then the whole constitution of the society is in crisis. On
Locke's account such crises are catastrophic. This sort of abuse amounts
to a dissolution of government and puts the legislature in a state of war
with the people. The legislature immediately forfeits its authority, and
that authority "devolves to the People, who have a Right to resume
their original Liberty, and, by the Establishment of a new Legislative,
(such as they shall think fit) provide for their own Safety and Security"
(ibid.). On Locke's account, then, the remedy for majoritarian abuse
seems to be more majoritarianism: the legislative majority forfeits its
power, and it is now up to the people (acting by majority rule) to set
things aright. And, one could say, this majoritarian motif permeates
Locke's whole theory of resistance and revolution: revolution – the re-
placement of one system of government by another – is only likely to
happen when "these illegal Acts have extended to the majority of the
People" (2nd T: 209).

---

[33] For the theorem (in social choice theory) that majority-decision alone satisfies elementary conditions of fairness and rationality, see May, 'A Set of Independent Necessary and Sufficient
Conditions for Simple Majority Decision.' See also Sen, *Collective Choice and Social Welfare*,
pp. 71–3.

I don't want to spend time here discussing the adequacy of this as a remedy for injustice: I have more faith in populist majoritarianism than most of my friends, and so I am more sympathetically disposed to Locke's account.[34] But I do want to ask why Locke did not accept the need for an extra layer of government – as I said, a counter-majoritarian power – to check legislation that might otherwise undermine people's natural rights.

There are two answers. First, inasmuch as he is open to the possibility of all sorts of mixed constitutions (2nd T: 132), Locke does not affirmatively rule this out: "[T]he Community may make compounded and mixed Forms of Government, as they think good" (2nd T: 132). His view is that any body with this function has to be regarded as a part of the legislature, rather than as an extra-legislative body. He specifically did not associate it with the judiciary,[35] but of course that's no reason why it should not comprise people who are judges. Insisting that it be regarded as part of the legislature is not just a matter of labeling. It reminds us, first, that such a body also may err in its decisions (or be complicit in the errant decisions of other institutions), and secondly, that the decisions that emerge from the legislative system as a whole (including the operation of this body) will have to be supreme in the political community "whilst the Government subsists" (2nd T: 150), so that it will pose exactly the same quandaries about superordinate control by the people through resistance and revolution as an untrammeled popular legislature would pose. Elsewhere I have argued that we should not make the mistake, when we interpret Locke's theory, of thinking that natural law and natural rights are available to Lockean legislators, judges, and other officials like the clear text of a written constitution, given in advance of anything they do.[36] Propositions of natural law and natural right are arrived at by fallible human reason, on Locke's account. They have an objective existence, to be sure: from a God's-eye point of view they are objective constraints on human political decisions. But objectivity is not the same as instant availability, nor is it the same as the absence of reasonable controversy. Since Locke rules out innatism, the only basis on which propositions of natural right become available to us is by our own reasoning (including reasoning from and about revelation), and that is a process that has to take place in real time, subject to all the vicissitudes of moral reasoning in real time by real human beings. I think one of the

[34] See Waldron, *Law and Disagreement*, Chs. 10–13.
[35] For Locke's view of the judiciary, see Waldron, *Dignity of Legislation*, pp. 85–6.
[36] See the chapter on "Locke's Legislature," in *Dignity of Legislation*, esp. pp. 68–85.

places where this reasoning is supposed to take place, in Locke's theory, is the legislature. For Locke thinks natural law reasoning carried out on an individual basis in the state of nature is problematic. Since each individual has the executive authority of the law of nature, and since each person's fallible real-time reasoning may come up with different results, each will face some chaotic uncertainty about whose idiosyncratic natural law reasoning they are at the mercy of; "for the Law of Nature being unwritten, and so no where to be found but in the minds of Men, they who through Passion or Interest shall miscite, or misapply it, cannot so easily be convinced of their mistake where there is no establish'd Judge" (2nd T: 136). And so Locke thinks it important that we establish a place where we do our natural law reasoning together, and come up with determinate (though of course still fallible) results which can stand in the name of us all. Now, if the suggestion that there should be a counter-majoritarian power in the legislature were accepted, then this body too might become one of the places where this collective reasoning takes place. But what we must understand is that the law of nature is no more easily available to such a body than to the majoritarian assembly. It is simply a matter of prudence whether we decide to have an extra layer of this kind.

The second point to note, however, is that it is not at all clear whether there is room in Locke's theory for the idea of special expertise in regard to natural rights, which counter-majoritarian institutional proposals often presuppose. (The idea is that we need to have panels of rights-experts as a check on the majoritarian decisions of ordinary inexpert legislators.) The tenor of our discussion towards the end of Chapter 4 was that Locke rejected the idea of moral experts. He doubted whether there was any expertise to be found in this field, at least any expertise that would not be available more or less as a matter of course to any ordinary person who turned his mind to natural law. Certainly natural law issues are sometimes complicated. This is particularly so in the Lockean theory of property, where one has to balance not only the labor theory, the market principle, and the operation of the various provisoes,[37] but also arrive at a proper distinction between the regulation and takings, which as Locke concedes in the *Second Treatise* is not always easy (2nd T: 139–40). Property is a troublesome case, moreover, because it requires people to adjust the claims on natural resources that they make on the basis of their own interests for the sake of the interests of others. The prominence of

---

[37] See Chapter 6, pp. 170–7.

interests and conflicts of interest is always likely to distort moral thinking
in this area. And so, some may say, an element of technical expertise
in unraveling complex argument, accompanied by a trained ability to
prescind from one's own interest in such a matter, might be the basis of
a special qualification to act as a legislator (or as a member of a counter-
majoritarian institution checking the activities of legislators). What is
remarkable, however, is that Locke makes no move in this direction at
all. Indeed, his account suggests that if anyone is specially qualified to
make morally reliable decisions in this area, it is the property-owners
themselves (2nd T: 140). Their qualification is certainly not that they
are disinterested, and despite Macpherson's argument, it is also not that
they have unusual moral expertise. On the contrary, Locke seems to
think that the need for special care in this fraught and complex area is
best served in a system in which decisions are taken by ordinary citizens
in a variable assembly. The capacity for natural law reasoning is widely
dispersed among ordinary folk, and Locke figures, rightly or wrongly
but certainly in an egalitarian spirit, that abuses are "not much to be
fear'd in Governments where the Legislative consists, wholly or in part,
in Assemblies which are variable, whose Members, upon the Dissolution
of the Assembly, are Subjects under the common Laws of their Country,
equally with the rest" (2nd T: 138).

VI

I have laid great stress in these last two chapters on the democratic
intellect, on Locke's faith in the political virtue of the ordinary person.
But in some areas, choices do have to be made. The people have to choose
a king or a president, if they think it desirable to have a monarchical
element in the constitution; certainly executive officers and judges have
to be appointed; and if there is an elective element in the legislature,
then those entrusted with the suffrage have to find some way of picking
and choosing among candidates for membership of the assembly. Since
we surely aim to choose the better rather than the worse person for
each of these offices, how are we to square the distinctions we draw with
the premise of basic equality. Is equality compatible with distinctions of
political virtue or merit? Are there some who are entitled to authority
by virtue of their merit alone?

   In various passages in the *Second Treatise*, Locke distinguishes between
those who are fit to be trusted with the authority of government and those
who are not fit to be trusted. He has in mind differences of excellence,

merit, political virtue. In Chapter 2 I mentioned Locke's anthropological speculation about "how easy it was in the first Ages of the World...for the *Father of the Family* to become the Prince of it" (2nd T: 74). It was important, he said, that people choose someone they trusted as their ruler for "without such nursing Fathers tender and careful of the public weal, all Governments would have sunk under the Weakness and Infirmities of Their Infancy" (2nd T: 110). In the first ages of the world, tribal patriarchs presented themselves to their extended families as "fittest to be trusted" (2nd T: 105), "fitter to rule them" (2nd T: 75), than anyone else in the group, "unless Negligence, Cruelty, or any other defect of Mind, or Body made him unfit for it" (2nd T: 105). And Locke goes on:

But when either the Father died, and left his next Heir, for want of Age, Wisdom, Courage, or any other Qualities, less fit for Rule: or where several Families met, and consented to continue together: there, 'tis not to be doubted, but they used their natural freedom, to set up him, whom they judged the ablest, and most likely, to Rule well over them. (2nd T: 105)

The people of America, Locke says, "commonly prefer the Heir of their deceased king; yet if they find him any way weak, or uncapable, they pass him by and set up the stoutest and bravest Man for their Ruler" (2nd T: 105). In all these passages, we seem to see Locke taking account of inequalities of political power predicated on virtue, strength, fitness, and capacity.

How is the significance of these differences made consistent with basic equality? It is made consistent in two ways. First, the leadership qualities in question are defined with reference to the interests of all members of the group, and those interests are equally considered. Locke is absolutely insistent on this when he talks in Chapter 14 of the *Second Treatise* about the leadership qualities exercised in connection with prerogative powers. Basic equality works here, as it does in many modern arguments about merit – not by insisting on equal outcomes, but by defining the range of interests that have to be consulted and considered *equally* when we are deciding what is to count as merit.[38]

Secondly, for Locke it is a matter of crucial importance that the virtues and qualities in question are connected to differential authority only via the notion of *consent* (or of some power of choice, like electoral suffrage, which has in turn been consented to). Political virtue is not inherently a

---

[38] See also Waldron, "The Substance of Equality," pp. 1361–3.

basis for power, and there is no direct inference from merit to authority.[39] Consent is the indispensable mediator between ability and superior status. Now admittedly, Locke says all sorts of things about consent: he talks about explicit consent, tacit consent, and (in the context of his anthropological speculations) "easie" and "scarce avoidable consent" (2nd T: 75). My point, however, is that whatever consent consists in, the upshot of its exercise is never directly defined by the qualities it responds to. Superior virtue and cleverness may be *reasons* for me to consent to your being in charge; but your superior virtue and intellect do not mean that my consent counts for less than yours, or that my consent is redundant in relation to the legitimacy of your authority. Even though you are my superior in these respects, and even though that is a reason for me to trust you with political authority, that reason has to be recognized *by me*. (And my recognition of such reasons, or my refusal to recognize them, counts for as much as yours or anyone else's.) In general, in Locke's theory, the fact that I am your inferior in political virtue does not mean that my consent to your political authority is dispensable. As Locke puts it, "no one can be ... subjected to the Political Power of another, without his own *Consent*" (2nd T: 95), and that applies to any pair of persons irrespective of the differences between them. Consent may be a rational response to perceived virtue. But so far as legitimacy is concerned, the moral force of consent itself is not differentiated by virtue – or by strength, power, or anything else. Nor is it dispensable in the face of the manifest differences in virtue or ability to which it is or would be a rational response.

VII

There is a passage towards the end of the *Second Treatise* where Locke seems to concede the legitimacy of something like an aristocratic component in a constitution – specifically the authority of the peerage in the English constitution, or as he calls it "our old Legislative of King, Lords and Commons" (2nd T: 223). A little earlier he talks in more abstract terms about the possibility that a legislature might comprise "[a]n Assembly of Hereditary Nobility" as well as representatives of the people (2nd T: 213). The self-understanding of the English aristocracy was then, even if it is not now, directly at odds with the principle of basic equality:

---

[39] As we saw in Chapter 2, however, Locke's view about the default authority of husbands appears to be unhappily inconsistent with this.

it was that there are certain lines of noble descent which confer upon their inheritors intrinsic superiority to all other humans, that this superiority is hierarchically organized with layers of peerage (princes are one another's peers, dukes are one another's peers, barons are one another's peers, and so on), and that it culminates in *royalty*, which is a noble lineage pre-eminently suited for final executive, maybe legislative, maybe even sacerdotal authority in a well-ordered community. Now, as I said, we do not believe this nonsense, and I don't think Locke did either. Part of me wants to rest content with noticing Locke's usage of "king" and "lord" to describe ordinary people in the state of nature – each individual "absolute Lord of his own Person and Possessions . . . subject to no Body," but surrounded by other individuals, "all being Kings as much as he, every Man his Equal" (2nd T: 123). This is how an egalitarian should talk of lordship and kingship. But the passages I have mentioned raise the possibility that there might be legitimate institutions and practices corresponding to this anti-egalitarian ideology of congenital nobility and royalty. So we need to say a little more about Locke's views on these matters.

I begin with some comments about the particular passages from the *Second Treatise* that I mentioned (2nd T: 213 and 223). First of all, both passages exemplify a feature of Locke's political theory that we have already noticed several times. Locke was not doctrinaire about political institutions. He thought the people were entitled to choose between a democracy, an oligarchy, and a monarchy, and if they chose either of the latter two, they could choose also whether appointment should be made electively or on an hereditary principle. Or he thought they could choose between "compounded or mixed Forms of Government, as they think good" (2nd T: 132). The form of government mentioned in the two passages is clearly a mixed form of government – that was what England had and thought of itself as having in Locke's day (for all that Englishmen disagreed about the balance of the mixture) – and for all its faults and all the abuses of those whom it empowered, it was not a form of government that Locke thought was in principle illegitimate. What he insisted on, however, was the point that such a constitution derived its legitimacy from having been chosen by the people, not from anything inherent in its character.

Secondly, the context of the particular passage in which Locke talks about "our old Legislative of King, Lords and Commons" (2nd T: 223) is an argument about the likely conservation of constitutional forms, despite their theoretical illegitimacy. The whole passage reads:

People are not so easily got out of their old Forms, as some are apt to suggest. They are hardly to be prevailed with to amend the acknowledg'd Faults, in the Frame they have been accustom'd to. And if there be any Original defects, or adventitious ones introduced by time or corruption, 'tis not an easy thing to get them changed, even when all the World sees there is an opportunity for it. This slowness and aversion in the People to quit their old Constitutions, has, in the many Revolutions which have been seen in this Kingdom, in this and former Ages, still kept us to, or, after some interval of fruitless attempts, still brought us back again to, our old Legislative of King, Lords and Commons. (2nd T: 223)

Nothing much can be inferred from this, since it is perfectly possible that the hereditary principle may be counted among the "acknowledg'd Faults" in this constitution. Moreover Locke's conservatism has virtually no normative flavor. It is not like Edmund Burke's affection for prejudice and tradition. The comment is intended as a reassurance to those who might be worried about the effects of his radicalism, not a suggestion that we ought to abandon our radicalism in favor of tried and true principles of hereditary nobility and royalty. It is an example of something I mentioned at the very beginning of Chapter 1 – Locke responding to the alarm that his radicalism was prone to generate, but responding this time not by flinching from his egalitarian commitments, but by offering real world reassurance about how the equals, whose authority he recognized, were likely to exercise that authority in times of crisis.

Thirdly, in the more abstract of the two passages, where we are asked to "suppose . . . the Legislative placed in the Concurrence of three distinct persons," i.e. king, nobility, and representative assembly (2nd T: 213), Locke's immediate purpose in this passage is actually to show how blame for a constitutional crisis might be allocated among the various layers of the legislature. "It is hard to consider it aright, and know at whose door to lay it, without knowing the Form of Government in which it happens" (2nd T: 213). This is Locke at his analytic best, using a complex example to show the careful and articulate application of the principles of his political theory. He mentions hereditary nobility in this passage, it is true. But one has to work pretty hard to extract from the context anything which would support the claim that aristocratic heredity is something that must be taken into account in the design of any well-ordered political society.

Is there anything anywhere else in Locke's political theory to support such a claim? Beyond saying that the people might have a monarchy, even an hereditary monarchy, if they want one, and that they may constitute an oligarchy too, if they like, by putting "the power of making Laws into the hands of a few select Men, and their heirs or successors" (2nd T: 132), does he offer any support to the anti-egalitarian view that there are royal and noble lineages in the world which any responsible political theorist must take seriously? Well, he accepts in the *First Treatise* that God might constitute a monarchy for some community. This is not just accepted for the sake of arguing with Filmer. Locke accepts that at various times God did establish a king in Israel, though he argues strenuously against Filmer that such kings were not always established on an hereditary basis and that certainly they were never established on the basis that the divine appointees were appropriately descended by primogeniture from Adam (1st T: 159–69). "That Regal Power was Established *in the Kingdoms of the World*, I think no body will dispute, but that there should be Kingdoms in the World, whose several Kings enjoy'd their Crowns, *by right descending to them from Adam*, that we think not only *Apocrypha*, but also utterly impossible" (1st T: 144). I guess we can't rule out the possibility that God might establish an hereditary royal line; but God of all people understands political theory and Locke thinks it is a mark of His not having done so that those who believe He has are embroiled in constant and internecine disputation about the appropriate heir to the divinely established lineage.[40]

On lineage generally, Locke's comments tend to be scathingly deconstructive. Responding to an assertion by Filmer that most of the civilized nations of the earth "fetch their Originall from some of the sons or Nephews of Noah,"[41] Locke responds first with the mischievous observation that this probably doesn't apply to "the *Chinese*, a very great and civil People," and then goes on to observe that this sort of lineage peddling is mainly the work of "Heralds and Antiquaries" and not really a preoccupation or even an interest of most people (1st T: 141). And mostly it's just idle boasting:

Whoever, Nations or Races of Men, *labour to fetch their Originall from*, may be concluded to be thought by them, Men of Renown, famous to Posterity for the Greatness of their Virtues and actions; but beyond these they look not, nor consider who they were Heirs to, but look on them as such as Raised themselves by their own Virtue to a Degree that would give a Lustre to those, who in future Ages could pretend to derive themselves from them. (1st T: 141)

[40] "But whatever our A. [i.e. Filmer] does, *Divine Institution* makes no such ridiculous Assignments: nor can God be supposed to make it a Sacred Law, that one certain Person should have a Right to something, and yet not to give Rules to mark out, and know that Person by ... 'Tis rather to be thought, that an *Heir*, had no such Right by *Divine Institution*, than that God should give such a right to the *Heir*, but yet leave it doubtful, and undeterminable who such Heir is." (1st T: 127)

[41] Filmer, *Patriarcha*, p. 7, cited by Locke in 1st T: 141.

It is possible, Locke concedes, that we might find such heroes among us – "God-like Princes . . . because such Kings partake of [God's] Wisdom and Goodness" (2nd T: 166). But far from establishing the legitimacy of an hereditary principle, such paragons are in fact dangerous to their subjects in the context of hereditary authority, for the subjects tend to allow them greater latitude than an ordinary official, and "when their Successors, managing the Government with different Thoughts . . . draw the Actions of those good Rulers into Precedent, and make them the Standard of their *Prerogative* . . . it has often occasioned . . . publick Disorders, before the People could . . . get that to be declared not to be *Prerogative*, which truly was never so" (2nd T: 166). Hence the truth in the paradox that "the Reigns of good princes have been always most dangerous to the Liberties of their People" (ibid.).

There is one other set of passages where Locke seems to lend a scintilla of credence to the suggestion that kings may be in some sense special, a different sort of breed from their subjects. At the end of *Second Treatise*, he says this: "[I]n some Countries the Person of the Prince by the Law is Sacred, and so whatever he commands or does, his Person is still free from all Question or Violence, not liable to Force, or any Judicial Censure or Condemnation" (2nd T: 205). The reason for this, he says, is to preserve "the security of the Government" as long as possible,[42] "[i]t being safer for the Body that some few private Men should be sometimes in danger to suffer than that the head of the Republick should be easily and upon slight occasions exposed" (2nd T: 205). That this is not a case of Locke finally recognizing the principle of royalty is indicated not just by the mischievous insertion of "Republick" in the passage just quoted, but by the generally pragmatic way in which this practice is defended. The most that Locke is prepared to say about the sanctity of monarchy is that, in a certain sort of mixed constitution,[43] the king may be thought to embody the legitimacy of the popularly established constitution, not vice versa. The king, for example, may be the recipient of "*Oaths of Allegiance* and Fealty" (2nd T: 151). Still, as Locke puts it,

---

[42] Obviously if the whole constitution collapses, then all bets are off so far as the sacredness of the prince's person is concerned.

[43] "In some Commonwealths, where the *Legislative* is not always in being, and the *Executive* is vested in a single Person, who has also a share in the legislative; there that single person in a very tolerable sense may also be called *Supream*: not that he has in himself all the Supream Power, which is that of Law-making: But because he has in him the *Supream Execution*, from whom all inferior Magistrates derive all their several subordinate Powers . . . having also no Legislative superior to him, there being no Law to be made without his consent . . . *he is* properly enough in this sense *Supream*." (2nd T: 151)

he has no right to Obedience, nor can claim it otherwise than as the publick Person vested with the Power of the Law, and so is to be considered as the Image, Phantom, or Representative of the Common-wealth, acted by the will of the Society, declared in its Laws; and thus he has no Will, no Power, but that of the Law. (2nd T: 151)

In the end, the king is just a man, and if he violates the laws, his will is not entitled to any obedience. It may not be necessary to physically resist him, "the harm he can do in his own Person not being likely to happen often, nor to extend itself far, nor being able by his single strength to subvert the Laws nor oppress the Body of the People" (2nd T: 205). But even there Locke has his doubts, and as the *Second Treatise* comes to an end, we find him making fun of, rather than subscribing to, the traditional monarchists' view that even *in extremis* the king is to be resisted "*with Reverence*" (2nd T: 235).

VIII

Finally in this chapter, I want to say something about criminals. In the work of John Locke, the transition from kings to criminals is not perhaps as abrupt as it might be in other contexts. Any comments we make about his theory of punishment should be framed with the reminder that, historically, most of what he wrote about criminality was oriented to the specific crimes associated with the establishment of or with attempts to establish absolute power. To put it another way, the crimes that particularly interested Locke were *crimes against equality*. I will return to this point at the very end of the chapter. But, for now, let's approach the discussion of Locke on punishment by considering his views about the forfeiture of rights.

I began this chapter with a discussion of the status of children. We saw that the relation of a child to the full condition of equality with all other persons is one of normative destiny (the child is "born to" equality, even though he is not "born in" it) and development and education. Now, once we recognize from the case of children that equality is not quite a matter of moral *stasis* and that an individual may stand in a dynamic relation to equality, we have to ask about whether a person's status as the bearer of rights is also something that the person in question can lose. There are two possibilities: renunciation and forfeiture. As to the first, Locke is adamant that one may not performatively renounce one's moral standing, by agreeing (say) to become another person's slave: "For a Man, not having the Power of his own Life, *cannot*, by Compact, or his own Consent, *enslave himself* to any one" (2nd T: 23). The argument for this stems directly from the God-given nature of our moral status. Our rights against others, to freedom, non-aggression, and mutual aid, are a reflection of the fact that having been "sent into the World by [God's] order, and about his business, [we] are his Property, whose Workmanship [we] are, made to last during his, not one anothers Pleasure" (2nd T: 6). Now exactly the same reasoning establishes that I am not made to last during my own pleasure, so that I do not have moral authority over my own life; having been made for God's pleasure I have no jurisdiction to upset that arrangement by electing to live at the pleasure of any human being, myself included. Alienability of life, liberty, and equality is of course the basis on which Locke erects his most powerful argument against absolutism. Political absolutism admits of no such contractarian defense as certain sixteenth-century thinkers imagined:[44] "For no Body can transfer to another more power than he has in himself; and no Body has an absolute Arbitrary Power over himself" (2nd T: 135). It's important also, as we shall see in Chapter 6, in Locke's argument about property: need cannot be the basis of slavery, for the necessitous man does not have any arbitrary right over his freedom to sell, not even for food (1st T: 42–3).[45]

But although Locke is adamant that one cannot performatively re-nounce one's moral status, he does toy with the idea that there are certain wrong things one can deliberately do which will have the moral effect that one's status is degraded. If done with that intention, they are wrong on that account; but they may still have the degrading effect. Locke plays the casuist a little with this position when he talks about an effective way by which a conquered aggressor, justly enslaved, may commit suicide, though he has no legitimate power over his own life: "For, whenever he finds the hardship of his Slavery out-weigh the value of his Life, 'tis in his Power, by resisting the Will of his Master, to draw on himself the Death he desires" (2nd T: 23). But this is not an endorsement of such forms of suicide, nor is it in any sense a recognition that the person in question does after all have the moral power to alienate life or liberty.[46]

---

[44] Tuck, *Natural Rights Theory*, pp. 49–59.   [45] See below, p. 179.
[46] For a particularly stringent version of this point, see Dunn, *Political Thought of John Locke*, p. 109. Dunn says that justly enslaved aggressors "are at liberty to terminate their slavery by death, not as a human moral right but as a behaviourial option – in the same way as an animal, kept obedient by fear, could be said to be at liberty to 'choose' death by behaving in such a way as to get killed." But if Dunn thinks this is the only way of reconciling the possibility Locke envisages – the slave's drawing on himself the death he desires by resisting the will of his master – with a normative natural law prohibition on suicide, I think he is mistaken.

This brings us to the issue of forfeiture. In his remarks about punishment Locke sometimes suggests that a person who violates a principle of natural law thereby forfeits his moral status of freedom and equality. This position of Locke's is highly problematic and in my view it is not carefully thought out. It is moreover inconsistent with some of the other things Locke says about punishment, particularly in his remarks about the prerogative power of pardon.[47] I am not sure I know how to deal with this tangle of issues; I certainly don't know how to reconcile it with the background theory of basic equality.

Let's consider first how a Lockean theory of violation and punishment would work in the absence of a theory of forfeiture and degradation. Let's investigate, in other words, what Locke's theory of violation and punishment would look like if he were to reject the inegalitarian theory that aggressors lose their human status. It would go something like this. Suppose X violates the natural rights of Y, and does so in a way that indicates that he might commit further violations against Y or against others in the future. It is fundamental to Locke's position that Y or anyone sympathetic to Y or anyone alarmed about the more general danger is entitled to respond punitively to this transgression, "[a]nd thus in the State of nature, *one Man comes by a Power over another*" (2nd T: 8). But it is

no Absolute or Arbitrary Power, to use a Criminal, when he has got him in his hands, according to the passionate heats, or boundless extravagancy of his own Will; but only to retribute to him, so far as calm reason and conscience dictates, what is proportionate to his Transgression, which is so much as may serve for *Reparation* and *Restraint*: for these two are the only reasons, why one Man may lawfully do harm to another, which is that we call *punishment*. (2nd T: 8)

This is a strong principle of limitation, and it is of course unintelligible unless associated with the view that X continues to have rights in the matter *subsequent* to his transgression. X's moral rights don't disappear from the picture, entitling Y or anyone else to treat X as though he mattered no more than an animal. True, Locke sometimes says that we can't even kill an animal "but where some nobler use, than its bare Preservation calls for it" (2nd T: 6), but the position about punishment goes well beyond that, in at least three respects. First, Locke insists on a principle of proportionality: X has the right, which an animal does not have, to be punished to no greater extent than is proportionate to his offence. Secondly, Locke insists that a legitimate aim of punishment is to

---

[47] There is an excellent discussion in Simmons, *The Lockean Theory of Rights*, pp. 148 ff.

make the criminal "repent" of his wrongdoing (2nd T: 8 and 12). And thirdly, and remarkably, Locke recognizes a power of pardon "to mitigate the severity of the Law . . . for the *end of Government* being *the preservation of all*, as much as may be, even the guilty are to be spared, where it can prove no prejudice to the innocent" (2nd T: 159).

These conditions – particularly the possibility of pardon – indicate that a theory of when to punish and how much to punish is to be guided by some sort of moral calculation that continues to include the violator, X, as a focus of concern. The passage just quoted is unintelligible unless "the preservation of all" includes X, as it included him before he became a transgressor. Now we may ask: must this calculation include X in exactly the same way that it included him before, or is X's standing in the equation now different from that of the other persons entitled to concern? Well, it is surely different in this respect: we are recalibrating our account of what people may do to one another *in light of the fact that X unjustly attacked Y.* X is now part of the problem, for all that his interests must continue to be borne in mind as we calculate the solution. But I don't think that point necessarily converts the situation into one of forfeiture of natural rights. For consider this: on Locke's account people do not have natural rights to unlimited liberty or any specified quantum of liberty (which they might then have to forfeit when they become bad guys). Liberty is not license (2nd T: 6 and 57), and even under the most favorable circumstances the extent to which each person is free to do as he wants must be determined systematically by a calculation that pays attention to the situation of each other person. We see this in the theory of property (e.g. 2nd T: 33); we see it in the theory of religious liberty (e.g. LCT: 42); we see it in regard to parents' rights (1st T: 100); we even see it in regard to free speech and freedom of the press.[48] Always, the extent of one's liberty is an artifact of a calculation that pays attention to the equal interest in liberty of others. The criminal, X, has a right to be treated as an equal in conducting this calculation; but he does not have the right that it be conducted without reference to the sort of person his violations have shown him to be; nor necessarily does he have a right to an equal share of liberty in the upshot of the calculation.[49] I am not saying that Locke's argument here is a utilitarianism of liberty[50] – i.e. that we are equals as inputs into the liberty equation, but there are no

---

[48] See Locke, "Liberty of the Press," p. 330.
[49] Once again, for the distinction between getting an equal share and being considered as an equal in the process by which shares are determined, see Dworkin, *Taking Rights Seriously*, p. 227.
[50] Cf. the discussion of "a utilitarianism of rights" in Nozick, *Anarchy, State and Utopia*, p. 28.

distributive constraints on the outputs that emerge. As well as an absolute insistence that we all be treated as equals in the process that allocates liberty, there may be a rough presumption that we will all end up with the same quantum of liberty, unless we have done something to defeat the presumption or unless some other peculiar circumstances obtain.[51] But defeat of that presumption is not the same as forfeiture of basic equality. The criminal retains the right, on this account, to be treated by all others as an equal in determining the particular demands of social life.

That's the version of Locke's theory of punishment most congenial to his underlying egalitarianism. By our lights, it is not necessarily an attractive account in Locke's hands. It provides for the possibility of capital punishment. The basic principle of the calculus is that as many persons as possible are to be preserved, and Locke reads this as permitting not just the restriction of some people's freedom, but the taking of some people's lives. It is also associated with a particularly ferocious account of self-defense. I am entitled to resist anyone who assaults me or robs me, and resist him with deadly force even if he has not offered deadly force, because "I have no reason to suppose that he, who would *take away my Liberty*, would not when he had me in his Power, take away everything else" (2nd T: 18).

What I have given so far is one side of Locke's account. Undeniably, however, there are also strands of much harder-line forfeiture theory in the *Second Treatise*. The harder-line theory presents itself in two versions. In the first or general version, it is an account of expulsion from the natural community. By the law of nature, says Locke, "*Mankind are one Community* . . . one Society, distinct from all other Creatures. And were it not for the corruption, and vitiousness of degenerate Men, there would be no need of any other; no necessity that Men should separate from this, and by positive agreements combine into smaller and divided associations" (2nd T: 128).[52] This "great and natural Community" (2nd T: 128) comprises initially the whole species, or – to put it in the language we developed in Chapter 3 – it comprises all those who can recognize in one another the special relation to God of which their capacity for abstract thought is a token. This is a community of people who understand

---

[51] I have in mind Locke's remarks about whether we may "pull down an innocent Man's House to stop the Fire, when the next to it is burning" (2nd T: 159).

[52] Compare natural community, in this sense, with Locke's conception of political community: "Since then those, who liked one another so well as to join into Society, cannot but be supposed to have some Acquaintance and Friendship together, and some Trust one in another: they could not but have greater Apprehensions of others, than of one another" (*Second Treatise*, 107).

that each of them has been "sent into the World by [God's] order, and about his business" and that they are "made to last during [God's], not one another's Pleasure" (2nd T: 6). As such, it is a community dedicated by natural law to mutual recognition, mutual respect, and mutual aid among equals. On any account of serious or endemic criminality, the criminal has distanced himself from the constitutive principles of this community, whether we see those principles as the norms of social peace or the values of equality and mutual respect that underlie those norms:

> In transgressing the Law of Nature, the Offender declares himself to live by another Rule, than that of reason and common Equity, which is that measure God has set to the actions of Men, for their mutual security: and so he becomes dangerous to Mankind, the tye, which is to secure them from injury and violence, being slighted and broken by him. (2nd T: 8)

Almost by definition, then, the offender is no longer a member (or now only problematically a member) of the natural community, for membership is defined by common acceptance of these rules and values. But Locke goes further and puts a bestial gloss on this loss of membership in natural community. By violating the natural law, "a Man so far becomes degenerate, and declares himself to quit the Principles of Human Nature, and to be a noxious Creature" (2nd T: 10).

> [H]aving renounced Reason, the common Rule and Measure God hath given to Mankind, hath, by the unjust Violence and Slaughter he hath committed upon one, declared War against all Mankind, and therefore may be destroyed as a Lyon or a Tyger, one of those wild Savage Beasts, with whom Men can have no Society nor Security. (2nd T: 11)

It is this bestialization of offenders, and the consequent insistence that they "may be treated as beasts of prey," that is the most difficult to reconcile with Locke's commitment to basic equality. Now, John Dunn believes that this need not be conceived as a literal or ontological bestialization, and I hope he is right. Dunn says:

> Those who by their aggression quit the law of reason do not of course by this behavior cease to be voluntary agents responsible to God for their misdeeds. But they become liable to be treated by other men, as though they were dangerous animals, as though they were no longer voluntary agents and hence had no rights against other men.[53]

---

[53] Dunn, *Political Thought of John Locke*, p. 107.

This may help a little bit in reconciling the two positions. For it seems to suggest that in an extreme case, even though X is a person, the way we are entitled to treat him may turn out to be indistinguishable from the way we are entitled to treat a beast of prey. We treat X, the person, as though he were (what he is not) a beast of prey. Still, the ontological point – that X really is a person, notwithstanding his transgressions – cannot be entirely irrelevant for us. For, first, we have to be very careful in our determination of whether it is appropriate to treat X in this way; we must not do so hastily or arbitrarily, or out of hostility to X. Furthermore, not all offending has this consequence: all offending may make a difference to how it is appropriate to treat the offender, but only in an extreme case will the appropriate way to treat him be like the appropriate way to treat a beast of prey. (Of course, opinions may differ as to where the threshold is drawn; and Locke – as I said in my comments about whether you are entitled to resist a robber with deadly force – holds very firm views about that. But that's another matter.) And so it is very important that care be taken in making this determination, and my point is of course that part of that care is oriented to X's moral standing. We take this care for the sake of X; it is partly for offenders' sakes that we are concerned "that Ill Nature, Passion and Revenge will carry [men] too far in punishing others" (2nd T: 13). Moreover, in deciding what is the appropriate level of response to X, we must consult again the calculus of concern for the whole species, and at that stage X's good must be included as an input along with the good of everyone else. It is not a case of X being expelled from the natural community first, and then the rest of us consulting our interests (exclusive of X's interests) in deciding how to treat X. We don't bestialize X first, and then decide how the rest of us are to respond to this animal. On Dunn's interpretation, we decide how it is appropriate to treat X and notice that, in an extreme case, this is tantamount to expulsion from the natural community. We decide how to respond to this being who is in fact a person, and then notice (again, in an extreme case) that the appropriate response is barely distinguishable from the appropriate response to a noxious animal.

The second strand of Locke's hard-line forfeiture theory has to do with the very specific relation between conqueror and aggressor in a just war; and this is where Locke's forfeiture thesis hooks up with what little there is in his political philosophy in the way of a theory of justified slavery. We are to imagine that X has mounted an attack on Y which may legitimately be responded to with deadly force, and now Y has X at the point of his sword. Locke says that X's situation is as follows:

having by his fault forfeited his own Life, by some Act that deserves Death; he, to whom he has forfeited it, may (when he has him in his Power) delay to take it, and make use of him to his own Service . . . This is the perfect condition of slavery, which is nothing else, but the state of war continued, between a lawful conqueror and a captive. (2nd T: 23–4)

The forfeiture here is *in personam*. It is a forfeiture *to* somebody in particular. Later in the *Second Treatise*, Locke goes to extraordinary pains to ensure that the "X" term of this relation – the captive – is strictly defined. The person who may be enslaved in this way is the actual aggressor, not his wife, not his children, not his descendants, not his co-nationals, often not even his accomplices, if they were conscripts (2nd T: 179 and 182). I shall argue in Chapter 7 that the effect of these restrictions is to place a huge distance between Locke's account of legitimate slavery and the institution of slavery as it actually existed in the seventeenth century. He is not quite as fastidious about the "Y" term. Is it only the intended victim of the aggressor to whom the aggressor's life and liberty is forfeit if he is conquered?[54] Or is it forfeit to anyone who has, justly, taken it on himself to resist the aggression? The answer depends a little bit on how tightly the forfeiture argument is tied to self-defense. If it is tied tightly to self-defense – my enslaving him is an aspect of my justly resisting him – then the furthest it can extend is to those that "joyn with [the intended victim of the aggressor], and espouses his Quarrel" (2nd T: 16). But if it is tied to punishment, then the provision that any man may treat an aggressor as he might treat a captured beast of prey would legitimize a more far-reaching doctrine of enslavement. I don't think Locke is in a position to extend it this far. For once the offender is subdued enough for there to be any question of punishment, the point-of-a-sword aspect of the situation has come to an end. "[W]hen the actual force is over, the state of war ceases" (2nd T: 20), and with its cessation, the particular forfeiture rights of the just conqueror come to an end as well. The same is true of virtually any attempt on the captor's part to regularize his relation with his slave, beyond merely delaying to take his life (2nd T: 28). As soon as the captor accords any rights to the conquered aggressor, then normal interaction between persons resumes:

if he be once allowed to be Master of his own Life, the *Despotical, Arbitrary Power* of his Master ceases. He that is Master of himself, and his own Life, has a right too to the means of preserving it; so that *as soon as Compact enters, Slavery ceases*, and he so far quits his Absolute Power, and puts an end to the State of War, who enters into Conditions with his Captive. (2nd T: 172)

---

[54] See 2nd T: 176, for Locke's account of the inheritability of just grievance against an aggressor.

I said before that there is a huge gap between Locke's very tight conditions for legitimate slavery and the way the institution actually operated in his time. And now we are starting to see a huge gap also between Locke's very tight conditions and the prospect of *any* stable or regularized system of slavery. And that of course was precisely what Locke intended, for remember his overarching intention was to defeat the claim that the "vile and miserable condition of slavery" could be the normal basis for organizing a political system (1st T: 1). I think we should read the connection between the theory of legitimate resistance to aggression and the theory of slavery as an attempt on Locke's part to minimize the scope that slavery would have for its legitimate operation in the world. Certainly, that is the tenor of Chapter 16 of the *Second Treatise*. For that reason alone, then, there is some merit in not exaggerating the hard-line tendencies of Locke's doctrine of forfeiture.

Clearly, this area of crime and punishment is a delicate terrain for the Lockean theory of equality. And there is always a temptation to sell the basic premise short at this stage in the heat of one's passionate indignation. It is, I think, worth remarking though that Locke's particular interest in this aspect of the argument is related to equality in another way. To the extent that Locke had a political interest in persuading people to bestialize offenders against the law of nature, his intended targets were not the idle poor, or the working class, or native Americans. His targets were absolutist kings and princes – those who in their actions and their politics violated (precisely) the principle of basic equality, and treated their subjects like slaves. These are the real animals, said Locke, and (in the words of the motto he chose for the *Two Treatises*) "*placari nequeant, nisi hauriendum sanguinem laniandaque viscera nostra praebuerimus.*"[55] Slavery does figure in Locke's argument about self-defense, but not merely as a fate that may befall the conquered aggressor. Slavery is often the aggressor's aim, "for no body can desire to have me in his absolute power, unless it be to compel me by force to that which is against the right of my freedom, i.e. make me a slave" (2nd T: 17). The point is pervasive in the *Second Treatise*. The violations of the law of nature from which we have most to fear are violations of the principle of basic equality; they are violations by people who treat other men, not as their equals, but as animals to be subjected and enslaved. And of course one of the reasons Locke has to spend time thinking about how crime is properly dealt with outside the

---

[55] The quotation is from Livy and was translated by Laslett as follows: "They are not to be placated unless we yield to them our blood to drink and our entrails to tear out" (Locke, *Two Treatises*, p. 136).

framework of politics and positive law is that often the criminals are in control of the positive legal apparatus, and those who are resisting them have no choice but to work outside it (2nd T: 20). The argument turns on itself in an intriguing way, when Locke notices that absolute monarchs in effect degrade their subjects, by denying them any redress:

the Subject, or rather Slave of an Absolute Prince . . . has not only no Appeal, as those in Society ought to have, but as if he were degraded from the common state of Rational Creatures, is denied a liberty to judge of, or to defend his Right; and so is exposed to all the Misery and Inconveniencies, that a Man can fear from one, who being in the unrestrained State of Nature, is yet corrupted with Flattery, and armed with Power. (2nd T: 91)

I am not saying that Locke's unfortunate tendency towards the bestialization of criminals is mitigated by the fact that the criminals he had in mind were mainly anti-egalitarian enslavers; but it is worth remembering that the overall drift of even this part of his argument is towards a robust vindication of equality against those who would act on the opposite principle.

6

"Disproportionate and Unequal Possession"

My aim in this book is not just to establish that Locke held a position on human equality, and that that position was held on theological grounds; I also want to show that this commitment to basic equality is an important working premise of his whole political theory, and that its influence is pervasive in his arguments about property, family, slavery, government, politics, and toleration. It is not just a piece of religiously inspired egalitarian rhetoric wheeled out up front as a sort of edifying decoration; if it were, its religious cast would be much less troubling. Basic equality operates for Locke as a premise and as a constraint. It is a premise for everything he says about authority, and it is also a premise for everything he says about our relations to each other, our concern for each other, and the extent to which our awareness of others' interests should affect our sense of what is reasonable in the pursuit of our own. And equality operates also in Locke's political philosophy as an on-going theoretical constraint, patrolling our derivations from the premises of the theory, checking not only that they are grounded in equality but also that their implications are broadly consistent with the idea that corporeal rational creatures are basically one another's equals. Both of these functions are apparent in the theory of property, and that is the subject of the present chapter.

I thought I should set aside a whole chapter to address the relation between Locke's argument about equality and his argument about property. Partly it is for personal reasons, for this is where I came in so far as my own particular interest in Locke's political philosophy is concerned.[1] But also it is because in the theory of property – in Chapter 5 of the *Second Treatise* – we really do see Locke's style of natural law argument at work. This is the chapter where he *shows* us, rather than just telling

---

[1] See Waldron, "Enough and as Good Left for Others"; "Two Worries About Mixing One's Labour"; "Locke, Tully and the Regulation of Property"; and especially *Right to Private Property*, pp. 137–252.

us, how a natural law argument would proceed from, and under the discipline of, a principle of basic equality.

I

The argument about property is a challenging case from the point of view of Locke's egalitarianism, because the aim of Chapter 5 of the *Second Treatise* seems patently inegalitarian. Locke is not only arguing for the legitimacy of private property; he is attempting to justify its "disproportionate and unequal" distribution (2nd T: 50). One gets a sense that his argument in this chapter would be a failure if inequality were not the outcome; and this makes all the more challenging the interpretive heuristic I am using – that a commitment to equality pervades Locke's work, and that it works throughout the theory as a premise and a constraint.

We should not exaggerate the problem, however. Though Locke's argument aims to explain and justify "disproportionate and unequal possession of the earth" (2nd T: 50), it is certainly not intended as a defense of the seventeenth-century status quo. Richard Ashcraft has drawn our attention to the contrast between Locke's work and that of his friend James Tyrrell in this regard.[2] Tyrrell was so eager to avoid any imputation of advocating a change in the system of property as it was already established that his argument amounted to a wholesale endorsement of existing property relations, whatever their form, distribution, or utility.[3] Locke on the other hand was quite critical of contemporary property arrangements, especially in the argument about inheritance and primogeniture in the *First Treatise* – an attack, by the way, which is very clearly grounded on principles of equality,[4] and which was well known in Locke's circle to lead in the direction of smaller estates, more equitably distributed.[5]

My aim in this chapter is to show that something like this egalitarianism pervades Locke's theory of property. It pervades the theory, in the story that Locke tells about the generation of private property rights by labor, and in his account of the limits on acquisition and the constraints on property, particularly in the controversial doctrine of charity in the *First*

---

[2] Ashcraft, *Revolutionary Politics*, pp. 282–3.
[3] See, for example, Tyrrell, *Of the Law of Nature*, Ch. 4, para. 8, pp. 162–3.
[4] Locke rejects as irrational the priority accorded to an eldest male child over the needs of his younger siblings: see *First Treatise*, paras. 87, 91, and especially 93. See also Waldron, "Locke's Account of Inheritance and Bequest," and Ashcraft, *Locke's Two Treatises*, pp. 93–6.
[5] Ashcraft, *Revolutionary Politics*, p. 283.

Treatise. Now to say that it is egalitarian is not to say that it leads to equal outcomes: we have seen that disparity often enough. Nor is it necessarily to say that the resulting theory is nice or congenial to our intuitions, for our intuitions are schooled also in other principles besides basic equality. When we look at the aspersions Locke casts on the mode of subsistence of aboriginal Americans, for example, and when we look at the way he modifies his doctrine of charity to accommodate some quite savage ideas about the best way to enforce the God-given duties of the poor, we see him taking positions that are unpleasant as well as unfamiliar. And it may seem a point against the more general thesis about a religious grounding for equality that I introduced in Chapter 1, and to which I will return at the end of Chapter 8, that the unpleasantness of Locke's position in these two regards is directly traceable to the particular religious conception that he accepted. But it is part of the aim of my book to caution against the reduction of religious argumentation in politics to cheerful anodyne positions that could be supported any way on any number of other grounds. In this chapter, we will see Locke's Protestant Christianity making contributions to his account of the implications of equality which are not only distinctive, but also quite counter-intuitive from the perspective of modern liberal egalitarianism.

II

If we say that Locke's aim is to defend unequal economic outcomes, we must remember the standpoint from which he is trying to defend that inequality. In the chapter on property, John Locke was responding to the very powerful critique put forward by Robert Filmer against those who claimed that all men were originally equal. On the egalitarian assumption that God gave the world to the whole human species (and not just to Adam), how was it possible, asked Filmer, that anyone could come to have private property in land or resources distinct from the claims of the rest of mankind? It seems strange, he said, that common property instituted by God should give way to private property instituted by man: "Doth it not derogate from the providence of God Almighty to ordain a community which could not continue? . . . [D]oth it not make the act of our forefathers, in abrogating the natural law of community by introducing that of property, to be a sin of high presumption?"[6] It was to answer this challenge – felt by politicians in his circle as difficult

---

[6] Filmer, "Observations Concerning the Originall of Government," p. 218.

and dangerous – that Locke produced the elaborate argument about initial acquisition in the *Second Treatise*. And the point I am making is that he would not have had to do so unless he had had what (in his opponents' eyes at least) was the foolish presumption to begin from a strong affirmative premise of equality: namely, the recognition that all men have initially "an equal Right to the use of the inferior Creatures, for the comfortable preservation of their Beings" (1st T: 87).

Indeed, Locke's premise is not just original equality, it is original communism – it is "very clear, that God, as King *David* says, *Psalm. CXV.* xvj. *has given the Earth to the Children of Men*; given it to Mankind in common" (2nd T: 25) – and even original community. By the law of nature, says Locke, "*Mankind are one Community* . . . one Society, distinct from all other Creatures. And were it not for the corruption, and vitiousness of degenerate Men, there would be no need of any other; no necessity that Men should separate from this, and by positive agreements combine into smaller and divided associations" (2nd T: 128).[7] That "great and natural Community" (2nd T: 128), whose margins we explored in our discussion of criminality at the end of Chapter 5, is a society dedicated by natural law to mutual aid and preservation among equals. The connection between equality and the mutual concern which is supposed to pervade such a natural community is developed by Locke very early in the *Second Treatise* with an argument he takes from his great sixteenth-century predecessor Richard Hooker.[8] The argument is developed immediately following Locke's initial statement of egalitarian principle:

> To understand Political Power right, and derive it from its Original, we must consider, what State all Men are naturally in, and that is, a *State of perfect Freedom* . . . A *State* also *of Equality*, wherein all the Power and Jurisdiction is reciprocal, no one having more than another; there being nothing more evident, than that Creatures of the same species and rank, promiscuously born to all the same advantages of Nature, and the use of the same faculties, should also be equal one amongst another without Subordination or Subjection, unless the Lord and Master of them all should, by any manifest Declaration of his Will, set one above another, and confer on him, by an evident and clear appointment, an undoubted Right to Dominion and Sovereignty. (2nd T: 4)

We are then told that "the Judicious *Hooker*" regarded this natural human equality "as so evident in it self, and beyond all question, that he makes

---

7 For Locke on natural versus political community, see 2nd T: 107, and Ch. 5, fn 52 above.
8 Spellman says that Locke cites Hooker in 2nd T: 5 to support the premise of equality (Spellman, *John Locke*, p. 112). Actually that's not true. What Locke does is cite the argument that Hooker built *upon* juridical equality – an argument from equal authority to equal concern.

it the Foundation of that Obligation to mutual Love amongst men, on which he Builds the Duties they owe one another" (2nd T: 5). This invocation of Hooker's *Laws of Ecclesiastical Polity* is also not just window-dressing on Locke's part: he reads Hooker's argument as a way of getting from basic equality of authority to what we call a principle of equal concern.

One way of understanding this is to say that Locke (with Hooker's help) is trying to unpack the case that may be made for the Golden Rule: "Love thy neighbor as thyself" or "Do unto others as you would have them do unto you."[9] In the *Essay Concerning Human Understanding*, in the course of his attack on innate moral ideas, Locke posed the following question. Let's say that "that most unshaken Rule of Morality and Foundation of all social Virtue, *That one should do as he would be done unto*, be propos'd to one, who never heard of it before, but yet is of capacity to understand its meaning; Might he not without any absurdity ask a Reason why?" (E: 1.3.4). Well, Richard Hooker's argument cited by Locke in section 5 of the *Second Treatise* is supposed to be the line of reasoning that would respond to that question. It is supposed to show that once we acknowledge that no human has a superior status, we have no choice but to treat the needs and desires of others as on a par with our own. Hooker says this:

[I]f I cannot but wish to receive all good, even as much at every Man's hands, as any Man can wish unto his own Soul, how should I look to have any part of my desire herein satisfied, unless myself be careful to satisfy the like desire, which is undoubtedly in other Men, we all being of one and the same nature? To have any thing offered them repugnant to this desire, must needs in all respects grieve them as much as me; so that if I do harm, I must look to suffer, there being no reason that others should shew greater measure of love to me, than they have by me shewed unto them. My desire therefore to be loved of my equals in nature as much as possible may be, imposeth upon me a natural duty of bearing to them-ward fully the like affection; from which relation of equality between ourselves and them that are as ourselves, what several Rules and Canons natural Reason hath drawn, for direction of Life, no Man is ignorant.[10]

There are several things going on here. One line of argument is simply instrumental: if I do not help others, I make it less likely that they will help me.[11] Or it might be an argument like that implicit in Kant's fourth

---

[9] See Harris, *The Mind of John Locke*, p. 309, for the significance of this in Locke's later moral theory.

[10] Hooker, *Laws of Ecclesiastical Polity*, Bk. I, sect. 8, p. 80.

[11] This depends of course on the others being aware of my selfishness. But as Thomas Hobbes remarked in a similar argument, it is foolish for anyone to rely on others' imperceptiveness in this regard: see Hobbes's response to "[t]he Foole" in *Leviathan*, Ch. 15, pp. 101–2.

example of the categorical imperative.[12] Each person, P, knows that he
is in various ways dependent on others' goodwill towards his interests,
and so he cannot but accept that this goodwill must be reciprocated by
him. Since there is no relevant difference between the call that another
person, Q, might make on P's goodwill, and the call that P might make
on Q's goodwill, the price of P's refusing any concern for others is that he
cannot reasonably expect others to show any concern for him. Certainly
the argument is supposed to turn on something like universalizability,
and on there not being any relevant difference from the moral point
of view between P's interest and Q's interest, or P's preference and Q's
preference. Locke's premise rules out any inherent superiority for P, and
since P must acknowledge Q as his equal, he must recognize Q's interests
and preferences too as the equals of his own.

But someone might say in response:

P's preferences have priority for P (over what P recognizes as Q's preferences) just
because they are *P's preferences*. Preferences don't float free of persons looking for
satisfaction, in a way that certain utilitarian conceptions suppose. A preference
is an orientation of a particular person to a state of affairs in the world, and we
cannot build an ethical theory on the assumption that the particularity of such
orientations is irrelevant.

How would Locke respond? I think he would say that the point is fair
so far as the primal psychology of preferences is concerned.[13] But the
Hooker argument kicks in as soon as one takes a step beyond that in the
direction of a moral theory of the reasonableness of seeking to satisfy
one's preferences. Morality has to do with the explanations one offers
to others, and with what they might reasonably be expected to accept
in a situation where their interests too are at stake.[14] As a moral matter,
P can hardly say to Q, "It is reasonable for me to pursue this interest of
mine, even at the expense of yours, just because it is *mine*." And again for
Locke, the religious dimension is important. What validates P's appetitive
behavior and his seeking for the satisfaction of any of his desires is not the
bare fact that he has preferences which move him, but that his obtaining
satisfaction of at least some of his desires is in accordance with God's
purpose in creating him. But then P can recognize also that this is exactly
true of Q's desires; they have their moral significance in the very scheme
that P's preferences have *their* significance in. So, for example, when

---

[12] Cf. Kant, *Grounding*, p. 32 (4: 423). This is how Ian Harris reads the passage: see Harris, *The Mind of John Locke*, p. 222.
[13] Cf. Locke, *Some Thoughts Concerning Education*, p. 77.
[14] Scanlon, *What We Owe to Each Other*, pp. 147 ff.

Locke says (in a passage we will examine in more detail in a moment) that someone taking resources from nature to feed himself is assured by reason that in "pursuing that natural Inclination . . . he followed the Will of his Maker" (1st T: 86), that person is not only given something to say to anyone who challenges him, but he is also given a basis on which he may recognize the importance, the equal importance – no, the *identical* importance – of others taking resources from nature to feed themselves. He cannot profess indifference to their endeavor and yet claim reason in support of his own.

Or suppose P gives priority to his own wishes, not because he thinks he is superior to Q, and not just because the wishes are his, but simply because he wills his own preservation in a situation of danger or scarcity. Locke actually recognizes a principle of self-preservation and he always conditions what he says about our duty to others with a self-preservation proviso: everyone ought as much as he can to preserve the rest of mankind, "when his own Preservation comes not in competition" (2nd T: 6). Doesn't this indicate that P need not always take others' interests as seriously as his own? Well, not quite. The first thing to note is that Lockean self-preservation is as much a duty as a right: "Every one . . . is *bound to preserve himself*, and not to quit his Station wilfully" (2nd T: 6). It is not a discretionary entitlement to give preference to self. P acknowledges that he owes a duty in respect of himself to his Creator. He knows that he has, in Locke's phrase, been "sent into the World by [God's] order and about [God's] business" (2nd T: 6), and that that is why he is entitled and required to preserve himself. Now, when he recognizes Q also as a being capable of apprehending the idea of God and His commands, P will see that Q also grasps this duty of self-preservation. Though the duty owed to God is owed uniquely by each of them – "the care of each man's salvation belongs only to himself" (LCT: 47) – each understands that their respective agent-relative duties have a common source. And that's important for Locke, for it goes to the basis of normativity in his moral theory. Part of the work done by the initial premise of equality is to establish, for each person, that there is nothing peculiar about his God-given moral status. God does not appear to have a purpose for him which is utterly different in character from His purposes for His other human creatures. Compare the moral situation here with the egoism of someone like Thomas Hobbes. Hobbes's theory treats P's survival as a *sui generis* source of normativity for P, something which is normatively quite opaque to Q, and it treats Q's interest as a *sui generis* source of normativity for Q, which is normatively quite opaque to P. The Lockean moral world, by contrast, involves not only a recognition that the source of the normativity of self-preservation in your case is similar to the source of the normativity of self-preservation in my case, but also a recognition of the fact that the source in the two cases is literally *the same*.

This affects how one views situations of scarcity, danger, and conflict. On Hobbes's scheme, there is nothing more natural than a competitive posture among rival interests.[15] For there is nothing about Q's interests that has any inherent interest to P except in the way of diffidence and competition. (Maybe it is sometimes instrumentally worthwhile for P to offer Q some satisfactions, but Q's satisfactions in themselves are quite alien to P.) Locke's scheme, by contrast, provides a basis for seeing competition as morally problematic: though the priority of self-preservation is agent-relative, and though sometimes this priority will require P to behave in ways in which a perfect altruist would not behave, still P's recognition of a common source for the normativity of P's self-preservation and Q's self-preservation means that both of them also have a duty to orient themselves if possible to a reconciliation of their interests in any circumstance where they tend to conflict. This, as we shall see, is the basis on which Locke requires individuals to form their conceptions of various constraints and limits on appropriation, imposed specifically in the interest of others.

III

I am not going to engage in any lengthy exposition or critique of Locke's labor theory – that is, his account of the generation of private property out of our original common endowment by people "mixing their labor" with natural resources. I did that *ad nauseam* in *The Right to Private Property*, and others have done it better in books published before and since.[16] But I want to make one or two observations about it, which will help us see the role of equality in the argument.

In modern philosophy it is tempting to treat Locke's labor theory as a secular piece of argumentation about entitlements accruing from labor.[17] It may be embellished up front with a bit of religious decoration (2nd T: 25–6), but it is tempting to say the main case could as easily be

---

[15] See also Waldron, "Self Defense," comparing Hobbes and Locke on self-preservation.
[16] Waldron, *Right to Private Property*, pp. 137–252; Ryan, *Property and Political Theory*, pp. 14–48; Kramer, *John Locke and the Origins of Private Property*; Sreenivasan, *Limits of Lockean Rights*.
[17] Cf. Nozick, *Anarchy, State and Utopia*, pp. 174 ff. See Waldron, "Religious Contributions," pp. 844–8, for a discussion of the significance of this choice as to how to interpret Locke's theory.

developed by an atheist. The argument may be treated simply as a suggestion about what happens morally speaking when you mix something you own (your labor) with something you don't own (a natural resource). Thus Robert Nozick asks the following question: "If I own a can of tomato juice and spill it in the sea so that its molecules (made radioactive, so I can check this) mingle evenly throughout the sea, do I thereby come to own the sea, or have I foolishly dissipated my tomato juice?"[18] And, in *The Right to Private Property*, I ask something similar: suppose there is a vat of wet cement that belongs to no one in particular, and I drop a diamond that I own into the vat just before the cement hardens; do I get to own the cement?[19] On this sort of approach, mixing my juice with the ocean or dropping my diamond into the cement is just something I happen to do, and we want to explore the moral difference that it makes. Now naturally I don't doubt the interest of this discussion, but whether it helps us understand Locke's account of appropriation depends on our being able to relate it to two aspects of his concerns that might not apply so easily to juice-in-the-ocean or diamond-in-the-vat. The first aspect is the teleology of the creation of natural resources, and the second is the special significance of labor in relation to that teleology. Both are essential to Locke's theory of property, and neither can be understood apart from his theological concerns.

The first aspect – the teleology of natural resources – reminds us that the argument about mixing one's labor is intended as a specific solution to a more general problem about humans' finding some way of satisfying their individual needs out of the material basis that God has provided.

The Earth, and all that is therein, is given to Men for the Support and Comfort of their being. And tho' all the Fruits it naturally produces, and Beasts it feeds, belong to Mankind in common, as they are produced by the spontaneous hand of Nature . . . yet being given for the use of Men, there must of necessity be a means *to appropriate* them some way or other, before they can be of any use, or at all beneficial to any particular Man. (2nd T: 26)

The "must" here is not merely a hypothetical imperative. It is driven by the teleology of our creation and that of the creation of the resources with which we find ourselves surrounded. That teleology is stated explicitly in an important passage in the *First Treatise*:

God having made Man, and planted in him, as in all other Animals, a strong desire of Self-preservation, and furnished the World with things fit for Food and Rayment and other Necessaries of Life, subservient to his design, that

[18] Nozick, *Anarchy, State and Utopia*, p. 175.   [19] Waldron, *Right to Private Property*, p. 188.

Man should live and abide for sometime upon the Face of the Earth, and not
that so curious and wonderful a piece of Workmanship by its own Negligence,
or want of Necessaries, should perish again, presently after a few moments
continuance: God, I say, having made Man and the World thus, spoke to him,
(that is) directed him by his Senses and Reason . . . to the use of those things,
which were serviceable for his Subsistence, and given him as means of his
Preservation . . . And thus Man's Property in the Creatures, was founded upon the
right he had, to make use of those things, that were necessary or useful to his
Being. (1st T: 86)[20]

The passage talks of our right to make use of things that are useful or
necessary to our being. But the right is one of those Lockean rights that
is also a duty.[21] Each person is directed "to the use of those things, which
[are] serviceable for his Subsistence" (1st T: 86). Each is required to help
himself. And so his having the right to help himself to natural resources
is intelligible not just in the light of his own purposes for himself, but in
the light of God's purposes for him. We shall see in a moment that this
also provides a theological context for the particular mode of helping
oneself – labor – that Locke thinks God has commanded. Laboring is
not just something we happen to do to resources (like happening to drop
a diamond in a vat of cement); it is the appropriate mode of helping
oneself to resources given what resources are *for*. Being permitted to help
oneself is not a divine indulgence of the self-interested inclination of
an acquisitive being. It is the naturally requisite next step following our
creation once we accept that we were created subservient to God's design
"that Man should live and abide for sometime upon the Face of the Earth,
and not that so curious and wonderful a piece of Workmanship by its
own Negligence, or want of Necessaries, should perish again, presently
after a few moments continuance" (1st T: 86).

In a footnote to his critical edition of the *Two Treatises*, Peter Laslett
cites this paragraph as an example of inconsistency between Locke's
political theory and the philosophical position set out in the *Essay*.[22] The
Essay repudiates the idea of innate practical principles, but here we have
Locke apparently saying that self-preservation is a principle implanted
in man by God.[23]

---

[20] See Taylor, *Sources of the Self*, p. 238, for helpful discussion of this passage.

[21] See Ryan, "Locke and the Dictatorship of the Bourgeoisie," p. 223.

[22] Locke, *Two Treatises*, p. 205.

[23] Another similar example might be Locke's account of the inclination to procreate: "God planted
in Men a strong desire also of propagating their Kind, and continuing themselves in their
Posterity" (1st T: 88).

For the desire, strong desire of Preserving his Life and Being having been Planted in him, as a Principle of Action by God himself, Reason, which was the Voice of God in him, could not but teach him and assure him, that pursuing that natural Inclination he had to preserve his Being, he followed the Will of his Maker. (1st T: 86)

Unfortunately Laslett has not read the passage (1st T: 86) carefully enough. Locke does not infer rightness directly from the existence of a natural inclination. He says humans find themselves with all sorts of inclinations: some of them nice, some of them nasty: "Nor can it be otherwise in a Creature, whose thoughts are more than the Sands, and wider than the ocean" (1st T: 58). As beings endowed with reason, we have to sort through our impulses and relate them to some rational understanding of our being and some experiential knowledge of our nature. Then and only then are we in a position to draw normative conclusions from the fact of their existence. Far from any inconsistency with Locke's philosophical argument, this is more or less exactly the point that is made in the discussion of innate ideas in the *Essay*. That discussion acknowledges the existence of natural inclinations:

I deny not that there are natural tendencies imprinted on the Minds of Men, and that from the very first instances of Sense and Perception, there are some things that are grateful and others that are unwelcome to them, some things that they incline to, and others that they fly: but this makes nothing for innate Characters on the Mind, which are to be principles of knowledge, regulating our practice . . . Principles of Actions indeed there are lodged in Men's Appetites, but these are so far from being innate Moral Principles that, if they were left to their full swing, they would carry Men to the over-turning of all Morality. (E: 1.3.3 and 13)

What we need, before we think it right to follow such an innate appetite, is some assurance that it guides us as we ought to be guided, and that assurance can only come from the exercise of our intellect. In the present context, we find that it is safe (and indeed requisite) to rely on our survival instinct only by relating it rationally to ideas like God, creation, and purpose. These are not given in the inclination themselves; they have to be brought to it by reason.

IV

A little later in this chapter, we will return to the *First Treatise* passage about the inclination to survive and therefore to appropriate. We will find that this line of argument about the teleology of appropriation is also key to Locke's doctrine of charity. But before I turn to that, I want to address the other aspect of Locke's account of initial acquisition that has, in my view, a theological significance not captured in the conventional philosophical treatment of these matters. I want to say a word or two about Locke's emphasis on labor, his insistence "that though the things of Nature are given in common, yet Man (by being Master of himself, and *Proprietor of his own Person*, and the *actions or labor* of it) had still in himself the great Foundation of Property" (2nd T: 44). I believe that this too has an important theological aspect, though I believe that aspect is often misunderstood.

It is sometimes argued that human labor is valued by Locke and accorded the significance he gives it because it is God-like in its creativity.[24] God is our maker and that is why we are his property: "being all the Workmanship of one Omnipotent, and infinitely wise Maker . . . [we] are his Property, whose Workmanship [we] are, made to last during his, not one anothers Pleasure" (2nd T: 6).[25] And *we* are the makers of the things *we* produce, and that is why they are *our* property. Labor or production confers on man a God-like authority over the thing that he makes. I have said that equality is fundamental in Locke's theory, but this line of thought seems to suggest that ideas associated with ownership may be even more fundamental than that. Since our relation to God (the relation which grounds our equality) is to be understood in terms of our being owned by Him, our being objects in which He has invested His labor, it looks as though the workmanship model is more fundamental than the basis we have identified for equality. But a moment's reflection reveals that *that* won't do. The lower animals are God's workmanship also, yet they are not our equals. Our equality stems not from our equally being God's workmanship but (in Locke's words) from "the *Idea* of ourselves, as understanding, rational Beings" (E: 4.3.18) capable of responding consciously, and recognizing in each other the ability to respond consciously, to God's will. Still even if it does not ground equality, the image of divine workmanship might still be thought of as the prototype for human ownership. A number of commentators have taken this view – and what a view it is! The normativity of the laborer's control

---

[24] Tully, *Discourse on Property*, pp. 35–8 and 116–24. Cf. Ashcraft's comment *Revolutionary Politics*, p. 259: "the Deity is the Great Property Owner."

[25] As Locke put it in the early *Essays on the Law of Nature*, "who will deny that the clay is subject to the potter's will?" Locke, *Essays on the Law of Nature*, IV, p. 105.

of his product is awesomely grounded on this interpretation: it is on a par with the primal normativity of God's command of his creation. On the basis of this, one might even be in a position to make an end-run around the constraints of equality. Though "different degrees of Industry were apt to give men Possessions in different Proportions" (2nd T: 48), that is not objectionable since the rights of industry are more fundamental than the basis of equality!

I believe the importance of this analogy in Locke's thought has been exaggerated. On the one hand, Locke makes it pretty clear that the fact of our being God's workmanship matters less for His authority than the fact that we are dependent on Him for our being. In the *Essay*, he seems to back both horses, saying that "[t]he *Idea* of a supreme Being . . . whose Workmanship we are, and on whom we depend" is one of the foundations of morality (E: 2.28.8). But in a fragment on "Law" dated 1693, Locke said that "[t]he originall & foundation of all Law is dependence. A dependent intelligent being is under the power & direction & dominion of him on whom he depends . . . If man were independent he could have noe law but his own will . . . He would be a god to himself."[26] On the other hand, it is simply not true that human labor is characterized as God-like in the *Two Treatises*. It does not give us God-like authority over what we produce: there are restrictions on our ability to destroy the products of our labor (2nd T: 6) or even to let it perish uselessly in our possession (2nd T: 31). And labor itself, though commanded of us, is seen as a burden, not a God-like privilege. Locke may not have held an orthodox position on original sin, but he accepted some association between labor and man's fallen condition. Refusing to infer any authority for Adam over Eve in their respective punishments at the Fall, Locke says of Adam that "God sets him to work for his living, and seems rather to give him a Spade into his hand, to subdue the Earth, than a Scepter to Rule over its Inhabitants" (1st T: 45). Nothing very God-like there, in the "toil" and "drudgery" to which Adam and his line are condemned. True, he insists in the *Second Treatise* that it is "*Labor . . .* that *puts the difference of value on everything*" (2nd T: 40) and that $9/10$ or $99/100$ of the value of the things useful to man – even land – "*must all be charged* on the account of *Labor*, and received as an effect of that: Nature and the Earth furnished only the almost worthless Materials, as in themselves" (2nd T: 43). Human labor

---

[26] Locke, *Political Essays*, p. 328. See also Colman, *John Locke's Moral Philosophy*, p. 45: "God is said not merely to initiate our existence: our continued existence is said to depend upon God's constantly preserving us."

is therefore quite appropriately the basis of property. But this is *not* because it has a God-like character.[27] This is not to deny the importance of labor. It is rather because labor is the appropriate mode of our participation in the creation and sustenance of our being. It is conceivable that rational beings could have been created without the need for nutrition and other material resources; or they could have been created in a way that secured the satisfaction of their material needs directly without any need for action on their part.[28] Humans could have been created in a way that did not require constant human effort to keep humanity alive. And perhaps that was our situation before the Fall. (Locke's view is that what humans lost in the Fall was their immortality (RC: 106), and he associates this with God's injunction specifically to labor: "*In the Sweat of thy Face thou shalt eat thy Bread*, says God" (1st T: 41).)[29] There are also hints in some of Locke's writings of a more narrowly ethical valorization of labor, in which the good thing about labor is taken to be the fact that it keeps us active and prevents us falling into idleness.[30] As we shall see, some hints of this come through also in Locke's attitude to the idle poor.[31] But it would be wrong to put too much weight on this. Labor is important for Locke not because it is activity but because of the sort of activity it is. God has commanded us not just to *do something* but to do something that will make use of His endowment and make it capable of supporting even greater numbers of the beings He might create (2nd T: 42).

v

Breaking down the analogy between human labor and divine creation helps put in perspective some of the things that Locke says about America – particularly about the modes of subsistence of its native inhabitants, which in Locke's opinion were not based on labor at all in the sense appropriate to the founding of private property.

[27] Divine workmanship would be conscious and insightful all the way down and it would understand every detail of its creation. In human labor by contrast, "what most of us do is to intervene in or originate processes whose complete operation we do not understand, yielding a response we could not completely design." Cf. Nozick, *Anarchy, State and Utopia*, p. 288, responding to Locke's point in the *First Treatise* about the non-Godlike character of the "creation" of a child by its parents (1st T: 52).

[28] Cf. Locke's comments on the relation between nutrition and action in 2nd T: 28.

[29] Citing Genesis 3:19. On the other hand, the injunction "Be fruitful and multiply, and replenish the earth and subdue it" (Genesis 1:28), of which Locke seems to make so much in his theory of property (2nd T: 35), is pre-lapsarian.

[30] See Locke, *Essays on the Law of Nature* ("God intends man to do something"), p. 105, cited by Ashcraft, *Revolutionary Politics*, at pp. 262 and 268.

[31] See below, pp. 186–7.

Labor begins life as a quite general category for Locke, including the work of hunters, gatherers, deep-sea fishermen, ploughmen, bakers and artisans. It seems to refer to any human means whereby objects are altered for the better satisfaction of human needs or wants.[32] However, when the discussion turns to the basis of property in land, labor takes on a new spin and a new significance. It is now specifically associated with cultivation: *"As much Land* as a man Tills, Plants, Improves, Cultivates, and can use the Product of, so much is his *Property"* (2nd T: 32). Locke concludes that if a man simply roams over unimproved land, hunting and gathering, or if he does nothing but pasture his flock on an unimproved meadow, he secures no property in the land that he uses.

The Canadian political philosopher James Tully has written an important article entitled, "Rediscovering America: The *Two Treatises* and Aboriginal Rights." I don't always see eye to eye with Tully on matters Lockean,[33] but I think he is right in this essay to draw our attention to the enormous significance of the distinction between cultivation and other modes of subsistence so far as seventeenth- and eighteenth-century thought about European settlement in the Americas is concerned. There is no doubt that something like the Lockean distinction was used to justify the displacement of native Americans; and I think Tully is absolutely right to insist that Locke was aware of this and may even have written Chapter 5 of the *Second Treatise* partly with this in mind. (He had interests of his own in America, and he was involved also in the plantation enterprises of others – something we will consider in Chapter 7, when we examine Locke's views about slavery.) Certainly nothing else can explain Locke's strident and repetitive insistence that uncultivated land is to be looked on as waste land, and may be the property of anyone with initiative enough to cultivate it.[34]

How does this hostility to aboriginal Americans stand with the premise of Christian equality? Does it mean that native Americans are less than our equals, on the Lockean account, because their mode of subsistence is dismissed and legitimately displaced in this way? Tully thinks the

---

[32] In one notorious passage, Locke even refers to the employment of labor as labor: "the Turfs *my Servant* has cut . . . become *my* property . . . The labor that was mine, removing them out of that common state they were in, hath fixed my property in them" (2nd T: 28). For rival views on the significance of this passage, see Tully, *Discourse on Property*, pp. 135 ff. and Waldron, *Right to Private Property*, pp. 224–32.

[33] See Waldron, *Right to Private Property*, pp. 198–200, 220–2, and 225–41.

[34] However, it may be a little far-fetched for Tully to argue also that Locke's chapter is intended to vindicate English agriculture in America against French fur-trading (Tully, "Rediscovering America," pp. 165–6). That really is pushing the *Québecois* line too far!

answer is "Yes."[35] He thinks Locke's aim in these passages is to put native Americans beyond the pale of the great natural human community I mentioned earlier, designating them as "wild Savage Beasts, with whom Men can have no Society nor Security" (2nd T: 11). The perhaps understandable attempts of native Americans to defend their traditional ways of life against European encroachment are seen as violent attacks on the very principle of property (which of course gives priority to a different mode of subsistence); "Indians" feature in one of Locke's paragraphs discussing the natural right of punishment (2nd T: 9); and even in the *First Treatise* Locke refers to the right of "a Planter in the West Indies" to muster up his friends and family "and lead them out against the *Indians*, to seek Reparation upon any Injury received from them" (1st T: 130). Tully is also quite right when he says that Locke is unacceptably offhand about the modes of subsistence which he envisages being displaced by European cultivation. In Tully's words:

Locke sets up cultivation as the standard of industrious and rational use, in contrast to the "waste" and lack of cultivation in Amerindian hunting and gathering, thus eliminating any title they might claim. The planning, coordination, skills, and activities involved in native hunting, gathering, trapping, fishing, and non-sedentary agriculture, which took thousands of years to develop and take a lifetime for each generation to acquire and pass on, are not counted as labor at all, except for the very last individual step (such as picking or killing), but are glossed as "unassisted nature" and "spontaneous provisions" when Locke makes his comparisons, whereas European activities, such as manufacturing bread are described in depth.[36]

He has in mind the long passages in paragraphs 40–4 of the *Second Treatise*, where Locke attempts to show in detail how much the value of a loaf of bread is due to the labor invested not only in cultivating the soil and planting and harvesting the wheat, but also in mining the metal to fashion the plough, and manufacturing and transporting all the implements of farming and baking and shipping and so on.

Certainly, it would seem that if anything like Lockean equality survives here, it is a concept of equality uncontaminated by what we would call respect for ethnic identity. For us, equal respect for individuals is sometimes seen as requiring equal respect for their diverse established ways of life. And Locke does not seem to be particularly sympathetic to that.

However, the picture may be more complicated than Tully allows. For there *are* passages in his later works where Locke comes close to a

---

[35] Tully, "Rediscovering America," pp. 142 ff.   [36] Ibid., p. 156.

norm of universal respect for ways of life, at least for those ways of life that do not impinge on others. These passages are to be found, as one would expect, in his writings on toleration and not only are they tolerant of difference, they are actually quite hostile to colonial or missionary imposition: "Not even Americans," Locke says, "are to be punished either in body or goods, for not embracing our faith and worship. If they are persuaded that they please God in observing the rites of their own country . . . they are to be left unto God and themselves" (LCT: 43). Then he adds this remarkable passage, which is hardly the epitome of colonial insensitivity:

Let us trace this matter to the bottom . . . [A]n inconsiderable and weak number of Christians, destitute of everything, arrive in a Pagan Country; these Foreigners beseech the Inhabitants, by the bowels of Humanity, that they would succor them with the necessaries of life; Those necessaries are given them, Habitations are granted, and they all join together, and grow up into one Body of People. The Christian Religion by this means takes root in that Countrey, and spreads itself; but does not suddenly grow the strongest. While things are in this condition, Peace, Friendship, Faith, and equal Justice, are preserved amongst them. At length the Magistrate becomes a Christian, and by that means their Party becomes the most powerful. Then immediately all Compacts are to be broken, all Civil Rights to be violated, that Idolatry may be extirpated: and unless these innocent Pagans, strict Observers of the Rules of Equity and the Law of Nature, and no ways offending against the Laws of the Society, I say unless they will forsake their ancient Religion, and embrace a new and strange one, they are to be turned out of the Lands and Possessions of their Forefathers, and perhaps deprived of Life it self. Then, at last, it appears what Zeal for the Church, joined with the desire of Dominion, is capable to produce; and how easily the pretence of Religion, and of the care of Souls, serves for a Cloak to Covetousness, Rapine, and Ambition. (LCT: 43)

In my opinion it is impossible to read that passage and say that Locke's aim in his mature work was to dehumanize the native Americans.

In fact, his position is quite complicated. The extent to which human equality requires equal respect for different ways of life is dominated (as everything in Locke's theory of equality is dominated) by his theological conception of natural law. So far as their religious practices are concerned, native Americans are to benefit from the same toleration as everyone else, for their pagan practices in matters of worship and ritual are of no prejudice to anybody else's salvation. "[S]eeing one man does not violate the right of another by his erroneous opinions and undue manner of worship, nor is his perdition any prejudice to another man's affairs, therefore, the care of each man's salvation belongs only to himself" (LCT: 46). Of course, practices like cannibalism or child sacrifice are to be prohibited in whatever cultural or religious context they occur: Locke is a straightforward natural law universalist so far as murder and infanticide are concerned.[37] And he was a connoisseur of contemporary anthropological stories about the various disgusting practices reported by travelers from America and Africa and Asia: the *Essay* offers some particularly choice examples,[38] illustrating not just the absence of innate moral principles but also, as Locke says elsewhere, how "far...the busie mind of Man [can] carry him to a Brutality below the level of Beasts," particularly where "Fashion hath once Established" and custom made sacred "what Folly or craft began" (1st T: 58). Locke's opposition to innatism does not lead him to relativism. He believed it was possible to use human reason – ordinary human reason – to sift through the customs of the world and determine at least for some of them whether or not they were in conformity with the requirements of natural law. And indeed, as we saw in Chapter 4, there are places in the *First Treatise* where Locke turns the universalist critique against European customs, and conjectures "that the Woods and Forests, where the irrational untaught Inhabitants keep right by following Nature, are fitter to give us Rules, than Cities and Palaces, where those that call themselves Civil and Rational, go out of their way, by the Authority of Example" (1st T: 58). So we cannot accept any simplistic version of Tully's hypothesis that has Locke reflexively investing the practices of his own culture with an aura of moral universalism, and nor I think can we accept any depiction of him as complicit in a deliberate attempt to dehumanize the peoples and practices that the colonists faced in the new world.

Even in his assertion that America is an unappropriated wilderness, Locke does not rest on European prejudice. He offers an extensive *argument* for this assertion, an argument which purports to take seriously both the commandments of God and the interests of all the humans affected. He relies on what he thinks we can figure out concerning the purposes of God in His original donation: "God gave the World to Men in Common; but since he gave it them for their benefit, and the greatest Conveniencies of Life they were capable to draw from it, it cannot be

---

[37] LCT: 39: "You will say, by this rule, if some congregations should have a mind to sacrifice infants, or (as the primitive Christians were falsely accused) lustfully pollute themselves in promiscuous uncleanness, or practise any other such heinous enormities, is the magistrate obliged to tolerate them, because they are committed in a religious assembly? I answer: No. These things are not lawful in the ordinary course of life, nor in any private house; and therefore neither are they so in the worship of God, or in any religious meeting."

[38] See E: 1.3.9.

supposed he meant it should always remain common and uncultivated" (2nd T: 34). God has commanded us to work hard and subdue the earth, making it bring forth just as much plenty and enabling it to sustain just as many people as it possibly can. "[T]he great Design of God, *Increase* and *Multiply*" (1st T: 41) and "the main intention of Nature, which willeth the increase of Mankind" (1st T: 59) are what drive Locke's sense of the importance of labor and cultivation. And he believes that these commands must be taken at face value, not filtered through any sort of independent principle of respect for existing cultures and practices. (If our response to divine command were modified by a principle of respect for existing culture or ethnicity, it would soon become impossible to use it as a basis for the critical evaluation of human societies.) The Americans, Locke says, live on top of the raw "materials of Plenty, *i.e.* a fruitful Soil, apt to produce in abundance, what might serve for food, raiment, and delight; yet for want of improving it by labor, have not one hundredth part of the conveniencies we enjoy" (2nd T: 41). Their lands are underpopulated and the lives of its few inhabitants are "needy and wretched" (2nd T: 37). Now if they really want to persevere in their mode of subsistence despite its wretched poverty, they can withdraw to some vacant inland place, or even coexist side-by-side with European agriculture (as Abel coexisted with Cain[39] – a rather unfortunate analogy, perhaps, for Locke to use), or they can take their chances in an economy dominated by agriculture, cognizant of the fact that, as things stood, even a landless day-laborer in England was fed, lodged, and clad better in a privatized economy than "a king of a large and fruitful [*un*cultivated] Territory" in America (2nd T: 41). But they are not entitled, Locke insists, to simply tie up in unproductive occupancy productive resources whose industrious cultivation could improve both their own prospects and those of a much greater population. This is in fact an application of something like his spoilation proviso (2nd T: 31), which we will discuss in a moment.

I am not saying that we – or the native Americans – should be convinced by this argument. (Tully may be right to reproach Locke for his failure to see that the native Americans also used land in efficient and ecologically benign ways.)[40] Often when Locke sees the need for an argument he produces a bad argument. And in our haste to refute it, we are wrongly tempted to say that his producing a bad argument is as good

---

[39] 2nd T: 38: "Thus, at the beginning, *Cain* might take as much Ground as he could till, and make it his own Land, and yet leave enough to *Abel*'s Sheep to feed on; a few Acres would serve for both their Possessions."

[40] Tully, "Rediscovering America," pp. 163 ff. and the passage quoted, above, at p. 166.

as thinking that no argument respecting equality needs to be produced
at all. That is a mistake, certainly in this context. For an argument which
purports to respect equality *has* been produced – an argument which
purports to pay attention to the interests of all, not just the colonists,
but also not just the native Americans and which claims that cultivation
makes everyone better off. We are not entitled to infer from the fact
that Locke produced a universalist argument purporting to favor modes
of subsistence familiar to us over modes of subsistence familiar to the
native Americans that therefore he intended to have them treated as
non-persons. If that were the case, he would not have felt the need for
an argument at all, any more than one needs an argument to justify the
killing of a deer or the extirpation of mosquitoes.

VI

Appropriation, Locke says, is necessary to consummate the usefulness
of God's bounty, and labor is the natural mode of appropriation: "God
commanded, and [man's] Wants forced him to *labor*" (2nd T: 35). But
appropriation by labor is confined within a framework dictated by the
overall teleology of Locke's account, and that confinement is represented
by the provisos and qualifications with which his account of appropriation
is hedged: the spoilation limitation, the so-called sufficiency limitation,
and the doctrine of charity.[41] These conditions are the shadows cast by
the principle of basic equality on the whole apparatus of property and
economy. They are the medium through which the principle of basic
equality patrols and disciplines the account.

Let's begin with the spoilation proviso: "Nothing was made by God
for Man to spoil or destroy" (2nd T: 31). It is widely believed – following
C. B. Macpherson's interpretation – that Locke set up the spoilation
proviso in the name of equality only to abandon it in order to vindicate
the inegalitarian effects of a money economy.[42] But this is based on a
mistaken account of the way in which the proviso is supposed to operate.
The best way to understand the spoilation proviso is as a reason for con-
demning any acquisition that has the effect of an appropriated resource
"perishing uselessly" in the possession of the appropriator (2nd T: 31

---

[41] The terms "spoilation limitation" – "As much as any one can make use of to any advantage of
life *before it spoils*, so much he may by his labor fix a Property in" (2nd T: 31) – and "sufficiency
limitation" – "at least where there is enough, and as good left in common for others" (2nd T: 27) –
were coined, I believe, by C. B. Macpherson in *Political Theory of Possessive Individualism*, pp. 204
and 211. My phrase "the doctrine of charity" refers to the doctrine set out in 1st T: 42.

[42] Macpherson, *Political Theory of Possessive Individualism*, pp. 203 ff.

and 46). Clearly, this represents the continuing importance for Locke's property theory of the basic teleology of nature I spoke about in section IV. Since "[t]he Earth, and all that is therein, is given to Men for the Support and Comfort of their being" (2nd T: 26), our use of it is at all times "subservient to [God's] design, that Man should live and abide for sometime upon the Face of the Earth, and not that so curious and wonderful a piece of Workmanship by its own Negligence, or want of Necessaries, should perish again, presently after a few moments continuance" (1st T: 86). To appropriate resources surplus to one's needs in a way that prevents their being used by anyone else runs directly counter to this principle, for "[n]othing was made by God for Man to spoil or destroy" (2nd T: 31). So understood, this principle respects basic equality in the most elementary sense: the natural resources are there for human use, where human use means use by any human – by someone or anyone who can use them. For *everyone* to be denied the use of them by someone who has no use for them himself, or does not propose to put them to human use, is a direct affront to the teleological relation in which each of us stands to the bounty provided by God. In those circumstances, the validity of their appropriation by labor (or by any other means) evaporates and the resources become common again.

Locke insists, however, that this is not what happens when the goods are sold in the market. If a man "bartered away Plumbs, that would have rotted in a Week, for Nuts that would last good for his eating a whole Year, he did no injury; he wasted not the common Stock; destroyed no part of the portion of Goods that belonged to others, so long as nothing perished uselessly in his hands" (2nd T: 46). It is no part of the spoilation proviso that appropriated goods must be used *by the particular person who appropriated them.*[43] The proviso is imposed in the interests of everyone, and their direct interest in the matter is simply that the humanly useful not be made humanly useless by human action. Locke does say that in the early ages of the world before the invention of money, the operation of this proviso had the effect of limiting each person's possessions to a (very) rough equality: "No man's Labor could subdue, or appropriate all; nor could his Enjoyment consume more than a small part" (2nd T: 35). But this was a superficial equality – what we might call "equality of outcome" – and not necessarily or in all circumstances a distributive pattern required by the deeper principle of equal concern

---

[43] Indeed there's no basis in the theory on which that could sensibly be required (as though consumption were a sort of liability that one took on in presumptuous act of appropriation – "You must eat up all the pudding that you took, every last spoonful!").

which generated the spoilation proviso. It is a superficial consequence of the operation of the spoilation proviso in circumstances where there is no systematic basis for allocating appropriated goods to the use of anyone other than the appropriator. But once such a basis becomes available, the superficial equality of outcomes vanishes. Macpherson thinks this means that the proviso has evaporated. But it hasn't. The proviso is served now by the market processes that allocate appropriated objects to human use. But if for some reason market processes didn't work to that effect, then the proviso would remain available as a basis for reproaching them.[44]

Locke is commonly said to have imposed a second condition on acquisition: it is sometimes called the "sufficiency proviso," after Locke's suggestion that unilateral appropriation is legitimate "at least where there is enough, and as good left in common for others" (2nd T: 27). In an article published more than twenty years ago, I suggested that this was not intended as a necessary condition on legitimate acquisition: after all, Locke could not possibly have meant that *no one* should appropriate any resources if there were not enough for everyone.[45] I believed then, and I still believe, that the sufficiency proviso is better understood as a *sufficient* condition[46] – no pun intended! – highlighting the point that there is certainly no difficulty with unilateral acquisition (which satisfies the other provisos) in circumstances of plenty, but leaving open the possibility that some other basis might have to be found to regulate acquisition in circumstances of scarcity. The former point already pays tribute to the underlying principle of equality by indicating that if the interests of others are *not* prejudiced by my acquisition then there can be no objection to it: "[H]e that leaves as much as another can make use of, does as good as take nothing at all . . . He that had as good left for his improvement, as was already taken up, needed not complain, ought not to meddle with what was already improved by another's labor" (2nd T: 33–4). The implication is informal, but clear: prejudice to others' interests is the main heading under which objections to acquisition can reasonably be lodged. Apart from that, there is no legitimate ground for complaint.

But suppose now that resources do become scarce and that land, especially, is no longer available for appropriation in such generous supply.[47]

---

[44] This is the force of my example in Waldron, *Right to Private Property*, p. 208, of the large-scale destruction of oranges to sustain market prices taken from Chapter 25 of John Steinbeck's *The Grapes of Wrath*.

[45] See Waldron, "Enough and as Good" and also *Right to Private Property*, pp. 209–18 and 280–3.

[46] Hence Locke's phrasing: "*at least where* there is enough, and as good . . . for others" (2nd T: 27 – my emphasis).

[47] See Nozick, *Anarchy, State and Utopia*, p. 176 and Waldron, *Right to Private Property*, p. 214.

The sufficiency proviso, as formulated, does not tell us what to do. It doesn't tell us that appropriation in these circumstances is illegitimate. But it suggests that there is a problem, and it tells us why: the interests of others are now in danger of being prejudiced by acts of individual acquisition, and the principle of equal concern, dominating the whole picture, requires that those interests should not simply be brushed aside for the sake of the interests, such as they are, of the appropriator.

But C. B. Macpherson seems to think that this is exactly what Locke does: he brushes their interests aside. He says that the sort of economy Locke favors tends to foster inequality and propertylessness among a large section of society, and to put people more or less completely at the mercy of those who are now in possession of the majority of society's resources. Their relation to the economy and to the basis of their subsistence is now through the wage relation, and Macpherson believes that Locke's understanding of the wage relation makes it incompatible with any thesis (of the sort that I have been pursuing) that the waged laborer is the equal of the man who pays his wages. In Chapter 4, we considered Macpherson's argument that Locke attributed different levels of rationality to the members of different classes, and different political rights on the basis of this differential rationality; I criticized, and I hope refuted, the main premise of that interpretation.[48] But now we are considering Macpherson's more inferential argument for the differential rationality reading – namely, that only this reading can salvage Locke's account of property and economy from manifest inconsistency. He says we can make no sense of Locke's theory of property except by supposing that those who end up with nothing are less than rational and therefore count as less than full moral members of the community. What else, he asks, could justify their being treated (as he thinks they are treated in Locke's account) as just "a commodity out of which riches and dominion might be derived, a raw material to be worked up and disposed of by the political authority?"[49] For Locke, free and equal individuals are owners of themselves (2nd T: 27); but wage laborers lack self-ownership, for they have alienated their labor. For Locke, the resources of the earth are given for the sustenance of all, and "Men, being once born, have a right to their Preservation" (2nd T; 25); but there cannot be a capitalist economy without the sustenance of millions being precarious enough to allow the wage relation to come into existence. So the potential laborers cannot

---

[48] For my criticism of Macpherson's take on the important passage from the *Essay* concerning the intellectual resources available to the day-laborer (E: 4.20.3) see, above, pp. 86–8.

[49] Macpherson, *Political Theory of Possessive Individualism*, p. 229.

be among those to whom God dedicated His largesse. Locke says that "God gave the World to...the Use of the Industrious and rational" (2nd T: 34), and Macpherson concludes that "those who are left with no land cannot be industrious and rational in the original sense."[50] And so on. The gist of the inference boils down to this: what Locke says about economic inequality implies that he cannot really take seriously the equal humanity of those whose position is prejudiced by the inequality that he countenances.

Macpherson's inference is riddled with mistakes, and it is hard to know where to begin.[51] We may start with what he says about labor and the position of the laborer. One point which relates to Locke's saying that "God gave the World to...the Use of the Industrious and Rational" (2nd T: 34) is that he never hesitates to call the poor day-laborer industrious. Consider his listing of the various factors that go into the production of a loaf of bread:

the Plough-man's Pains, the Reaper's and Thresher's Toil, and the Baker's Sweat, is to be counted into the *Bread* we eat; the Labor of those who broke the Oxen, who digged and wrought the Iron and Stones, who felled and framed the Timber employed about the Plough, Mill, Oven, or any other Utensils, which are a vast Number, requisite to this Corn, from its being feed to be sown to its being made Bread, must all be charged on the account of Labor. (2nd T: 43)

There may be an economic sense in which the labor mentioned here is owned by those who employ the baker and the ploughman, etc.[52] But the pains, the toil and the sweat remain attributable to the laborer, and so is the attendant rationality and virtue (or at least that part of it that has to do with actual performance of and attention to the task, even if some aspect of the planning is attributed to a manager or entrepreneur). Macpherson thinks that all the rationality associated with labor must be imputed necessarily, on Locke's account, to the person who gets the benefit of the acquisitions or profits that accrue from its exercise. But there is no reason to suppose that Locke thought this. On the contrary

---

[50] Ibid., p. 234.

[51] In an effective early critique, Alan Ryan made this observation: "Although Macpherson's theory about Locke's doctrine is thus falsified in so many details, it still presents a challenge to any critic. For its overall coherence and interest is extremely impressive." See Ryan, 'Locke and the Dictatorship of the Bourgeoisie," p. 227.

[52] Compare Tully, *Discourse on Property*, pp. 135–45 and Waldron, *Right to Private Property*, pp. 228–32. See also Wood, *John Locke and Agrarian Capitalism*, pp. 85–90. (Part of this has to do with the way we read 2nd T: 85 – "[A] Free-man makes himself a Servant to another, by selling him, for a certain time, the Service he undertakes to do, in exchange for Wages he is to receive" – and how much weight we put on its particular phraseology.)

he makes it plain that labor's association with rationality is separable from labor as a process of acquisition. "[T]he Turfs my Servant has cut" (2nd T: 28) may be my property, but the cutting of them – which on Locke's account makes up the overwhelming proportion of their value – is an action attributed to the servant. It does not cease to be the servant's action or to be industrious and rational as an action by the servant simply by virtue of the fact that the servant works for hire and both the raw materials and the finished product of his labor belong to someone else.[53]

Nor is Locke anywhere near being driven to such a pass in order to rationalize the inequality and deprivation of members of the laboring class. On the contrary, he is at pains to show that they are among the beneficiaries of the sort of unequal money economy that he envisages. The day-laborer may own no property except his wages and the bread and rented housing that he buys with them; but still, compared to a person living as a free man in an undeveloped (and largely egalitarian) economy, he is better off. This is the gist of the famous passage comparing the agricultural economy of England with subsistence economies of the native Americans:

> There cannot be a clearer demonstration of any thing, than several Nations of the *Americans* are of this, who are rich in Land, and poor in all the Comforts of Life; whom Nature having furnished as liberally as any other people, with the materials of Plenty, *i.e.* a fruitful Soil, apt to produce in abundance, what might serve for food, raiment, and delight; yet for want of improving it by labor, have not one hundredth part of the Conveniencies we enjoy: and a King of a large and fruitful Territory there, feeds, lodges, and is clad worse than a day Laborer in *England*. (2nd T: 41)

Far from treating the laborer as a commodity, this passage seeks to justify the Lockean economy with reference to the laborer's own interest. Notice also that although what is being justified here is an unequal outcome – "disproportionate and unequal Possession" (2nd T: 50) of land in England as opposed to somewhat more equal common rights in America – the form of the justification uses a particularly strong version of the egalitarian principle of maximin.[54] Locke actually seeks to show that the poorest participant in the English economy is better off than the *best*-off participant in the native American economy, from which it certainly follows that the poorest participant in the English economy is better

---

[53] See also Ashcraft, *Revolutionary Politics*, pp. 269–70.
[54] See Rawls, *Theory of Justice*, pp. 152–7, for a defense of the maximin principle.

off than the worst-off participant in the native American economy. Again, it's a familiar contrast between equal outcomes, on the one hand, and an egalitarian argument, from a deeper premise of equal concern and respect, on the other. Maximin may not be palatable to all egalitarians; but it is hard to deny that it is fundamentally an egalitarian approach to justification.

The maximin argument of 2nd T: 41 is not the only way in which we see Locke taking seriously the interests of members of the laboring class in his argument about economic inequality. We see him doing something similar in his argument about money (2nd T: 45–50). There too Locke feels the need to constrain his account of "disproportionate and unequal Possession" (2nd T: 50) with an extra layer of argument to vindicate the claims of basic equality. He sees that it is not enough to show that the introduction of money makes the accumulation of more than one can use compatible with the spoilation proviso. The extra accumulation that this permits does adversely affect others' interests; others are now "straitened" by one's larger possessions (2nd T: 36). And he argues therefore that in addition to the maximin argument that I discussed in the previous paragraph, the resulting equality also needs to be ratified by consent. Now this is a remarkable move in the context of the Lockean theory of property, for early on in the chapter on property the whole tendency of his approach was to set his face *against* consent as a basis for legitimate acquisition: "If such a consent as that was necessary, Man had starved, notwithstanding the plenty God had given him" (2nd T: 28). Nevertheless, consent is demanded at this point precisely to vindicate the interests of those whom Macpherson believes Locke has an interest in marginalizing. Locke discerns their consent in the conventional basis of the assignment of value to money: "[S]ince Gold and Silver . . . has its *value* only from the consent of Men . . . it is plain, that Men have agreed to a disproportionate and unequal Possession of the earth, they having by a tacit and voluntary consent found out a way how a man may fairly possess more land than he himself can use the product of" (2nd T: 50). Now I am not saying this is a *convincing* argument. In my opinion, it is one of the worst arguments in the *Second Treatise*, for this reason: those who are likely to be most prejudiced by the inequality are those who (on account of their poverty) will be participating least in monetary conventions, and so least likely to be involved as tacit consenters in assigning conventional value to gold and silver.[55] Still, as I said a moment ago, the production of

---

[55] See Waldron, "Property, Justification and Need," pp. 198–202.

a bad argument purporting to respect equality is not the same as Locke's thinking that equality does not need to be respected at all. I believe he was quite proud of this argument – it is not presented casually or dismissively – and the impulse to base the argument at this point on *consent*, an idea that only makes sense for free and equal individuals, is already at odds with the tenor of Macpherson's interpretation.

VII

Beyond all these arguments about sufficiency, spoilation, money, and maximin, there is also a much more fundamental condition on Locke's theory of property. This is a principle of charity, a principle which requires property-owners in every economy to cede control of some of their surplus possessions, so that they can be used to satisfy the pressing needs of the very poor, when the latter have no way of surviving otherwise. In this section, I want to focus on the work that this principle does explicitly for the idea that the rich and the poor are fundamentally one another's equals in spite of their disparities of wealth. As we shall see, charity introduces further religious and indeed specifically Christian considerations into the picture in a quite striking and still largely unexplored way.

The principle of charity is not introduced in the *Second Treatise* chapter on property. It is introduced in paragraph 42 of Locke's argument against Filmer in the *First Treatise*. There Locke insists that anyone who is in desperate need has "a Title to so much out of another's Plenty, as will keep him from extreme want, where he has no means to subsist otherwise" (1st T: 42). It is not an original doctrine: there are versions of it in Aquinas and in most natural law theories.[56] But if it is taken at face value, it changes the complexion of Locke's theory of property quite significantly. As I said earlier, the theory in the *Second Treatise* appears to be aimed at a legitimation of inequality, of the "disproportionate and unequal Possession of the Earth" which a labor theory – or at least an historical entitlement version of a labor theory[57] – generates once money is introduced. But the *First Treatise* doctrine mitigates that inequality by providing in effect a right to a "safety net" for the poorest members of

---

[56] See Aquinas, *Summa Theologica*, II. q. 66; Waldron, "Enough and as Good," p. 327; Finnis, *Aquinas*, pp. 191–3. For the reception of these ideas in early modern England, see Horne, *Property Rights and Poverty*, pp. 9–72.

[57] See Nozick, *Anarchy, State and Utopia*, pp. 150–3 for the structure; but see Dunn, *Political Thought of John Locke*, p. 6, for a discussion of the (until recently) quite common socialist interpretation of Locke's labor theory.

society, if they have no other means of subsistence. The theory in the *Second Treatise* appears to be intended, like Robert Nozick's theory, as a hard-headed (hard-hearted?) defense of private property against redistribution by the state.[58] But if poor people have the rights which the *First Treatise* says they have, then in order to uphold all property entitlements a Lockean government may have to be continually interfering to redistribute surplus goods from the rich to the most needy.[59]

The immediate context of Locke's introduction of the principle is his attack on the claim made by Robert Filmer that God's donation of the world and everything in it to Adam and his male heirs entitled Adam's heirs to absolute political authority (which the Filmerites rather ingenuously thought included the later Stuarts – Charles II and his brother James, Duke of York). Now Locke, as we have seen, denied that there was any such specific donation to some humans at the expense of others (1st T: 30). But his strategy in the *First Treatise* is that of a lawyer – resisting each step in his opponent's argument, by showing successively that even if the previous step is conceded, the next step does not follow, and so on.[60] So even were he willing to concede the donation, he insists nevertheless that there is a difference between *property* and *sovereignty*: "[I]f after all, any one will needs have it so, that . . . *Adam* was made sole Proprietor of the whole Earth, what will this be to his Sovereignty? . . . [H]ow will the Possession even of the whole Earth, give any one a Sovereign Arbitrary Authority over the Persons of Men?" (1st T: 41). Property could become sovereignty only if the proprietor were able to exploit his position to coerce obedience. But Locke dismisses this out of hand: "The most specious thing to be said, is, that he that is Proprietor of the whole World, may deny all the rest of Mankind Food, and so at his pleasure starve them, if they will not acknowledge his Soveraignty and Obey his Will" (1st T: 41). We will examine Locke's reasons for calling this specious in a moment. But it is worth noting that a paragraph or two later, he argues that even if Adam *could* use his rights in this way, even this, he insists, would not show what Filmer wanted to show:

[58] Cf. Nozick, *Anarchy, State and Utopia*, p. 238: "The major objection to speaking of everyone's having a right to various things such as . . . life, and so on, and enforcing this right, is that these 'rights' require a substructure of things and materials and actions; and other people may have rights and entitlements over these . . . There are particular rights over particular things held by particular persons . . . No rights exist in conflict with this substructure of particular rights. Since no neatly contoured right to achieve a goal will avoid incompatibility with this substructure, no such rights exist. The particular rights over things fill the space of rights, leaving no room for general rights to be in a certain material condition."

[59] See Waldron, *Right to Private Property*, pp. 282–3.

[60] See especially 2nd T: 1 for a summary of his use of this strategy in the *First Treatise*.

Should anyone make so perverse a use of God's Blessings poured on him with a liberal Hand; should anyone be Cruel and Uncharitable to that extremity, yet all this would not prove that Propriety in Land, even in this Case, gave any Authority over the Persons of Men, but only that Compact might; since the Authority of the Rich Proprietor, and the Subjection of the Needy Beggar began not from the Possession of the Lord, but the Consent of the poor Man, who preferr'd being his Subject to starving.

In other words, this argument of Filmer's fails to dislodge political authority from its basis in the consent of the governed. It simply rests on a Hobbesian view of consent;[61] and it leaves as free as before the man who refuses (even suicidally) to be humbled by his needs in this way.

In fact, Locke is insistent that property rights cannot be exploited in the way we have been discussing. What are his reasons? Why does he think it is "specious" to say that the owner of the world may let others starve if they will not acknowledge his authority? He offers two connected arguments. The first is a rather weak utilitarian argument. Locke suggests that the inclusion of this power in the right of property would tend in practice to lead to economic stagnation rather than "to promote the great Design of God, *Increase* and *Multiply*" (1st T: 41). A man with this sort of dominion, Locke implies, is likely to exploit it inefficiently with all men as his slaves, rather than promoting a liberal economy: "He that doubts this, let him look into the Absolute Monarchies of the World, and see what becomes of the Conveniences of Life and the Multitudes of People" (1st T: 41). The second argument, by contrast, is based on elementary natural right. Instead of saying that absolute rights of property are economically and demographically counter-productive, Locke now invokes the doctrine of charity directly:

God the Lord and Father of all, has given no one of his Children such a Property, in his peculiar Portion of the things of this World, but that he has given his needy Brother a Right to the Surplusage of his Goods; so that it cannot justly be denied him, when his pressing Wants call for it. As *Justice* gives every Man a Title to the product of his honest Industry, and the fair Acquisitions of his Ancestors descended to him; so *Charity* gives every Man a Title to so much out of another's Plenty, as will keep him from extream want, where he has no means to subsist otherwise. (1st T: 42)

This is something, Locke says, that "we know." How we know it, we are not told. In a footnote to his edition Laslett suggests Locke has biblical authorization in mind here – Luke 11.41: "But rather give ye alms of such

---

[61] Hobbes, *Leviathan*, pp. 97–8 (Ch. 14) and 141–2 (Ch. 20).

things as ye have; and behold, all things are clear unto you."[62] There
is, however, no textual basis for this attribution; and we must remember
that in the *First Treatise* Locke is in a mood to actually cite chapter and
verse whenever he feels the need to do so.

The language of this passage is extremely interesting. In modern liberal
theory, charity is usually seen as a duty,[63] but not a matter of right: to
give of one's wealth to the poor is something one ought to do, but not
something one owes to any assignable individual. It is often presented as
a paradigm of a moral duty that ought not to be enforced.[64] Poor people
should be grateful for charity, but they may not demand it or claim it
or justify it as rightfully theirs. Some of what Locke says is suggestive
of this tradition. He says that God requires us to attend to the wants of
others and that it would be *a sin* to let a poor man perish for want of
necessities. (In a moment or two I want to say something about this in
relation to Locke's views about law and the specifically Christian virtues.)
He distinguishes the demands of charity from those of justice, drawing
at least at a verbal level the distinction that libertarians have made so
much of. But it is clear that subscription to that position will not get
him what he wants in this argument. For his argument against Filmer to
succeed, he needs to be able to show not only that it is wrong to withhold
charitable assistance but that the rich man has no right to do so, no right
even to offer it subject to conditions like political submission. For the
most part, then, his language is emphatically stronger than the liberal
tradition on this subject. Though charity is contrasted with justice, still
charity "cannot justly be denied." If it cannot justly be denied, then
anyone who denies it cannot claim to be exercising his property rights.
The sin of uncharitableness simply vitiates the exercise of the rights in
question. A man in need has "a Right" to another's surplus goods: indeed
Locke twice talks of his having "a Title," in a way that suggests that this
too is to be regarded as a property entitlement.

It is also noteworthy that Locke goes out of his way to present this as
a quite general doctrine. To answer the Filmer position, he needed to
establish no more than that *Adam* could not exercise the property rights
given specifically to him by God in this way. But Locke generalizes and
says it is *always* wrong for the rich to withhold goods from the poor, and

---

[62] Locke, *Two Treatises*, p. 170 n.

[63] An imperfect duty at that: for a discussion of imperfect duties, see Buchanan, "Justice and
Charity," pp. 569 ff.

[64] For a discussion, see Waldron, "Welfare and the Images of Charity," pp. 226–30, and "On the
Road," pp. 1062–88.

that "*Charity* gives every man a title" to the surplus goods of another when he is desperately in need of them (1st T: 42). The doctrine of rights generated by need, then, is set out as explicitly and as generally as could be.

The fact that charity is regarded as a specifically Christian virtue is for Locke no reason for thinking that it is unenforceable, or anything less than a duty. In the *Reasonableness of Christianity*, Locke argues that one of the things that Jesus Christ clarified was the imperative nature of his commandments (and responding to the needs of others was certainly one of those). Philosophers, he said, might be able to show that a virtue like charity is *a rather good idea*; but only the commandments of Christ the lawgiver can present it as directly obligatory (RC: 141–6). Admittedly, not all commandments by Jesus can or should be enforced by the state. His most fundamental commandment is to believe in him as the Messiah.[65] But the central argument of the *Letter Concerning Toleration* is that such belief cannot be enforced. But there we have a specific reason (or pair of reasons) for non-enforcement: (1) belief is not subject to the will, and coercion works only through the will;[66] and (2) what I believe (e.g. about Jesus being the Messiah) does not affect the well-being of anyone else.[67] Neither of these applies to charity, and it is noteworthy that when Locke talks in *The Reasonableness of Christianity* about the difference between what Christ requires us to *believe* (where uncoerced sincerity is of the essence) and what he requires us simply to *do*, it is charity he mentions. He cites the charitable requirements of the sheep and goats story in Matthew 25:31–46 – feed the hungry, give water to the thirsty, shelter the homeless, and visit those who are in prison – as his prime examples of what we are commanded to do as opposed to what we are expected to believe (RC: 127). However, there are passages in the *Letters Concerning Toleration*, and in the *Reasonableness of Christianity*, which hint at the possibility that charity may be a virtue that state power *could* be used to uphold but shouldn't. Thus for example, Locke presents Jesus' commandment to the rich young man "sell all you have and give to the poor" (Matthew 19:21) as a test only. It is Christ's test to see whether the young man

---

[65] Locke spends most of *The Reasonableness of Christianity* arguing that nothing else is necessary for salvation (RC: 17–112).

[66] LCT: 18: "[T]he care of souls cannot belong to the civil magistrate, because his power consists only in outward force; but true and saving religion consists in the inward persuasion of the mind, without which nothing can be acceptable to God. And such is the nature of the understanding, that it cannot be compelled to the belief of anything by outward force." (See also Waldron, "Locke, Toleration and the Rationality of Persecution.")

[67] LCT: 46: "[O]ne man does not violate the right of another by his erroneous opinions."

in question really would be willing to follow his commandments, not a genuine imperative addressed to all of us:[68]

[O]ur Saviour, to try whether in earnest [the young man] believed him to be the Messiah, and resolved to take him to be his king, and to obey him as such; bids him give all that he has to the poor, and come and follow him; and he should have treasure in heaven. This I look on to be the meaning of the place; this, of selling all he had, and giving it to the poor, not being a standing law of his kingdom; but a probationary command to this young man; to try whether he truly believed him to be the Messiah, and was ready to obey his commands, and relinquish all to follow him, when he, his prince, required it. (RC: 120)

Selling all you have and giving it to the poor would be a form of what I want to call *radical* charity – giving away what you actually have a moral right to keep, giving away enough to impoverish yourself. This is not what Locke is arguing for; it goes way beyond the charity which he argues for in the *First Treatise* – the charity that he thinks should be enforced. Radical charity may be a particular requirement imposed on particular people, but it is not intended as a general command.

Certainly, too, there is a strand of argument in the later *Letters Concerning Toleration* from the 1690s which insists, against Locke's opponent Jonas Proast, that the mere fact that something morally good *could* be enforced is not itself a reason for saying that it *ought* to be enforced by the state. Locke uses the example of lying: "[I]f it be his duty to punish all offences against God; why does the magistrate never punish lying, which is an offence against God, and is an offence capable of being judicially proved?"[69] The answer Locke gives to his own question is that a state enforcement of lying is not necessary for any of its recognized functions. That may not be an entirely satisfactory answer, but it is sufficient to establish a contrast with the principle of charity. For Locke is convinced that charity – in the 1st T: 42 sense – *is* necessary, for the proper limitation of property, and for the prevention of economic inequality turning into political inequality. So it is the proper business of the commonwealth.

The doctrine we have been discussing – the doctrine of charity – is not mentioned explicitly in the *Second Treatise*. We know that the *Two Treatises* were written at different times and for somewhat different purposes.[70] Is there any reason to believe that the author of the chapter on property

---

[68] It seems the young man failed the test: "[W]hen the young man heard that saying, he went away sorrowful: for he had great possessions" (Matthew 19:22). (Note that Locke cites the version of the story told in Luke 18:18–30.)

[69] Locke, *Third Letter*, p. 295.

[70] For a cross-reference from the discussion of property in the *First Treatise* to the theory of property in the *Second*, see 1st T: 87.

intended the theory he set out there to be qualified by the doctrine we have been discussing? The strongest evidence for the independence of the two *Treatises* in this regard is Locke's silence on the matter in the chapter on property. There are several places where one would expect him to mention such a proviso (if he believed in it); and he doesn't, or at least not in so many words. When he is defending unequal possessions, he mentions that people in the first ages of the world had enough in the way of land and natural resources for their own acquisitions. And a little later, he writes

This I dare boldly affirm, That the same *Rule of Propriety*, (viz.) that every Man should have as much as he could make use of, would hold still in the World, without straitning any body, since there is Land enough in the World to suffice double the Inhabitants had not the *Invention of Money* . . . introduced (by Consent) larger Possessions, and a Right to them. (2nd T: 36)

The clear implication is that some people *are* "straitned" by the inequality that money introduced. If so, it seems odd not to mention the natural law doctrine of charity by which such straitening might be mitigated. Sure, this does not actually contradict the charity doctrine; but the passage is remarkable for the omission of the doctrine, if we assume it was one that Locke had in mind when he wrote it.

I used to think there was a more substantial difficulty in accommodating the charity doctrine.[71] The basis on which Locke argues for individual acquisition is the idea of mixing one's labor with resources or land – "joyn[ing] to it something that is his own, and thereby making it his *Property*" (2nd T: 27). On a literal interpretation of this argument, the laborer transfers to the object the inviolable right he has in his own person. If this is so, it is hard to see how that right can be overridden by the mere fact of another's need. Either the object contains the owner's labor or it does not: the other's need cannot as it were drive the labor, and the entitlement, out. The objection poses a substantial difficulty for the doctrine of charity; but it is worth noting that it also would pose a difficulty for the other restriction on property rights that Locke *does* mention explicitly in the *Second Treatise* – namely, the spoilation proviso.[72] This equally implies the defeasibility of the title conferred by labor on natural law grounds that have a lot to do with respect for the equal interests of others. I used to think that what was going on here was that Locke

---

[71] I am grateful to G. A. Cohen for helpful discussion of this question. See also Cohen, *Self-Ownership, Freedom, and Equality*, pp. 189–90.

[72] 2nd T: 31 and 37–8.

was running two different lines of argument to justify private property in the *Second Treatise*: one which was entitlement-based, deriving from the exclusive right one has in one's person and one's labor (2nd T: 27), and the other based broadly on the notion of human need and what must happen in order for mankind to prosper. The provisions and limitations imposed in the name of equality make sense primarily in relation to the second of these arguments; and the same is true of the principle of charity. But I am no longer convinced that it makes sense to see the mixing of labor as a separate line of argument, less hospitable to modification by charity or the other provisos. For as we saw in section III, the labor theory works only against the background of labor's significance in God's plan for the survival of the human beings He has created. If labor were not presented against that background, if it were just something I happen to own, there would be no answer to Nozick's embarrassing question, "Why isn't mixing what I own with what I don't own a way of losing what I own rather than a way of gaining what I don't?"[73] Any account of the significance of labor rich enough to answer this question will hook up easily with the account based on need, and will be naturally subject to the principle of charity.

Bearing all that in mind, I think we can say that the substantive case for importing the *First Treatise* doctrine of charity into the *Second Treatise* theory of property revolves around the premises of Lockean natural law. Locke was emphatic about the basic principle of the law of nature being the preservation of as many people as possible: "Everyone as he is *bound to preserve himself* . . . so by the like reason when his own Preservation comes not in competition, ought he, as much as he can, *to preserve the rest of Mankind*" (2nd T: 6). What are the implications of this fundamental requirement? It sounds like an active and positive duty to do whatever will promote the preservation of as many people as possible. True, in some passages it is discussed as though Locke has in mind only negative duties of non-aggression. For example, the passage just quoted continues: "and may not unless it be to do Justice on an Offender, take away, or impair the life, or what tends to the Preservation of the Life, the Liberty, Health, or Good of another" (2nd T: 6). But elsewhere in the *Second Treatise*, Locke makes it clear that the duty goes far beyond this. It includes the power to pardon offenders and to save them from their deserved punishment – "for *the end of Government* being the *preservation of all*, as much as may be, even the guilty are to be spared, where it can prove no prejudice to

---

[73] Nozick, *Anarchy, State and Utopia*, p. 175.

the innocent" (2nd T: 159). And it may even include a duty to infringe property rights in an emergency, like "pull[ing] down an innocent Man's House to stop the Fire, when the next to it is burning (2nd T: 159). Anyway, it has never been clear to me that the duty of charity – at least as Locke presents it – *is* a purely positive as opposed to a negative duty. I think it is extremely significant that Locke's language in paragraph 42 of the *First Treatise* involves a denial that property-owners have the right to *withhold* their surplus goods from the poor. In other words, he seems to be committed not to a view about *giving* but to the view that neither the rich nor civil society on their behalf is entitled to *resist* the poor when the poor attempt to seize their surplus goods for themselves. It is not a question of forcing the rich to do anything: it is enough that they be compelled simply to stand back and let the poor take what (on account of their "pressing Needs") is rightfully theirs.[74] The needy have a right to surplus goods, and the rich have no right to withhold them. Though Locke does not talk at this stage of the role of the state in these matters, it is clear that what he has in mind are not so much affirmative charitable obligations (which, once introduced into the picture, might have to be enforced) but unjust and uncharitable withholding and denying (which may have to be prevented by the state).[75]

More specifically, at the beginning of the chapter on property, we are told in very general terms that "[m]en, being once born, have a right to their Preservation, and consequently to Meat and Drink, and such other things, as Nature affords for their subsistence" (2nd T: 25). Now, that might be construed as mere meaningless rhetoric, except that Locke quickly puts it in play to do some rather important work. For when he defends the legitimacy of unilateral appropriation, he raises the specter of starvation as a basis for his rebuttal of any consent requirement: "[W]ill any one say [that a man] had no right to those Acorns or

[74] See generally Waldron, "Welfare and the Images of Charity."

[75] Though it implies all this, it is worth noting what Locke's doctrine of charity does *not* imply. James Tully uses the passage as a basis for attributing to Locke the view that "property is not only conditional on the owner's performance of a social function, but is held specifically for the sake of the performance of a social function: to preserve mankind" (Tully, *Discourse on Property*, p. 99). This is a suspect interpretation. Locke is insisting that goods surplus to an owner's needs be made available to the pressing needs of others. He is not setting up any theory of social function to govern property in goods in general. If there is no surplus or no desperate need there is no requirement in this passage or anywhere else in Locke that individual property should serve a social function. Indeed in other passages he contradicts Tully's interpretation directly, saying in 1st T: 92, for example, that "Property is for the Benefit and sole Advantage of the Proprietor." In the enthusiasm of discovering that Locke held something less than a Nozickian theory of absolute entitlement, we must beware of interpreting him out of all recognition as some sort of social democrat. (See also Waldron, *Right to Private Property*, pp. 157–8.)

Apples he thus appropriated, because he had not the consent of all Mankind to make them his? . . . If such a consent as that was necessary, Man had starved, notwithstanding the Plenty God had given him" (2nd T: 28). The prospect of starvation and the straightforward need to take care of it simply short-circuit any complaint based on the illegitimacy of appropriation without consent. Since the rights which are rebutted in this way are real rights – each person's right to partake in God's original donation – Locke is saying, in effect, that the right to consent or withhold consent can be trumped by desperate need. And he cannot consistently maintain that without also maintaining what I have called the doctrine of charity.

One last hurdle. Those who want to portray an uncharitable Locke are fond of telling us about the John Locke who was the author of an essay on the Poor Law – a draft of a representation concerning methods of employing the poor. That is not early Locke; it is dated 1697, from the period of our interest. And it certainly seems to be devoid of the sort of compassion that one would associate with a generous spirit of charity. Locke talks about "begging drones" and "superfluous brandy shops,"[76] and he suggests that the idle poor should be whipped and mutilated if they go begging, instead of doing the work assigned to them.[77] Even little children should be given two or three hours of labor useful to the parish per day.[78]

There are four things I want to say about this. First, as a matter of personality, we should observe that Locke actually had a reputation for being charitable (though those who mention it also mention its limits):

He was very charitable to the Poor, except such Persons as were Idle or Prophane, and spent the Sunday in the Alehouses, and went not to Church. But above all he did compassionate those, who after they had labour'd as long as their Strength wou'd hold, were reduced to Poverty. he said it was not enough to keep them from starving, but that such a Provision ought to be made for them, that they might live comfortably.[79]

Secondly, moving now to Locke's political position, we must bear firmly in mind that the paper on the Poor Law *does* assume that the poor have a right to subsistence. Locke insists that "everyone must have meat, drink, clothing, and firing."[80] And he says that "if any person die for want of due relief in any parish in which he ought to be relieved, the said parish [must]

---

[76] Locke, "An Essay on the Poor Law," p. 184.   [77] Ibid., pp. 186–7.   [78] Ibid., p. 190–2.
[79] Masham, "The Life and Character of Mr Locke," p. 350. The bequests in his will bear this out:
      see Locke, "Last Will and Testament," pp. 355–6.
[80] "Essay on the Poor Law," p. 189.

be fined according to the circumstances of the fact and the heinousness of the crime."[81] Thirdly, we have already seen that Locke is in favor of charity being enforced, but not *radical* charity.[82] Well, now we may think of a *second* form of radical charity that Locke is not prepared to enforce. This would be charity to someone who refuses to work when he *could* work, charity to someone who does not make any efforts to provide for himself or work to subsidize the cost of his provision. And Locke is no more in favor of enforcing this than he is of enforcing the other sense of radical charity – "sell all thou hast and give to the poor."

A final point returns us to the issue of labor. Locke really took seriously the injunction to labor – and a poor man with an offer of gainful employment was not a person who had no means to subsist (within the meaning of 1st T: 42). His view that the "true and proper relief of the poor . . . consists in finding work for them"[83] is not contrary to the egalitarian premise of the doctrine of charity. Quite the reverse: it is what that premise amounts to against the background of what he regards as God's manifest purpose for man, and what reason reveals as the benefit to all of labor.

---

[81] Ibid., p. 198.   [82] See above, p. 182.   [83] "Essay on the Poor Law," p. 189.

7

"By Our Saviour's Interpretation"

Anyone who reads the *Two Treatises of Government*, alert to their religious and theological character, will find it quite striking how much is made of Old Testament sources and how little of any teaching or doctrine from the Christian Gospels and Epistles. I mentioned at the very beginning of this book John Dunn's claim that Locke's whole frame of discussion in the *Two Treatises* is "saturated with Christian assumptions – and those of a Christianity in which the New Testament counted very much more than the Old."[1] Well, if Dunn is right, the saturation is so complete as to be virtually invisible. Jesus and St. Paul may be there in the background of Locke's theory of equality. Maybe. But they are *well* in the background, and their specific teachings are not appealed to at all, not even to resolve any of the conundrums which, in Chapter 3, we found associated with what Dunn calls "the normative creaturely equality of all men in virtue of their shared species-membership."[2]

By contrast, the Old Testament is all over the *Two Treatises*, the *First Treatise* especially. Actually, it may be a mistake to phrase this as a simple contrast between *Old* and New Testaments. In the Old Testament or Hebrew Scriptures – what Locke calls "the sacred ancient writings of the Jewish nation allowed by the Christians to be of divine original" (P&N: ii.483) – there is a considerable amount of legal, social, and political material (in the Mosaic law) that can safely be disregarded by non-Jews, as it was intended for the governance of the nation of Israel alone: "For no positive law whatsoever can oblige any people but those to whom it is given. 'Hear, O Israel,' sufficiently restrains the obligations of the law of Moses only to that people" (LCT: 42). This, however, does not apply to the natural law material in Genesis and to a lesser extent the

---

[1] Dunn, *Political Thought of John Locke*, p. 99. He writes: "Jesus Christ (and Saint Paul) may not appear in person in the text of the *Two Treatises* but their presence can hardly be missed when we come upon the normative creaturely equality of all men in virtue of their shared species-membership."
[2] Ibid.

Psalms – that's of general application. And it's mainly that which I have in mind when I talk about the imbalance of Old Testament over New Testament material – the teachings of general application in the Hebrew scriptures and the Christian scriptures respectively.[3]

I

The imbalance is most apparent of course in the *First Treatise*, where Locke is tracing "*Sir* Robert [Filmer] . . . *through all the Windings and Obscurities which are to be met with in the several Branches of his wonderful System*," and taking "*pains to shew his mistakes, Inconsistencies, and want of (what he so much boasts of, and pretends wholly to build on) Scripture-proofs.*"[4] In fact the balance between Old and New Testament-based arguments is somewhat more even in Filmer's *Patriarcha* than it is in Locke's *First Treatise*,[5] as is the balance between biblical citation and theoretical argument more generally. Indeed, anyone who took their view of Filmer's work from Locke's *First Treatise* would get quite a wrong impression. In the blue Cambridge edition of Filmer's writings, the argument from Genesis is found on just six of the sixty-eight pages that *Patriarcha* comprises, and the history of Israel apart from Genesis is cited on only two or three pages beyond that. Filmer mentions Aristotle more than Adam, and Bellarmine, Bodin, and Suarez are discussed in much greater detail than Noah or Abraham. A lot of the time, Filmer is simply doing political philosophy in his own voice, to refute the propositions of Grotius, Milton, and Hobbes. Perhaps we can read the *Two Treatises* as a whole as responding to the different kinds of argument in Filmer's writing. The *Second Treatise* may be read as a reply to Filmer's theoretical arguments (and to the use that was being made of them around the Exclusion Crisis), while the *First Treatise* disposes of Filmer's biblical arguments. Even so, it is intriguing that Locke chose to devote 120 pages of biblical refutation to Filmer's six pages of biblical argument;[6] and even that estimate of Locke's 120 pages takes no account

---

[3] Locke thinks there's also a distinction to be drawn within the New Testament: he insists that the Epistles are of secondary importance since "[t]hey were to those who were in the faith and true christians already: and so could not be designed to teach them the fundamental articles and points necessary to salvation" (RC: 152). As a result Locke was accused of contempt for the Epistles: for his rebuttal of this charge see Locke, *Second Vindication*, 249–50.

[4] Locke, *Two Treatises*, Preface.

[5] Here are some examples of Filmer's use of New Testament material. He cites St. Paul concerning submission to the powers that be (and the similar injunctions in the Epistle general of St. Peter) and he also cites the equivalent Gospel passage about rendering to Caesar the things that are Caesar's (Matthew 22: 21). See Filmer, *Patriarcha*, pp. 4, 38, 39, 40, and 43.

[6] Indeed the only sustained passage of the *First Treatise* that is not scriptural in focus is the core passage on inheritance in Chapter IX, about ten pages at most.

of the amount of Old Testament argument that figured in the pages that were lost, "and were more than all the rest," i.e. more than the *Second Treatise* and *First Treatise* put together.[7]

To be sure, these crude quantitative measures tell us little about the substance or character of Locke's scriptural argument. He says again and again that he is having to take time and space out of all proportion to Filmer's provocation simply to expose the fallacies of Filmer's exegesis. Paragraph 20 of the *First Treatise* is typical. Concerning a passage from Filmer on Adam's title to sovereignty by creation, Locke writes:

> I fear I have tired my Reader's Patience, by dwelling longer on this Passage than the weightiness of any Argument in it, seems to require: but I have unavoidably been engaged in it by our A____'s [Filmer's] way of writing, who hudling several Suppositions together, and that in doubtful and general terms makes such a medley and confusion, that it is impossible to shew his Mistakes, without examining the several Senses, wherein his Words may be taken, and without seeing how, in any of these various Meanings, they will consist together and have any Truth in them. (1st T: 20)

The point, says Locke, is to show the difference between genuine argument and the mere accumulation of biblical verses. For though Filmer's assertion, that Adam was king of the world from the time of his creation, is patently false, yet, says Locke, Filmer presents it

> as an evident Conclusion drawn from preceding words, though in truth it be but a bare assertion joyn'd to other assertions of the same kind, which confidently put together in words of undetermined and dubious meaning, look like a sort of arguing, when there is indeed neither Proof nor Connection: A way very familiar with our A____, of which having given the Reader a taste here, I shall, as much as the Argument will permit me, avoid touching on hereafter, and should not have done it here, were it not to let the World see, how Incoherencies in Matter, and Suppositions without Proofs put handsomely together in good Words and a plausible Style, are apt to pass for strong Reason and good Sense, till they come to be look'd into with Attention. (1st T: 20)

It is noticeable that Peter Laslett's Cambridge edition is quite silent on this passage – no footnotes, no historical references, no bibliographical apparatus. I think Locke's insistence here that he is having to take time in this passage to show the difference between rigorous and fake argument is really quite an embarrassment to those historians who try to bully us into reading the *Two Treatises* as purely political pamphlets, having nothing to do with philosophical rigor. Philosophical rigor in the

---

[7] Locke, *Two Treatises*, Preface, p. 137.

context of "*Scripture-proofs*" – or in Filmer's case, the lack of it – is exactly what the *First Treatise* is about. The scriptural character of Locke's writing might suggest that he is doing something different from philosophical argumentation. In fact Locke is trying to give the world a lesson in the difference between *arguing* from scriptural revelation and simply assembling various verses and catch-phrases in an opportunistic political tract. Much of Locke's philosophical argument in the *First Treatise* is hermeneutical in character: he is wrestling philosophically with the problem of interpreting biblical texts. The fact that it is *about* scripture doesn't make it any the less philosophical, any more opportunistic or occasional. Indeed, Locke's observations on interpretation are, I think, of enormous interest to us – for whom hermeneutics, the problem of interpretation, looms almost as large in theology, in jurisprudence, and in philosophy generally as it did in Locke's day.[8] I don't know whether these lessons were of much interest to Locke's patron, Anthony Ashley Cooper, and his political cronies. They might perhaps have been satisfied with "counter-arguments" as philosophically disreputable as Filmer's, if they would do the political trick. But it evidently mattered to the historical author John Locke. His claims about good and bad reasoning in the *First Treatise* show very little sign of any concession to political exigency.

I emphasize these points about the difference between political philosophy (even scripturally based political philosophy) on the one hand, and the publication of a mere political pamphlet on the other, because again and again in the *First Treatise* Locke rails against the tricks and sloppiness that are exactly what one would expect as the characteristics of a political tract. For the purposes of his "scripture-proofs," says Locke, Sir Robert Filmer just seizes on words, without any consideration of their context or their logical role in argument. "Let the words *Rule* and *Subject* be but found in the Text or Margent, and it immediately signifies the Duty of a Subject to his Prince, the Relation is changed, and though God says *Husband*, Sir Robert will have it *King*" (1st T: 49). And people do this all the time, Locke says, even when they are reading him or other contemporary authors. (He is constantly testy about such insensitive readings of his own works by his own critics.)[9] But it is a particular sin in the context of revelation:

---

[8] I particularly recommend the disquisition on interpretation in the Preface to Locke's *Paraphrase and Notes on the Epistles of St. Paul* (P&N: i.103–16). Some of this material is also prefigured in *The Reasonableness of Christianity* (RC: 152).

[9] See, for example, Locke's comments on Thomas Burnet's "Third Remarks" in Burnet, *Remarks on John Locke*, pp. 57, 61 and 66. He attempted to head off such criticism in his Preface to the *Two Treatises*, p. 138: "*Cavilling here and there, at some Expression, or little incident of my Discourse, is not an answer to my Book.*"

God, I believe, speaks differently from Men, because he speaks with more Truth, more Certainty: but when he vouchsafes to speak to Men, I do not think, he speaks differently from them, in crossing the Rules of language in use amongst them. This would not be to condescend to their Capacities, when he humbles himself to speak to them, but to lose his design in speaking, what thus spoken, they could not understand. (1st T: 46)[10]

If an understanding of revelation required us to assume that the words meant something other than what they ordinarily mean, then we might as well not have the revelation at all, for we would then be at the mercy of interpreters whose own credentials may be much more of an issue than anything they might try to convince us of on the basis of the gloss they impose on scripture.

Nowhere, by the way, is this point about directness more important than in Locke's view of the specifically Christian revelation. It is connected to the points about ordinary intelligence and "the democratic intellect" that I made towards the end of Chapter 4. The whole purpose of Christ's teachings was to clarify the moral law – in Locke's words, "clearing it from the corrupt glosses of the scribes and pharisees" (RC: 122), and "giving plain and direct rules of morality and obedience" (RC: 146). To this end, Jesus chose as his apostles and messengers not a company of learned doctors and scholars – "abler men of higher birth or thoughts," or "men of letters, more studied in their rabbins" (RC: 83) – but (as Locke puts it) "a college made up, for the most part, of ignorant, but inspired fishermen" (RC: 140), "poor, ignorant, illiterate men" (RC: 83), who could be relied upon simply to report what they were told. This is consistent with Locke's general suspicion of learned commentary – "What have the greatest part of the comments and disputes upon the laws of God and man served for, but to make the meaning more doubtful, and perplex the sense?" (E: 3.10.12) – including the cautions he registered for himself in the Preface to the *Paraphrase*, a caution against reading the Bible through philosophical eyes.[11] If anything, Locke suggests, we are

---

[10] At the beginning of *The Reasonableness of Christianity*, Locke describes the New Testament as "a collection of writings, designed by God, for the instruction of the illiterate bulk of mankind, in the way to salvation; and therefore generally to be understood in the plain and direct meaning of the words and phrases: such as they may be supposed to have had in the mouths of the speakers, who used them according to the language of that time and country wherein they lived; without such learned, artificial, and forced senses of them, as are sought out, and put upon them, in most of the systems of divinity, according to the notions that each one has been bred up in" (RC: 5).

[11] "'Tis plain that the teaching of Men Philosophy, was no part of the Design of Divine Revelation; but that the Expressions of Scripture are commonly suited in those Matters to Vulgar Apprehensions and Conceptions of the Place and People where they were delivered" (P&N: i.114).

to read our philosophy in the light of the direct words of scripture, rather than the other way round.[12]

What I want to emphasize, then, is Locke's insistence on the integrity of textual argument, an integrity which rises above political and historical occasion. Think back to our discussion of Locke's views on women in Chapter 2. Filmer cites the Fifth Commandment "Honor thy Father," as a basis for patriarchal authority. But Locke complains that the words "*and Mother*, as Apocriphal Words, are always left out" (1st T: 60). And he cites chapter and verse to refute Filmer on this. "Had our A. set down this Command without garbling, as God gave it, and joyned Mother to father, every Reader would have seen that . . . it was so far from establishing the Monarchical Power of the Father, that it set up the Mother equal with him" (1st T: 61). This is actually one of the rare occasions in the *First Treatise* when Locke also cites the New Testament, in references to Ephesians 6:1 and Matthew 15:4.[13] And the correction of Filmer on this particular point goes on and on.[14] The point is to criticize the poor intellectual standards that Filmer displays in his exegesis: Filmer seems to have thought, says Locke, that the goodness of the royalist political cause was sufficient to justify "warp[ing] the Sacred Rule of God, to make it comply with his present occasion" (1st T: 60); and Locke wants to resist that. Once again I am unable to resist a kick at the Cambridge school: historians of ideas do their students no favors at all by ignoring the significance of these passages, and by teaching them to read the *Two Treatises* as though Locke himself were uninterested in the difference

[12] However, Harris, "The Politics of Christianity" suggests that Lockean political theory might also provide a basis for the intelligent theology. In the seventeenth century, the usual line on original sin was that Adam's fall rendered his descendants liable to punishment, either by analogy with corruption of the blood in cases of treason, or on the basis of some theory of representation. Harris says that Locke's political theory made both analogies impossible. Locke insisted on each person's individual responsibility for their own salvation: "every one's sin is charged upon himself only" (RC: 7), "none are truly punished, but for their own deeds" (RC: 8). He said the sins of the father were not to be visited on their children (2nd T: 182), which – as we shall see – led him to condemn certain justifications of slavery. And he was quite scathing about theories of representation which "would have all Adam's posterity doomed to eternal, infinite punishment, for the transgression of Adam, whom millions had never heard of, and no one had authorized to transact for him, or be his representative" (RC: 4). Representation in Locke is always based on consent; hence his insistence in 2nd T: 151 that the king represents the whole society only in the sense that they agree to have him as executive of what is ultimately *their* will, declared in the laws *they* have enacted.

[13] The verse from Matthew, 15:4, to which Locke refers, but which he does not quote, is: "For God commanded, saying, Honour thy father and mother: and, He that curseth father or mother, let him die the death." That passage is quoted again in 1st T: 66. The verse from Ephesians 6:1 is: "Children, obey your parents in the Lord . . ."

[14] See 1st T: 60, 61, 62, 64, 65, 66, and 67; 2nd T: 52, 65, 66, and 69.

between a good argument and a merely partisan one, as though he too were merely trying to make political argument comply with the exigencies of the present occasion.

II

Let us return now to this question of the balance between Old Testament and New Testament passages in Locke's political writings. There is, as I have said, precious little mention in the *Two Treatises* of anything from the teachings of Jesus Christ. Even in the more argumentative and less biblical *Second Treatise* the balance is between about twenty-five citations from the Hebrew scriptures and just two from the New Testament. Those two consist of a rather vacuous observation from 1 Timothy in support of the spoilation proviso (in 2nd T: 31), and again some New Testament material (in 2nd T: 52) on honoring your mother as well as your father. How are we to explain this paucity?

One promising clue is Locke's well-attested opinion that the coming of Jesus Christ made no difference to the content of natural law,[15] and that indeed Christ "prescribed unto His followers no new and peculiar form of government" (LCT: 43).

[T]here is absolutely no such thing under the Gospel as a Christian commonwealth . . . There are, indeed, many cities and kingdoms that have embraced the faith of Christ, but they have retained their ancient form of government, with which the law of Christ hath not at all meddled. He, indeed, hath taught men how, by faith and good works, they may obtain eternal life; but He instituted no commonwealth. He prescribed unto His followers no new and peculiar form of government, nor put He the sword into any magistrate's hand, with commission to make use of it in forcing men to forsake their former religion and receive His. (LCT: 43)

This is reinforced too in *The Reasonableness of Christianity*, where one of the major themes is the non-political nature of Christ's mission and the great care taken by Jesus to avoid until the very end of his ministry any preaching or self-proclamation that could be construed as subversive of

---

[15] "[T]hat eternal law of right, which is holy, just, and good; of which no one precept or rule is abrogated or repealed; nor indeed can be, whilst God is a holy, just, and righteous God, and man a rational creature. The duties of that law, arising from the constitution of his very nature, are of eternal obligation; nor can it be taken away or dispensed with, without changing the nature of things, overturning the measures of right and wrong, and thereby introducing and authorizing irregularity, confusion, and disorder into the world. Christ's coming into the world was not for such an end as that; but, on the contrary, to reform the corrupt state of degenerate man." (RC: 112)

Roman or Jewish secular authority.[16] In fact, this silence of the Gospels on matters political is an insistent theme in Locke's political theory from start to finish. In an early work, the *First Tract on Government*, written around 1660, Locke wrote:

The Scripture speaks very little of polities anywhere (except only the government of the Jews constituted by God himself over which he had a particular care) and God doth nowhere by distinct and particular prescriptions set down rules of governments and bounds to the magistrate's authority, since one form of government was not like to fit all people, and mankind was by the light of nature and their own conveniences sufficiently instructed in the necessity of laws.[17]

The magistrate, Locke said, needed no "commission from Scripture," any more "than a Master is to examine by Scripture what power he hath over his servant."[18]

Now, in response to this, someone versed in the New Testament might say: "Well, whether or not the magistrate *needs* a commission from God, he surely gets one in the Epistles." Consider this well-known passage from St. Paul's Epistle to the Romans:

Let every soul be subject unto the higher powers. For . . . the powers that be are ordained of God. Whosoever therefore resisteth the power, resisteth the ordinance of God: and they that resist shall receive to themselves damnation. For [the ruler is] not a terror to good works, but to the evil . . . [H]e is the minister of God to thee for good. But if thou do that which is evil, be afraid; for he beareth not the sword in vain: for he is the minister of God, a revenger to execute wrath upon him that doeth evil. Wherefore ye must needs be subject, not only for wrath, but also for conscience sake . . . For this cause pay ye tribute also: for they are God's ministers, attending continually upon this very thing. Render therefore to all their dues: tribute to whom tribute is due; custom to whom custom; fear to whom fear; honour to whom honour.[19]

At first glance this certainly appears to represent a Pauline endorsement of existing political authority. But Locke goes beyond first glance. His note on this passage in the *Paraphrases and Notes on the Epistles of St. Paul* is quite complicated and, I think, very significant for the theoretical enterprise. He says this:

Whither we take powers here in the abstract for political authority, or in the concrete for persons de facto exercising political power and jurisdiction, the sense will be the same (viz) that Christians by virtue of being Christians are

---

[16] See esp. RC: 81; also more generally RC: 35–100.
[17] Locke, *First Tract on Government*, p. 51.   [18] Ibid.   [19] Romans 13:1–5.

not any way exempt from obedience to the civil magistrates, nor ought by
any means to resist them, though by what is said ver. 3 it seems that St Paul
meant here magistrates having and exercising a lawfull power. But whither the
magistrates in being were or were not such, and consequently were or were
not to be obeyed, that Christianity gave them no peculiar power to examine.
They had the common right of others their fellow citizens, but had no distinct
priviledg as Christians. And therefore we see ver. 7 where he enjoyns the paying
of tribute and custome etc It is in these words. Render to all their dues; Tribute
to whom tribute is due; honor to whom honor etc. but who it was to whom any
of these or any other dues of right belonged he decides not, for that he leaves
them to be determined by the laws and constitutions of their country. (P&N:
ii.588)

In other words, Locke reads St. Paul as saying something genuinely
neutral, non-committal so far as the tasks of political philosophy are
concerned. If it has a point, says Locke, the passage from Romans is
directed against the Jews – Locke tends to make the Epistles a little more
anti-Semitic in flavor than they need to be – since above all others

the Jews were apt to have an inward reluctancy and indignation against the
power of any heathen over them, takeing it to be an unjust and tyrannical
usurpation upon them, who were the people of god, and their betters... The
doctrine of Christianity was a doctrine of liberty...from the Mosaical law.
Hence corrupt and mistakeing men espetialy Jewish converts impatient, as we
have observed, of any heathen dominion might be ready to infer that Christians
were exempt from subjection to the laws of heathen governments. (P&N: ii.588)

This is the inference which Locke says St. Paul is anxious to resist. The
idea is that opposition to Mosaic law is not opposition to law as such.
More generally, though, Locke does not gloss the passage from Romans
as requiring Christian support for *de facto* authority. On the contrary, he
reads it as requiring support for whatever authority is legitimate in the
world. "Obey the powers that be," therefore, is not to be interpreted as
a commission for magistrates, on Locke's view; it is to be interpreted
instead as an assertion of the autonomy of at least the political part of
political theory from the teachings of the New Testament. The theology
tells us nothing affirmative about the substance of political theory.

Let me repeat this, for it is important to grasp what St. Paul's teaching
in Romans entails on Locke's reading. *It does not entail that existing political
power is to be treated as legitimate.* Whether the powers that be are exercising
legitimate authority, and consequently whether we ought to obey them,
is something that our Christian faith gives us no particular basis for
examining. We must examine it using other resources – like ordinary

reason, as encapsulated in good political theory.[20] If reason shows that some *de facto* ruler is *not* exercising legitimate authority, then Romans 13 gives the ruler no support. But if reason shows that a *de facto* ruler *is* exercising legitimate authority, then the fact that some of his subjects are Christians (while the ruler perhaps is not) does not detract from his authority.

In the long and inutterably tedious *Third Letter for Toleration*, Locke puts a slightly different spin on the text "The powers that be are ordained of God." But it's a different spin which if anything reinforces the main point. People set up governments by consent to avoid the inconveniences of the state of nature. These governments, Locke says, "may very fitly be called powers ordained of God," in the following indirect sense: they are "chosen and appointed by those who had the authority from God so to do" – i.e. ordinary consenting people – "for he that receives commission, limited according to the discretion of him that gives it, from another who had authority from his prince to do so, may truly be said, so far as his commission reaches, to be appointed or ordained by the prince himself."[21] Again, this is a clear indication that the passage from Romans 13 is to be read in the light of Locke's theoretical (indeed his contractarian) argument, rather than the other way round.

III

Locke uses exactly the same interpretive maneuver in the *Paraphrases* so far as St. Paul's comments on slavery are concerned. This might be as good a time as any to say something about Locke's problematic relation to slavery and his personal involvement in the slave trade and the slave economies of some of the American colonies.

The New Testament passage on slavery, on which Locke is commenting, is 1 Corinthians 7:20–3, where Paul says (in Locke's paraphrase)

Wert thou called being a slave, think thy self not the less a Christian for being a slave: but prefer freedom to slavery if thou canst obtein it. For he that is converted to Christianity being a bond-man is Christs freed-man. And he that is converted being a free man, is Christ's bond-man under his command and dominion. (P&N: i.201–2)

John Dunn sees here the presence in Locke's thought of something like the Protestant doctrine of *the calling*: a theological basis on which everyone

---

[20] Hence there is no substitute for good political theory: see 2nd T: 4 and 111.

[21] Locke, *Third Letter*, p. 224.

is to be reconciled to his given position in life. "Men are put into the world in particular social situations and with particular individual talents. They are called by God to fill a particular role."[22] I am not sure about this as a general theme in Locke's work, but I am certain there is nothing at all of that flavor in his note on the passage from 1 Corinthians. For what Locke says there is the exact equivalent of what he said about the passage from Romans 13: civil slavery, he says, was "not dissolved by a mans becomeing a Christian" (P&N: i.202n). And in general, Locke goes on, Paul tells us that "noething in any man's civil estate or rights is altered by his becoming a Christian" (ibid.). This is quite different from the idea of a calling; indeed it does not even amount to a recommendation of quietism or acceptance. It is a pure negative. *If* slavery is legitimate, then Christians may be slaves; and then they should obey their masters on account of its legitimacy, not on account of Christian quietism. But if slavery is illegitimate, then Christians, like everyone else, may not be slaves and need not and probably should not obey their *de facto* masters. That is the gist of what Locke wrote at the end of his life. And that is exactly what he wrote also some thirty years earlier in the "Second Tract on Government": "[B]ondservants, even though they were made subject to Christ . . . owe the same obedience as before to their masters."[23] If moral and political theory could establish that they already owed no obedience to their masters, then that would remain their position after the coming of, or their conversion to, Christianity.

So the Christianity of the alleged slave (or of the society in which slavery purports to exist) makes no difference. Now, it's important to see that this does not mean theology is irrelevant to the issue of the legitimacy of slavery. On the contrary, Locke is adamant that it is because we are, each of us, responsible to God for our own freedom that we are not entitled to sell ourselves into slavery, i.e. to alienate the stewardship of our freedom to anybody else. "A man . . . *cannot*, by compact, or his own Consent, *enslave himself* to any one" (2nd T: 23). In the same passage, he goes to considerable lengths to show that a practice among the Jews that *looks* like people selling themselves into slavery was in fact not that at all, but instead a rather oppressive form of employment. And of course this position – against the possibility of alienating one's freedom – is crucial to Locke's argument against political absolutism: "[N]o Body can transfer to another more power than he has in himself; and no

---

[22] Dunn, *Political Thought of John Locke*, p. 222.   [23] Locke, "Second Tract on Government," p. 72.

Body has an absolute Arbitrary Power over himself... A Man, as has been proved, cannot subject himself to the Arbitrary Power of another" (2nd T: 135). Thus the legislature, which is constituted by nothing more than the transfer of powers from individuals, cannot acquire arbitrary authority on any consensual basis. This is absolutely fundamental to Locke's political argument, and it represents a decisive siding of Locke against those who, like Luis de Molina and Francisco Suarez, associated a radical theory of rights with the possibility of contractarian defenses of slavery and absolutism, in what Richard Tuck has shown was one of the great controversies of sixteenth- and seventeenth-century rights-theory.[24] (Notice also that it makes nonsense of the idea that Locke thought of all rights on the model of property.[25] Property can be alienated by gift or sale in the marketplace, but many of our most important rights are, in the strictest sense, inalienable on Locke's account.)

In general opposition to slavery is the leitmotiv of Locke's *Two Treatises*. The *First Treatise* opens the batting against Filmer with an announcement which reads rather like a chorus from "Rule, Britannia!":[26] "Slavery is so vile and miserable an Estate of Man, and so directly opposite to the generous Temper and Courage of our Nation; that 'tis hardly to be conceived, that an *Englishman*, much less a Gentleman, should plead for't" (1st T: 1). Still, showing that *Britons* cannot be slaves, and also that slavery cannot be based on consent, is not enough to complete a comprehensive case against this peculiar institution. For there are other possibilities: one is that slavery might be appropriate for human beings of certain natures – Aristotle's "natural slaves"[27] – and the other is that slavery might be based on some legitimate form of captivity. What has Locke to say about these possibilities?

So far as natural slavery is concerned, Locke's egalitarianism will not permit it, and he dismisses it out of hand. (Incidentally, Sir Robert Filmer also dismisses this possibility in *Patriarcha*.)[28] Nature, Locke says, "has made no such distinction between one Man and another" (2nd T: 172). Ian Harris points rather ingenuously to a passage in the *Second Treatise* which he thinks shows that Locke *did* accept the possibility of natural slaves.[29] Locke writes of latter-day Filmerians:

[24] See Tuck, *Natural Rights Theories*, pp. 49–57.   [25] Macpherson, *Democratic Theory*, p. 235.
[26] I owe this characterization to Farr, "So Vile and Miserable An Estate."
[27] Aristotle, *The Politics*, Bk. I, Chs. 4–6, pp. 5–9.
[28] Filmer, *Patriarcha*, p. 15. (See Chapter 1, p. 17 above, for the full text of Filmer's rejection of Aristotle's doctrine of natural slavery.)
[29] Harris, *Mind of John Locke*, p. 172.

their Civil Policy is so new, so dangerous, and so destructive to both Rulers and People, that as former ages never could bear the broaching of it; so it may be hoped, those to come, redeem'd from the Impositions of these *Egyptian* Under-Task-masters, will abhor the Memory of such servile Flatterers, who whilst it seem'd to serve their turn, resolv'd all government into absolute Tyranny, and would have all Men born to, what their [own] mean Souls fitted them for, Slavery. (2nd T: 239)

But I think it is pretty clear Locke means this as simple vituperation, and not at all as a serious philosophical claim that some men (e.g. Filmerians) are slavish by soul or by nature.

That leaves slavery by captivity, and here there is no doubt: Locke *is* prepared to say that humans who are conquered as unjust aggressors by those who are defending themselves or their property in a just war may be enslaved. The argument is that since they may legitimately be put to death, they may therefore legitimately be subjected by their conquerors to any indignity short of death, including forced labor. "[H]aving by his fault forfeited his own Life, by some Act that deserves Death; he, to whom he has forfeited it, may (when he has him in his Power) delay to take it, and make use of him to his own Service, and he does him no injury by it" (2nd T: 23). This is the only form of legitimate slavery that Locke is prepared to acknowledge. But it is an extraordinarily limited acknowledgment.

For one thing, Locke insists that this is not a relationship in which the slave has any obligation: it is a pure case of legitimate power – one of those interesting cases where legitimacy and obligation come apart.[30] No doubt the legitimate slave had a duty not to engage in aggression in the first place. But he has violated that, and he now deserves death; and that is all there is to say on his side of the equation. He can choose at any time whether to obey the master or risk the death he deserves; and if he has an obligation to obey I suspect it is nothing more than an artifact of his general duty to God to remain alive (even when he deserves death), and not risk the indirect suicide of resistance, a prospect about which Locke is somewhat equivocal in the chapter on slavery.[31] It is *not* a matter of his conqueror having offered him a bargain and his being bound by a contract. Locke is emphatic about that: a bargain based on

---

[30] See Waldron, "Theoretical Foundations of Liberalism," pp. 49–50. See also Dworkin, *Law's Empire*, p. 191.

[31] See 2nd T: 23: "whenever he finds the hardship of his Slavery outweigh the value of his Life, 'tis in his Power, by resisting the Will of his Master, to draw on himself the Death he desires."

force has no validity,[32] nor does a bargain to dispose of one's freedom (2nd T: 186).[33]

Also the conditions are themselves very restrictive. We are talking only about the enslavement of captives taken in a *just* war, and only captives who were *actual participants* in the aggression that made the just war necessary. Locke insists that this applies only to those who actually participated in the unjust aggression – not their wives, not their children, not their fellow-countrymen.[34] And he is emphatic also that only actual deliberate participation counts; tacit or presumed consent to an involvement in the aggressive enterprise is not enough. All this is explicit and insistent in the chapter on conquest.[35] If someone is attacked unjustly by a king and his army, then he – the person who is attacked – may enslave the king and the soldiers "who have actually assisted, concurrd, or consented to that unjust force" (2nd T: 179). But he is *not* entitled to enslave a whole people simply because they were subjects of an unjust aggressor. The ordinary subjects of an aggressor cannot be assumed to have given their consent to the aggression. On the contrary, the hypothesis goes the other way: this is not the sort of thing for which consent can ordinarily be assumed (2nd T: 179).

Seymour Drescher has suggested that beyond natural slavery (which Locke rejects) and slavery by just captivity (which he acknowledges, but only on the most severely restricted basis), there might also be a third category: slavery by purchase.[36] He observes that Locke seems to acknowledge this in a passage towards the end of the *First Treatise*, where he speaks of a "Planter in the *West Indies*" having "Power in his Family over Servants born in his House, and bought with his Money" (1st T: 130). And he compares this with the practice in ancient Israel: "Those who were rich in the *Patriarchs* days, as in the *West Indies* now, bought Men and Maid Servants, and by their increase, as well as purchasing of new, came to have large and numerous Families" (1st T: 130). The passage is certainly a challenging one. James Farr believes that Locke is simply noticing the existence of a common practice and that this does not amount to an endorsement of slavery-by-purchase: "His recognition of it is on a par with his recognition of, say, suicide or absolute monarchy

---

[32] Compare the *First Treatise* passage on coercive agreements (1st T: 43) which we discussed in Chapter 5 above, pp. 178–9.
[33] See also the discussion at the end of Chapter 5 above.   [34] See 2nd T: 178, 182, and 189.
[35] Locke, *Second Treatise*, Chapter 16.
[36] Drescher, "On James Farr's 'So Vile and Miserable an Estate.'"

or the ravages of lions and tigers."[37] But this won't quite do, since Locke
is explicitly talking about entitlement here: the context is an argument
that not all power descends by inheritance from Adam, since some is
acquired through purchase.

A Mans Riding, in an expedition against an Enemy, his Horse bought in a
Fair, would be as good a Proof that the owner enjoyed the Lordship which
Adam by command had over the whole World, by Right descending to him, as
Abraham's leading out the Servants of his Family is, that the Patriarchs enjoyed
this Lordship by descent from Adam: since the Title to the Power the Master
had in both Cases, whether over Slaves or Horses, was only from his purchase;
and the getting a Dominion over any thing by Bargain and Money, is a new way
[i.e., a preposterous way] of proving one had it by Descent and Inheritance.
(1st T: 130)

Farr, I think, takes the wrong tack. We need not read an egalitarian
Locke as utterly rejecting the possibility that Drescher notices. It is just
conceivable that a slave *may* legitimately be sold on Locke's account. But
that can happen only if the slave in question was justly captured in a
just war (and, as we have seen, Locke regards this as a severely limited
though not necessarily empty category) and only if there is also some
way of getting round the point we noticed at the end of Chapter 5, that
certain ways of regularizing the relation between master and servant
are inconsistent with the basis of slavery (2nd T: 172).[38] On the other
hand, Farr is right to emphasize that the legitimacy of the enslavement of
someone not justly captured in a just war can never be established by the
mere fact of purchase. The logic of this aspect of a master's entitlement
is simply Nozickian, on Locke's account. Defects in the application of
the principle of justice-in-acquisition cannot be cured by any subsequent
applications of the principle of justice-in-transfer.[39]

And, of course, Farr is also right to emphasize in a general way the
difference in Locke's work between noticing the existence of some practice and according it legitimacy. Many people may act as though their
power over slaves is justified purely by purchase without regard to the
justice of the initial enslavement of the individuals in question; but the
noticeable prevalence of that wouldn't make it right. Locke did not, as
Jacqueline Stevens alleges, "believe that the existence of a practice validates it."[40] His books are replete with reports of existent practices that
he condemns. I can't resist citing what I think is the clearest example of

---

[37] Farr, "Slaves Bought with Money," p. 472.   [38] See above, p. 148.
[39] See Nozick, *Anarchy, State and Utopia*, pp. 150–3.   [40] Stevens, *Reproducing the State*, p. 100n.

Locke's insistence on the distinction between fact and right, which is in a passage from the *Letter on Toleration*. It has nothing to do with slavery, but it goes as follows:

There are two sorts of Contests amongst men, the one managed by Law, the other by Force; and these are of that nature that where the one ends, the other always begins. But it is not my business to inquire into the Power of the Magistrate in the different Constitutions of Nations. I only know what usually happens where Controversies arise without a judge to determine them. You will say then the Magistrate being the stronger will have his Will and carry his point. Without doubt; but the Question is not here concerning the doubtfulness of the Event, but the Rule of Right. (LCT: 49)

That's the spirit in which Locke writes almost all of his political philosophy. It's the spirit in which he comments on the prospects for resistance to tyranny by an isolated individual at the end of the *Second Treatise* (2nd T: 208).[41] And it's also the spirit in which he ends his discussion of slavery in the *Second Treatise*. Locke acknowledges that men generally ignore the natural law principles he has set out: "Conquerours, 'tis true, seldom trouble themselves to make the distinction, but they willingly permit the confusion of War to sweep altogether" (2nd T: 179). But, he goes on,

this alters not the Right: for the Conquerours Power over the Lives of the Conquered, being only because they have used force to do, or maintain an Injustice, he can have that power only over those, who have concurred in that force, all the rest are innocent; and he has no more Title over the People of that Country, who have done him no Injury, and so have made no forfeiture of their Lives, than he has over any other, who, without any injuries or provocations, have lived upon fair terms with him. (2nd T: 179)

We have then a severely limited case for slavery, together with a quite rigorist attitude to the conditions that must be met before enslavement can possibly be legitimate.

Now I want to venture a risky hypothesis. Nobody who thought this carefully about the relation between practice and justification and also about the one limited case in which slavery *might* be justified – nobody who announced the restrictions on the legitimacy of slavery that Locke announced and made them bear so much weight in his theory of politics – could possibly have believed in the moral legitimacy of African slavery as an institution in the English colonies in America.[42]

---

[41] Thus I disagree with Stevens, "The Reasonableness of John Locke's Majority," pp. 443–7.

[42] Locke, as James Farr has noted in "So Vile and Miserable an Estate," was unwilling to provide any actual historical examples of justified slavery.

Historically, the hypothesis is risky because of what we know of John Locke's own involvement with American slavery. Locke invested money personally both in plantation enterprises and in an enterprise (The Royal African Company) that had a monopoly in the slave trade. In the late 1660s and the 1670s Locke worked as a secretary to the Lords Proprietors of Carolina, and in that capacity – due partly to his association with Shaftesbury, chief among the Lords Proprietors – he certainly transcribed, and perhaps played a large part in drafting, what came to be known as *The Fundamental Constitutions of Carolina*. (Scholarly opinions differ about the exact extent of his involvement.)[43] *The Fundamental Constitutions of Carolina* clearly assume slavery as an institution and they say things like "Every freeman of Carolina shall have absolute power and authority over his negro slaves,"[44] though they also insist that "[s]ince charity obliges us to wish well to the souls of all men, . . . it shall be lawful for slaves, as all others, to enter . . . and be of what church any of them shall think best, and thereof be as fully members as any freemen."[45]

Much of this description of Locke's involvement I have taken from an article by Jennifer Welchman. Professor Welchman concludes that part of her article by saying: "The man whose career I've just described to you is not a man likely to construct or defend a theory of political or natural rights incompatible with slavery."[46] Let us think about that. What does Welchman's comment assume about the notion of a life or a career? What does it assume about integrity and about the unity of a political and intellectual life? I suspect it depends on quite modern twentieth- or twenty-first-century notions of career and integrity – notions that are underwritten in our lives by a certain amount of prestige, safety, and independent prosperity (not to mention academic tenure). Paradoxically they are underwritten also by our political impotence. We who have no power can afford to cultivate a fastidious unity (or appearance of unity) in the theories we espouse and the political actions we undertake, for our political actions are nothing more than the casting of a secret ballot or the signing of an open letter.[47] (Is it putting it too meanly to say that, for us, the integrity of theory and practice means at most some sort of continuity between what we write in an academic journal and what we write in the *New York Review of Books*?) At any rate, these notions of integrity

---

[43] For doubts about Locke's actual involvement as an author, see Milton, "John Locke and the Fundamental Constitutions of Carolina," pp. 469 ff.

[44] Locke, "Fundamental Constitutions of Carolina", p. 180.   [45] Ibid., p. 179.

[46] Welchman, "Locke on Slavery and Inalienable Rights," p. 75.

[47] See Posner, *Problematics of Moral and Legal Theory*, Ch. 1; and Waldron, "Ego-Bloated Hovel," pp. 619–24.

and the unity of a life are arguably anachronistic in terms of seventeenth-century intellectual culture.[48] Certainly what I have referred to as their underpinnings (in our case) have little application to the material and career circumstances of a man who did not make a living as a university scholar with tenure, who was involved in deadly political conspiracy, and who often – as when he fled Oxford in 1683, his books blazing behind him – could not even guarantee his physical *safety* as a scholar, let alone his livelihood. Let me add that I am not trying to *excuse* Locke's investment in slavery. I am simply resisting an inference from something he did to something he "must have" thought. No doubt there is something to be said, too, about the role of Locke's own character in all of this: he was not the sort of man one would expect to dissociate himself fastidiously from power and patronage in order to vindicate his own moral views. But it's not just a matter of character. Historians of ideas need to be sensitive to the historical events of Locke's life, certainly; but they also need to be sensitive to the historically specific idea of what it is to *make a life for oneself* out of such events. The symbolic politics familiar to us – the politics of disinvestment, conscientious refusal, and righteous dissociation – are not unproblematically available as an ahistorical matrix on which we can infer what Locke must have thought from the company he kept and the investments he made.[49]

As a matter of fact, I think we *can* see our author slipping in some distinctly Lockean ideas into the *Constitutions of the Carolinas*. The stuff about slaves going to whatever church they like is clearly Locke, as is the comment he adds to it – "religion ought to alter nothing in any man's civil estate or right" – which (as we have seen) is exactly what he was writing around the same time in the *First* and *Second Tracts on Government*. Be that as it may, it is obvious that any seventeenth-century constitution for the Carolinas (for that matter any eighteenth- or early nineteenth-century constitution for the Carolinas) was going to include a clause permitting slavery. I don't think we can infer anything about the personal politics let alone the political philosophy of the transcribing secretary from the fact that he failed to persuade the Lords Proprietors of the colony to take the slavery clause out (and abolish the institution). Indeed I doubt that we can infer very much about Locke's political theory from the fact that he probably didn't even try.

[48] My point is not that it is anachronistic to reproach Locke for not holding opinions like ours about slavery (cf. Ashcraft, "Simple Objections and Complex Reality," p. 109). I am saying that it is anachronistic to use our concept of political or scholarly integrity as a heuristic for determining whether he in fact did hold anything like our position.

[49] I am grateful to Karma Nabulsi for conversations on this topic.

If we read the theory as it is written in the *Two Treatises* then the position is clear. There is simply no possibility of reconciling Locke's very limited theory of legitimate enslavement with the reality of the institution in the Carolinas or anywhere else in the Americas. Locke was well aware of the methods of the slave-hunters and could have been under no illusion that the slaves they trafficked in were aggressors defeated in a just war. Englishmen at that time had no interest in establishing agriculture in Africa and so they could not construct a plausible defense of a just war against its native inhabitants along the lines that James Tully suggests Locke contemplated against native Americans.[50] Also Locke was perfectly familiar with the fact that women and children were also enslaved, in proportions that suggest patent violations of the natural law principle he insisted upon – that the just captivity of an aggressor does not implicate his family (2nd T: 182). He was well aware, too, that slavery in the Americas was an inherited status, that slaves were bred; and of course, this straightforwardly contradicts the moral individualism which is as crucial to his moral and political theory generally as it is to his opposition to specific theories about corruption of the blood and the posterity of those who have engaged in aggression.

So what can I say? Two facts are clear: (1) There is nothing in Locke's theory that lends an iota of legitimacy to the contemporary institution of slavery in the Americas; and (2) African slavery in the Americas was a reality and Locke himself was implicated with it, in the ways that I have described. I prefer to leave those facts where they lie, sitting uncomfortably together, than to try and resolve a contradiction between them, a contradiction which exists only by virtue of our own late twentieth- or early twenty-first-century ideas about the political integrity of an intellectual life.

IV

I have been proceeding, as I hope the reader can tell, on the basis of theme and digression. I want to return now from this digression about slavery to the main theme that I introduced at the beginning of this chapter: the comparative absence of any New Testament references, material, and argumentation in John Locke's *Two Treatises of Government*.

We have pursued a partial explanation. Locke did not believe that there was any specifically *political* theory contained in the teachings of the Gospels; and to the extent that he drew anything political from the

---

[50] Tully, "Rediscovering America," pp. 142 ff. See also my discussion in Chapter 6, above.

Epistles it was precisely to reinforce that point. Christianity changes nothing so far as the legitimacy of terrestrial political institutions is concerned. But this will not do as a complete explanation. For although the *Second Treatise* is an attempt "to understand *Political* Power" and distinguish it from other forms of power, it does so on the basis of natural law theory, to which the whole first half of the *Second Treatise* is devoted and which, if the Locke of *The Reasonableness of Christianity* is to be believed, has nowhere been better and more forcefully expounded than in the teachings of Jesus Christ (RC: 133 ff.). Admittedly, we must take care not to exaggerate the continuity between the *Treatises* and the *Reasonableness*. Depending which view you accept about the composition of the *Second Treatise*, there might be as many as fifteen years between them. It is often suggested that the key contrast is between the *Essay* and the *Reasonableness* – *The Reasonableness of Christianity* being a sort of apology for the failure of the *Essay* to demonstrate the foundations of morality. (I said in Chapter 4 that I had my doubts about that picture, and I won't repeat them here.)[51] Where there is a striking dissonance, however, is in the way in which natural law foundations are set out in the *Second Treatise* and the way in which they are discussed in *The Reasonableness* of Christianity. For Locke is purporting to *do* in the *Second Treatise* what he was prepared to say in the *Reasonableness* had never in fact been done successfully without the aid of the Gospels.

It is true, there is a law of nature: but who is there that ever did, or undertook to give it us entire, as a law; no more, nor no less, than what was contained in, and had the obligation of that law? Who ever made out the parts of it, put them together, and showed the world their obligation? (RC: 142)

In context, Locke's rhetorical question is directed at the pre-Christian philosophers. But a lot of what he says in the *Reasonableness* seems to suggest that it would be hopeless to attempt a systematic and compelling exposition of natural law, even in the post-Christian era, except on the basis of the teachings of Christ.[52] From this point of view, then, the *Second Treatise* – with its lack of Gospel-based argument – is at odds with the sort of pessimism about unaided reason that suffuses *The Reasonableness of Christianity*.[53]

---

[51] See above, p. 99.

[52] See also Locke's note in P&N: ii, p. 499 (commenting on Romans 2:14): "For though from Adam to Christ there was noe revealed positive law but that given to the Israelites yet it is certain that by Jesus Christ a positive law from heaven is given to all mankind, and that those to whom this has been promulgated by the preaching of the gospel are all under it and shall be judged by it." (I am indebted for this citation to Spellman, *John Locke*, p. 48.)

[53] Incidentally, the common view – that Locke's *Reasonableness of Christianity* is an attempt to vindicate religion in rationalistic terms (along the lines of Kant's *Religion Within the Limits of Reason Alone*) – is

Is it perhaps just a matter of genre – that the *Second Treatise* simply reflects the way natural law treatises were written in the sixteenth and seventeenth centuries? I am not sure. It is worth noting that Locke also eschewed the use of biblical material in his early *Essays on the Law of Nature* (from around 1663–4), as did Samuel Pufendorf in his treatise *On the Duty of Man and Citizen According to Natural Law*. Hugo Grotius, on the other hand, *did* make use of New Testament material in *The Rights of War and Peace*. He cited the teachings and example of Christ in his discussion of oaths and truth-telling, and most notably and extensively in developing his theory of punishment.[54] And it's not just rhetoric: Grotius feels impelled to ask, for example, whether the Christian teaching of forgiveness confines the right to punishment "within closer bounds," and he has to go through some quite considerable contortions to salvage the idea of retribution.[55] (In this connection, it is surely interesting that Locke argued in the *Reasonableness* that the idea of redemption could be arrived at in principle by the same sort of reasoning that arrives at the idea of God; and that Locke also thought, like Grotius, that reason, not just Christian revelation, showed that "the infliction of punishment, only to gratify resentment" was something repugnant to the law of nature.)[56]

v

Specifically Christian arguments are not always absent from Locke's mature political thought. They are in fact quite prominent in the *Letters Concerning Toleration*. The original *Letter*, Locke says, contains "my Thoughts about *the mutual Toleration of Christians* in their different Professions of Religion" (LCT: 23 – my emphasis) and the thesis is set out quite explicitly: "The Toleration of those that differ from others in Matters of Religion is so agreeable to the Gospel of Jesus Christ . . . that it seems monstrous for Men to be so blind, as not to perceive the Necessity and

---

quite mistaken. It seems to be based on a reading of nothing more than the title of the work. For an accurate account, see Tully, "Governing Conduct," pp. 225 ff.

[54] See Grotius, *Rights of War and Peace*, Bk. II, Chs. 13 (pp. 161 and 164–5) and 20 (pp. 223, 231–2, 239, and 254); and Bk. III, Ch. 1 (pp. 292, 297, and 300).

[55] Ibid., pp. 230–2 (Bk. II, Ch. 20, para. x).

[56] Compare Locke, *Reasonableness*, pp. 7–10 with Grotius, *Rights of War and Peace*, p. 230: "For the infliction of punishment, only to gratify resentment, so far from being conformable to the Gospel, has been shewn above to be repugnant even to the law of nature." See also Locke, 2nd T: 8, "And thus in the State of Nature, *one Man comes by a Power over another*, but yet no Absolute or Arbitrary Power, to use a Criminal when he has got him in his hands, according to the passionate heats, or boundless extravagancy of his own Will, but only to retribute to him, so far as calm reason and conscience dictates, what is proportionate to his Transgression, which is so much as may serve for *Reparation and Restraint*."

Advantage of it in so clear a Light" (LCT: 25). This is not just happy talk. Locke reverts to the Gospels many times to bolster particular points he wants to make about toleration. For example, in his observations about ecclesiastical organization in the *Letter*, he makes it clear that Gospel authority is crucial. To the defenders of episcopacy, he says

let them show me the edict by which Christ has imposed that law upon His Church. And let not any man think me impertinent, if in a thing of this consequence I require that the terms of that edict be very express and positive; for the promise He has made us (Matt. 18.20), that "wheresoever two or three are gathered together" in His name, He will be in the midst of them, seems to imply the contrary. (LCT: 21)

But he also invokes the example of Jesus and the spirit of Christian charity as a matter of general liberal ethos, as in this passage: "[T]he Gospel frequently declares that the true disciples of Christ must suffer persecution; but that the Church of Christ should persecute others . . . I could never yet find in any of the books of the New Testament" (LCT: 22). In another passage, he declares:

If, like the Captain of our salvation, they sincerely desired the good of souls, they would . . . follow the perfect example of that Prince of Peace, who sent out His soldiers to the subduing of nations, and gathering them into His Church, not armed with the sword, or other instruments of force, but prepared with the Gospel of peace and with the exemplary holiness of their conversation. (LCT: 16)

How bracketable is this Christian material in the *Letter Concerning Toleration*?[57] I had always assumed it could be bracketed off and that a substantial argument for toleration would remain – namely the argument based on the fact that belief is not subject to the will, and that therefore coercion, which works on the will, is inappropriate for producing true belief. I argued that in a 1988 paper on toleration, suggesting that as well as the Christian argument there was also a general argument for toleration that might be persuasive to anyone.[58] I didn't intend to infer from this that a secular Lockean argument could be extended to free speech generally or to toleration of differing life-styles. John Dunn is quite right to insist on "the yawning chasm between the implications of Locke's argument for tolerating varieties of Christian belief and practice within a Christian state and society and the implications . . . for freedom

---

[57] Compare the discussion about "bracketing" at the beginning of Chapter 3.

[58] Waldron, "Locke, Toleration and the Rationality of Persecution," pp. 89–90. For an effective critique, see Fish, *Trouble with Principle*, pp. 176–8.

of thought and expression more broadly within a secular state or a more intractably plural religious culture."[59] Nothing can get the benefit of Locke's argument unless it is a "religion in which authentic belief is a precondition for valid religious worship and religious worship is a central duty for man."[60] Still, even within the realm of religion, Locke himself did seem to think that there was something in his argument that might appeal to a Mahometan mullah or a Hindu prince contemplating the enforcement of their own religious views; and presumably he would have to accept that in that regard they might be impervious to any argument based on the teaching or example of Jesus Christ and his apostles.

But in fact I think now that the main argument of the *Letter* does have to rest on its distinctively Christian foundations. This becomes apparent once we take into account the concessions that Locke is forced to make in the *Second, Third* and *Fourth Letters Concerning Toleration*. The argument in the original *Letter* of 1689 had been that "true and saving religion consists in the inward persuasion of the mind . . . And such is the nature of the understanding, that it cannot be compelled to the belief of anything by outward force" (LCT: 18). But Locke's critics – notably Jonas Proast – had argued and argued persuasively that force may work indirectly to inculcate beliefs or to make the mind receptive to beliefs, even if it does not work directly on the understanding. Locke accepted this. There is no denying, he said, that in particular cases force may work to procure salvation. God himself makes use of all sorts of things to save men's souls – "as our Savior did of clay and spittle to cure blindness."[61] God *might* have ordained the general use of force in religious matters in the way that he gave specific commandments to the Israelites to punish idolatry with death. As a matter of fact, he says, that was a positive law specifically addressed to the Jewish nation, and not to us.[62] But things could have been different. (And if they *had* been different we would know about it only through revelation, which means we are held hostage in our theory of toleration to what revelation actually tells us about the use of force in matters of worship and belief.) "If God thought it necessary to have men punished to make them" pay attention to the Gospel teaching, says Locke, "he could have called magistrates to be

---

[59] Dunn, "What is Living and What is Dead in the Political Theory of John Locke?" p. 19.
[60] Dunn, *Locke*, p. 57.   [61] Locke, *Second Letter Concerning Toleration*, p. 68.
[62] "For no positive law whatsoever can oblige any people but those to whom it is given. 'Hear, O Israel,' sufficiently restrains the obligations of the law of Moses only to that people. And this consideration alone is answer enough unto those that urge the authority of the law of Moses for the inflicting of capital punishment upon idolaters" (LCT: 42).

spreaders and ministers of the Gospel, as well as poor fishermen."[63] So
the position to which Locke retreats is that even though force may work in
some cases and even though it may be ordained for some specific nation,
it has not generally been ordained by God as a means of conversion: "It
is not for the magistrate, or any body else, upon an imagination of its
usefulness, to make use of any other means for the salvation of men's
souls than what the author and finisher of our faith hath directed."[64]
And although this is bolstered with other, somewhat more ecumenical
arguments about force being counter-productive as well as productive,
and about the poor likelihood that magistrates will have the discernment
to discover what is "true religion" before deploying force – the main line
of argument in Locke's case for toleration that survives Proast's critique
is dominated by his sense of what God has and has not ordained; and
for that the specific biblical evidence of the life and teaching of Jesus is
indispensable.

I am mindful that there is no reason to think that in the 1680s Locke
had already seen his way through to what we can discern as the outcome
of his exchange with Proast. (If the *Third* and *Fourth Letters for Toleration*
of the 1690s are any indication, I'm not sure he ever accepted that his
secular argument had been knocked down.) And as I have already said,
we should not assume that he held in the early 1680s the pessimistic view
of the natural law argument that he expounded in *The Reasonableness of
Christianity*. So we should be careful not to phrase our problem – about the
absence of New Testament materials from the *Two Treatises* – as though
it were a question of why Locke failed to deploy resources the need for
whose deployment only became apparent to him later.

VI

I have often wondered whether the absence of New Testament materials
from the *Two Treatises of Government* has any connection with the fact that
the latter work also says nothing at all on the subject of religious toleration. Religious toleration was one of Locke's abiding preoccupations,
and from a purely philosophical point of view it is odd that he should
make no mention of it in a treatise concerned with the functions and
limits of government. If anything, the occasional references to religion in
the *Second Treatise* seem to indicate that the legitimate Lockean polity need

---

[63] Locke, *Second Letter Concerning Toleration*, p. 84.   [64] Ibid., p. 81.

not be a secular one at all.[65] In the chapters on resistance and revolution, Locke suggests that a people may be entitled to rise up against their prince if he has by his actions or negligence endangered "their Estates, Liberties, Lives . . . and perhaps their Religion too" (2nd T: 209) and he speaks darkly too of a "Religion underhand favored (though publickly proclaimed against)" (2nd T: 210). I am not saying that the doctrine of toleration is incompatible with the general argument of the *Second Treatise*. It certainly is not, despite these superficial indications. Still, the omission *feels* significant.

Historically and politically, the omission of tolerationist argument from the *Second Treatise* is perhaps not difficult to explain. James II was trying to enlist the support of Dissenters in favor of the repeal of Test Acts against Catholics, which meant that during the mid-1680s, tolerationist rhetoric was being used against the Whigs. So there was every reason for those opposed to James, whether immediately before or after his succession, to play down this aspect of their overall position. As John Marshall has argued, support for resistance to James's succession was so precarious that Locke and his circle recognized the inadvisability of entangling the case for resistance, argued in the *Second Treatise*, with an argument about toleration that might diminish the breadth of its appeal.[66]

I suspect, however, that there were also intellectual reasons for Locke's hesitation. We catch a glimpse of these, I think, when we compare the definitions of "church" and "commonwealth" provided in the *Letter Concerning Toleration*:

The Commonwealth seems to me to be a Society of Men constituted only for the procuring, preserving, and advancing their own Civil Interests. *Civil Interests* I call Life, Liberty, Health, and Indolency of Body; and the Possession of outward things, such as Money, Lands, Houses, Furniture, and the like . . . *Let us now consider what a Church is*. A church, then, I take to be a voluntary Society of Men, joining themselves together of their own accord in order to the publick worshipping of God in such manner as they judge acceptable to Him, and effectual to the Salvation of their Souls. (LCT: 26 and 28)

Now the temptation is to say that the key difference here is in the allocated functions – protection of civil interests, as defined, versus worship and salvation of the soul. But notice another cardinal difference: churches are defined as voluntary organizations whereas the commonwealth is

---

[65] Waldron, "Locke, Toleration, and the Rationality of Persecution," p. 100.
[66] Marshall, *John Locke*, pp. 288–9.

not. (I don't mean the commonwealth is defined as involuntary; I mean that it is not defined here by reference to its being *voluntary*.) Consider what Locke goes on to say about a church:

I say it is a free and voluntary Society. Nobody is born a member of any Church; otherwise the Religion of Parents would descend unto Children by the same right of Inheritance as their Temporal Estates, and everyone would hold his Faith by the same Tenure he does his Lands, than which nothing can be imagined more absurd. Thus therefore that matter stands. No Man by nature is bound unto any particular Church or Sect, but everyone joins himself voluntarily. (LCT: 28)

There are two striking things in this passage. First, almost everything Locke says here about a church, he says about the commonwealth in the *Second Treatise*. Here he says a church is a free and voluntary society; there he says that political power is established by consent:

Men being, as has been said, by Nature, all free, equal, and independent, no one can be put out of this Estate, and subjected to the Political Power of another, without his own Consent. The only way whereby any one divests himself of his Natural Liberty, and puts on the bonds of Civil Society, is by agreeing with other Men to joyn and unite into a community . . . This any number of men may do, because it injures not the freedom of the rest; they are left as they were in the liberty of the State of Nature. (2nd T: 95)

Secondly, the disanalogy that Locke raises in the passage cited above from the *Letter* is precisely the source of some difficulty for him in the *Second Treatise*. If a person was born into a church, Locke says, his religion would descend to him by inheritance as his property does (LCT: 28). But in the *Two Treatises*, Locke has to scramble to sort out the relation between inheritance of land and membership of civil society. Since "*a Child is born a Subject of no Country or Government*" (2nd T: 118), his property is in principle free of any political entanglement. However,

because Commonwealths not permitting any part of their Dominions to be dismembered, nor to be enjoyed by any but those of their Community, the Son cannot ordinarily enjoy the Possessions of his Father, but under the same terms his Father did, by becoming a Member of the Society; whereby he puts himself presently under the Government he finds there established, as much as any other Subject of that Common-wealth. (2nd T: 118)

Locke emphasizes in the *Treatise* that this question has caused difficulty – "this has generally given the occasion to mistake in this matter" (2nd T: 118) – and I believe that the presence of exactly this issue in the passage from the *Letter* indicates that Locke was actually quite unsure in the 1680s how exactly to characterize civil society. Was it voluntary? Was it in that respect just like a church? In that case, what would be the objection to a group of people banding themselves together in an all-purpose association, since they were entitled to band together voluntarily in a state and entitled also to band together voluntarily in a religious association? Clearly something had to give, and we are alerted to this anyway in the quite different issue of property and inheritance and their tortured relationship to the basis of civil society. Locke cobbles together a solution in the *Second Treatise*, but it's not at all clear he's entitled to it: by what right may a society insist that a man attach political conditions in perpetuity to the property – *his* property – that he brings to it? Also, a similar set of conundrums arises at the end of the *Second Treatise*, where Locke has to scramble to explain why grounding the right of resistance on the voluntary nature of civil society doesn't generate an all-purpose right of exit. In the *Letter* we are told that the voluntary nature of a church means that people can leave it when they like and take their property with them (LCT: 30–1). Why isn't this equally true of the voluntary nature of civil society? Is it because civil society is not really a voluntary organization at all? Locke's omission of any reference to consent in its definition in the *Letter* indicates that he was toying with that position. What I am saying, then, is that I don't believe Locke had sorted these things out in his own mind, and he certainly did not want to contaminate the tentative settlement he had reached in the *Second Treatise* with the somewhat different tentative settlement he seems to have reached in the *Letter*.

VII

Well, once again we have circled several times around the question of the absence of New Testament material from the *Two Treatises of Government* without really answering it. The *Letter Concerning Toleration* uses New Testament material; the *Treatises* don't. And not only the New Testament material, but also the positions in the *Letter* that the New Testament material is used to support are absent from the *Treatises*. There is doubtless some connection, but that still doesn't explain why Locke didn't use New Testament material to support the positions that he did want to argue for in the *Treatises*.

Maybe I am making too much of this question and it is not really a problem, any more than there is a problem about the fact that Locke offers virtually no discussion of Aristotle in the *Two Treatises*,[67] whereas Filmer spends a very considerable amount of time in his company. Or maybe I have pursued the inquiry at too superficial a level. Remember that John Dunn's claim was that "Jesus Christ (and Saint Paul) may not appear in person in the text of the *Two Treatises* but their presence can hardly be missed" in the grounding of Locke's theory of human equality.[68] Certainly there is something right about that – just as there *is* something distinctively Christian (maybe even distinctively Protestant) in flavor about Locke's insistence in the *Treatises* and in the *Letters on Toleration* that *each* of us – each *one* of us – has been sent in to the world specifically by God "by his order and about his business" (2nd T: 6) and that it is not for any other to meddle with or denigrate that individual commission. It is certainly true that the Lockean argument for creaturely equality will not work unless man's relation with God is understood in that way; or at least it amounts to something quite different if man's relation with God is understood in some other way or left out of the picture altogether. And all that is true, though the New Testament is barely cited explicitly.

Still, I have not been able to resolve the question of why Locke offered no *explicit* Christian argument for the specifically individualist way in which he understood man's relation to God's commission and God's purposes. I *suspect* – though I have nothing to offer in support of this, and this is the last strand of explanation that I shall venture – that as well as the issue of political strategy, there might also have been some reluctance on Locke's part to entangle his political arguments in the *Treatises*, which were already strange and radical enough by contemporary standards,[69] with the various issues of Christology which we know he was wrestling with in the 1680s. We know that at that period, he was toying with various Socinian and unitarian possibilities.[70] Certainly if he had mingled in the sort of arguments we find ten years later in *The Reasonableness of Christianity*, he would have virtually guaranteed hostile misunderstanding of the *Second Treatise* (and indeed we have reason to think that his Christological views were more rather than less controversial than this in the 1680s when the *Two Treatises* were put together). So this might have led him to shy away from using any New Testament

---

[67] See 1st T: 154, where Aristotle is mentioned together with Homer as "Heathen poets and philosophers"; and 2nd T: 74, where Locke quotes from Hooker who mentions "the Arch-Philosopher" (i.e. Aristotle). Cf. Filmer, Patriarcha, pp. 12–18 and 44–7.

[68] Dunn, *Political Thought of John Locke*, p. 99.

[69] For the "strange" arguments of the *Second Treatise*, see 2nd T: 9, 40, 180; see also Waldron, *Dignity of Legislation*, pp. 74–5.

[70] See Marshall, *John Locke*, pp. 337–50 and Spellman, *John Locke and the Problem of Depravity*, pp. 129 ff.

material. So – again, quite apart from the political considerations that John Marshall and others have mentioned – if John Dunn is right and if a specific Christian flavor is there anyway, perhaps the best explanation of Locke's failure to make it explicit (in the way that the much less fraught Old Testament material was made explicit) was a desire on Locke's part to avoid unnecessary controversy in respect of a work that he knew was likely to be controversial enough already.

8

Tolerating Atheists?

I began this book by addressing the theme of inclusion and exclusion in John Locke's political theory – in particular his views about the contemporary exclusion of women from politics and social power.[1] I mentioned Locke's attack on Robert Filmer's excision of "mothers" in his account of the significance of the Fifth Commandment, and Locke's failure to subscribe to the explicit position of his friend James Tyrrell that "women are commonly unfit for civil business." Still, it appeared that Locke was not consistent on the application of basic equality to women; his position seems to have been one of clear philosophical commitment to equality tarnished by a theoretically unmotivated presumption in favor of wives' being subordinate to their husbands. As I said in Chapter 2, I don't think this turned Locke's theory into well-worked-out patriarchalism disguised beneath a liberal egalitarian veneer; it still seemed to strike many of his contemporaries as more rather than less egalitarian than one would expect to find in the late seventeenth century.

Since then we have pursued the theme of inclusion more generally, considering not just the case of women, but the whole basis of Locke's egalitarianism in politics, religion, and morality, and especially what I called in Chapter 4 his democratic conception of the human intellect – his notion that the capacity for responsible participation in the moral and political realm is available on much the same basis as Christian faith is available. Christianity is, in Locke's words, "a religion suited to vulgar capacities" (RC: 157), preached by its founder as something intelligible to "a company of poor, ignorant, illiterate men" (RC: 83). By the same token, the natural law which Christianity clarifies, and knowledge of which is the basis of responsible participation in politics, is no less available to "the illiterate and contemned Mechanick" and the "unscholastick Statesman" as it is to the "learned Disputants and

---

[1] See Chapter 2 above.

all-knowing Doctors" (E: 3.10.9), who are all too often privileged in philosophical accounts of politics. And I have argued that this conception of the adequacy of the ordinary intellect is itself driven by Locke's sense of each person's relation to God and his ability to consider his own actions in the light of that relation.

In this final chapter, I want to consider a particular aspect of the *limits* of this egalitarian political inclusiveness in Locke's philosophy. I believe (as I have said) that his politics, particularly when read in the light of his discussions of religion, are much more accommodating than many commentators suppose. But the inclusiveness and the accommodation are not unlimited. So now I want to take a look at the limits that Locke argues for, particularly in his explicit comments on the social and political exclusion of atheists in the *Letters Concerning Toleration*.

I

It is commonly said that Locke intended to exclude Catholics and atheists from the benefit of the otherwise very broad toleration for which he argued in the 1689 *A Letter Concerning Toleration*. As the title of this chapter suggests, most of what I want to say is about atheists. But before I get on to that, let me ask whether it is accurate to say that Locke excluded Roman Catholics from religious toleration. It is commonly supposed that he did; but I have my doubts.

The only explicit reference to Roman Catholicism in the *Letter* – that is, the only passage that actually uses that term – seems to argue exactly the opposite. Locke says:

> the Magistrate ought not to forbid the Preaching or Professing of Any Speculative Opinions in any Church because they have no manner of relation to the Civil Rights of the Subjects. If a *Roman Catholick* believe that to be really the Body of Christ, which another man calls Bread, he does no injury thereby to his Neighbor. (LCT: 46)

And he adds, for good measure: "If a *Jew* do not believe the New Testament to be the Word of God, he does not thereby alter anything in mens Civil Rights" (ibid.). Locke continues: "I readily grant that these Opinions are false and absurd. But the business of Laws is not to provide for the Truth of Opinions, but for the Safety and Security of the Commonwealth, and of every particular mans Goods and Person" (ibid.). That is the only occasion, as far as I am aware, when he uses the term "Roman Catholic." He does use the term "papist" in the *Letter*; again it is without any indication that papist religion is intolerable:

I am doubtful concerning the Doctrine of the *Socinians*,[2] I am suspicious of the way of Worship practised by the *Papists*, or *Lutherans*; will it be ever a jot safer for me to join either unto the one or the other of those Churches, upon the Magistrate's command, because he commands nothing in Religion but by the Authority and Counsel of the Doctors of that Church? (LCT: 37)

Here papist religion is simply used as a routine example – among others like Lutheranism and Socinianism – in the argument for toleration.[3] And the same is true of Locke's use of the term "Vatican" in an analogy he develops between the inappropriateness of public force in religious matters and its inappropriateness in matters of personal health:

Let us suppose … that some Prince were desirous to force his Subjects … to preserve the Health and Strength of their Bodies. Shall it be provided by Law that they must consult none but *Roman* Physicians … What, shall no Potion, No Broth, be taken, but what is prepared either in the *Vatican*, suppose, or in a *Geneva* Shop? (LCT: 35)

When Locke sums up his position on toleration at the end of the *Letter* – "The *Sum of all* we drive at is, *That every Man may enjoy the same Rights that are granted to others*" (LCT: 53) – we find that Rome is included effortlessly along with Geneva: "Is it permitted to worship God in the *Roman* manner? Let it be permitted to do it in the *Geneva* form also. Is it permitted to speak *Latin* in the Market-place? Let those that have a mind to it be permitted to do it also in the Church" (ibid.). This reciprocity or equivalence, back and forth, between Rome and Geneva is repeated several times also in the *Second* and the *Third Letters Concerning Toleration*. For example, Locke illustrates his point about every prince being "Orthodox to himself" (LCT: 42) by saying that if an English prince is entitled to enforce his orthodox Anglicanism, then equally "king Louis of good right comes in with his dragoons; for it is not much doubted that he as strongly believed his popish priests and Jesuits to be the ministry which our Lord appointed, as either king Charles or king James the Second believed that of the church of England to be so."[4] And he cites as a benefit of the toleration he proposes that in countries like Italy, Spain, and Portugal "such a toleration, established there, would permit the doctrine of the

---

[2] As we saw in Chapter 7 (p. 215), Socinianism was a creed to which Locke himself was accused of subscribing. See also Marshall, *John Locke*, pp. 419 ff. and Spellman, *John Locke*, p. 130.

[3] See also LCT: 56, "The *Papists* and the *Lutherans*, tho' both of them profess Faith in Christ and are therefore called Christians, yet are not both of the same Religion: because These acknowledge nothing but the Holy Scriptures to be the Rule and Foundation of their Religion; Those take in also Traditions and the Decrees of Popes and of these together make the Rule of their Religion."

[4] Locke, *Third Letter for Toleration*, p. 151.

church of England to be freely preached, and its worship set up, in any popish, Mahometan, or pagan country."[5]

Indeed, in the later *Letters*, papists are routinely referred to by Locke as being well within the pale. Richard Ashcraft may be right to say that "there is no reason to believe that, in the whole of his life, Locke ever doubted that Catholicism was a theologically ridiculous...doctrine."[6] But of course that doesn't establish its intolerability. Locke's strategy in the *Letters* is always to acknowledge the absurdity of various beliefs which at the same time he insists are nevertheless to be given the benefit of toleration. When he makes a long list of doctrines or practices whose evident perversity should not disqualify them from toleration, it reads something like this: "socinians, papists, anabaptists, quakers, presbyterians," as well as "jews, mahometans, and Pagans."[7] Or, again, consider this phrasing from the *Second Letter Concerning Toleration*: "Suppose the controversy between a Lutheran and a papist; or, if you please, between a presbyterian magistrate and a quaker subject..."[8] Here papism is included in the examples Locke uses in his defense of toleration as effortlessly and as casually as you please. When he argues for the civil rights of Jews in the *Third Letter*, Locke asks : "[W]hy might not Jews, pagans, and Mahometans be admitted to the rights of the commonwealth, as far as papists, independents, and quakers?"[9] This pervasive affirmative evidence in favor of Catholicism's inclusion within the breadth of Lockean toleration is very seldom cited by those who have convinced themselves somehow that he *must* have found the Roman Catholic religion intolerable.

I guess that what people *read* as Locke's rejection of the toleration of Roman Catholics is a passage like the following:

That Church can have no right to be tolerated by the Magistrate which is constituted upon such a bottom, that all those who enter into it do thereby, *ipso facto*, deliver themselves up to the Protection and Service of another Prince. For by this means the Magistrate would give way to the settling of a foreign jurisdiction in his own country. (LCT: 50)

---

[5] Locke, *Second Letter Concerning Toleration*, pp. 64–5. Conversely, he says to his opponent, "your way of applying force will as much promote popery in France, as protestantism in England" (ibid. p. 77).

[6] Ashcraft, *Revolutionary Politics*, p. 99.

[7] Locke, *Third Letter for Toleration*, p. 229. This is not to mention the use he makes of lists like "transubstantiation, consubstantiation, real presence" (ibid., p. 240) – a list which comprises not only Roman doctrine but also doctrines of the holy sacrament that have at various times been orthodoxy in the Church of England.

[8] Locke, *Second Letter Concerning Toleration*, p. 100.   [9] Locke, *Third Letter for Toleration*, p. 231.

Though the point is described here in purely abstract terms, we are all supposed to know to whom he is referring. In fact, an example *is* given. However, it is not the example of Catholics, but rather of certain Muslim persuasions:

It is ridiculous for any one to profess himself to be a *Mahumetan* only in his Religion, but in everything else a faithful Subject to a Christian Magistrate, whilst at the same time he acknowledges himself bound to yield blind obedience to the *Mufti* of *Constantinople*; who himself is intirely obedient to the Ottoman Emperor, and frames the feigned Oracles of that Religion according to his pleasure. (LCT: 50)

Richard Ashcraft thinks it obvious that "a Mahumetan" here is a metaphor for James II (and "the Mufti of Constantinople" presumably a metaphor for the Pope). I'm not sure how we are supposed to know this: presumably it is on the basis of other passages in the *Letters*, but since there is no direct textual support for the exclusion of Catholics, presumably the passages that this interpretation relies on *also* have to be given a non-literal interpretation to constitute evidence which might persuade us to read this passage metaphorically. Notice also that this passage cannot even be read as a denial of toleration to Muslims. Throughout the *Letters*, Locke is firm and explicit: "neither Pagan nor Mahometan, nor Jew, ought to be excluded from the civil rights of the commonwealth because of his religion" (LCT: 56). The example is used rather to show that if someone *did* combine faith in Islam with political allegiance to the Mufti of Constantinople, he would put himself beyond the pale of toleration *by virtue of the combination*, not by virtue of his Muslim faith alone. And that I believe is the same as his position on Catholics; more of that in a moment.

Besides this passage about allegiance to a foreign power, Locke also talks about the danger posed by men who "attribute unto the Faithful, the Religious and Orthodox, that is, in plain terms, unto themselves, any peculiar Privilege of Power above other Mortals, in Civil Concernments" (LCT: 50). He mentions, for example, the rule that "*Faith is not to be kept with Hereticks,*" or the principles that "*Dominion is founded in Grace*" and that "*Kings excommunicated forfeit their Crowns and Kingdoms*" (LCT: 50). These, Locke says, have no right to be tolerated by the magistrate.[10] It is well known that doctrines like these have been associated with Roman

---

[10] Also there is to be no toleration for those "that will not own and teach the Duty of tolerating All men in matters of meer Religion" (LCT: 50). Again, this can't be applied exclusively to Roman Catholics. It evidently applies to many Protestant sects, including of course the Church of England in Locke's lifetime.

Catholicism; and they were the professed basis of the *de jure* exclusion of
Catholics from English public life in the 1689 settlement. But again, what
is striking in the *Letter* is how careful Locke is to characterize these views
in general terms, so that their link with Rome or with any particular
religious sect is understood as contingent rather than necessary.

True, Locke does refer to some of these doctrines as "secret Evil"
(LCT: 49), and he does sometimes see the secretive character of Roman
Catholic political practice as a threat.[11] So maybe in these passages he
is matching that secretiveness with his own esoteric specifications. But
I don't think we should be too Straussian about this.[12] There was no
particular reason for Locke to talk in code about the refusal of toleration
to Catholics if that is what he believed. It was orthodox state practice
in England at the time the *Letter Concerning Toleration* was published and
the later *Letters*, which I have cited extensively, were written.[13] Moreover
Locke had no qualms about speaking explicitly about these issues in his
early works on toleration, when he did clearly hold this view. "Papists,"
he said in *An Essay on Toleration* published in 1667, "are not to enjoy
the benefit of toleration" – which is, he adds, no less than they de-
serve, because of their own pitiless cruelty.[14] And in that 1667 essay, he
argues explicitly against trying to disaggregate the different strands of
Catholicism:

> Since men usually take up their religion in gross, and assume to themselves the
> opinions of their party all at once in a bundle, it often happens that they mix
> with their religious worship and speculative opinions other doctrines absolutely
> destructive to the society wherein they live, as is evident in the Roman Catholics
> that are subjects of any prince but the Pope.[15]

Now even there, where he is explicitly taking this very hard line, Locke
concedes that the magistrate *may* tolerate the Catholic religion if he has
some assurance "that he can allow one part without the spreading of
the other," and that the subversive opinions "will not be imbibed and
espoused by all those who communicate with them in their religious
worship."[16] And he thought in 1667 that securing that assurance, that

---

[11] See Ashcraft, *Revolutionary Politics*, pp. 502–3.
[12] Cf. Rabieh, "Reasonableness of Locke," defending the argument of Strauss, "Locke's Doctrine
of Natural Law," pp. 499–501.
[13] Historically, Locke was well known to be associated in the 1680s with a faction opposed to the
repeal of the Test Acts; and he was associated with the success of the Revolution which embedded
the Acts even more firmly in English public life. There was no political reason whatever for him
to conceal or keep implicit his opposition to the toleration of Roman Catholics, if that was really
his position.
[14] Locke, "Essay on Toleration," p. 152.   [15] Ibid., p. 146.   [16] Ibid.

disaggregation of opinions, would be very difficult. But by the 1690s, when the first *Letter Concerning Toleration* is published, and the subsequent *Letters* written, Locke evidently has less difficulty with disaggregation, and he is therefore not prepared to say that papists *as such* may not be tolerated. The most he is prepared to say is that certain specific political doctrines may not be tolerated. So, although Catholicism does spring to mind as an example of such political subversiveness, Locke is also able to cite Catholicism as a routine example of one tolerable religion among others in a multi-faith society.

II

By contrast, in Locke's mature thought on these matters, the refusal of toleration to atheists is as explicit as one could wish. Locke says, "those are not at all to be tolerated who deny the Being of a God. Promises, Covenants, and Oaths, which are the Bonds of Humane Society, can have no hold upon an Atheist. The taking away of God, tho but even in thought, dissolves all" (LCT: 51). That sounds pretty apocalyptic: "The taking away of God . . . even in thought, dissolves all." Maybe John Dunn puts it a little too strongly when he writes that Locke saw atheism "as a sort of spiritual equivalent of AIDS in the most hysterical contemporary understandings."[17] But Locke did see atheists as some sort of all-purpose menace, and this precisely because of what they did and did not believe. What is it exactly about religious skepticism[18] that posed this menace for Locke? What is it about atheism that poses such a menace, according to the author of the *Letter Concerning Toleration*?[19]

One reason Locke gives in the passage just quoted is that promises, covenants, and oaths, which he says "are the Bonds of Humane Society," can have no hold upon an atheist (LCT: 52). He is assuming that the social fabric depends on commitments underpinned by the fear of God – people's ability to give undertakings to one another that can be relied on (even in the face of great danger and temptation) because they were given in the presence of God – undertakings that can lend some stability and predictability to human affairs. (I don't just mean commercial contracts, but also things like the Mayflower Covenant: a few people on the edge

---

[17] Dunn, "What is Living and What is Dead," p. 19.

[18] For the equation of "atheism" and "scepticism," see Locke, *A Third Letter for Toleration*, p. 415.

[19] Locke himself was sometimes accused of a form of Socinianism bordering on atheism. W. M. Spellman notes that "[i]n 1697 the Grand Jury of Middlesex presented as a nuisance *The Reasonableness of Christianity* on the grounds that it denied the Trinity and forwarded Arianism, Socinianism, atheism, and Deism" (Spellman, *John Locke*, p. 130).

of a wilderness pledging their support to one another in circumstances where they will die without it.)[20] In this connection, we must remember that Locke is not relying on traditional forms of hierarchy for stability and social cohesion in his politics: he has to make promissory undertakings, and the spirit of such undertakings among otherwise free and equal individuals do an amount of work in moral and political philosophy that his more conservative critics regarded as reckless, to say the least. Promises and contracts cannot do that work unless they are backed up with the fear of God, in whose presence the undertakings in question have been given.

Intriguingly, in Book I of *The Essay Concerning Human Understanding*, Locke considered possible alternative reasons why people might think that they ought to keep their promises. (In context, this is intended to illustrate the point that moral rules are not self-evident, but always based on reasons.)

> That Men should keep their Compacts, is certainly a great and undeniable Rule in Morality: But yet, if a Christian, who has the view of Happiness and Misery in another Life, be asked why a Man must keep his Word, he will *give* this as a *Reason*: Because God, who has the Power of eternal Life and Death, requires it of us. But if an *Hobbist* be asked why; he will answer: Because the Publick requires it, and the *Leviathan* will punish you if you do not. And if one of the old *Heathen* Philosophers had been asked, he would have answer'd: Because it was dishonest, below the Dignity of a Man, and opposite to Vertue, the highest Perfection of humane Nature, to do otherwise. (E: 1.3.5)[21]

It's an interesting passage, first because it seems to illustrate, in Locke's work, something like a Rawlsian *overlapping consensus*,[22] and secondly because it seems to represent a much more generous overlapping consensus than Locke is prepared to acknowledge in the *Letter Concerning Toleration*. For here we are to imagine that a Hobbist (whom Locke certainly regarded as pretty much equivalent to an atheist) might yet have some reason for keeping his promises; and if that is so, it is not at all clear that the atheist (at least of the Hobbist persuasion) is the sort of general menace that the Locke of the *Letter* says he is. I guess it is possible to reconstruct an argument to reconcile the two passages. The Hobbist relies on fear of Leviathan to motivate promise-keeping. Yet, as Locke and

---

[20] "This whole adventure," said the Mayflower compactors, "growes upon the joint confidence we have in each others fidelity and resolution herein, so as no man of us would have adventured it without assurance of the rest." (See Arendt, *On Revolution*, p. 173.)

[21] Marshall, *John Locke*, p. 302, reckons that "Heathen Philosophers" is a reference to Cicero.

[22] Compare Rawls, *Political Liberalism*, pp. 133 ff. (I shall return to this theme of overlapping consensus later in the chapter: see pp. 230–1 and 236–40.)

Hobbes both know, Leviathan or organized civil society is supposed to be constituted by promises and contracts, and *those* promises, by definition, cannot themselves be supported by the power of the state. As I said before, Locke's particular worry about atheists may have less to do with their day-to-day involvement in social and commercial life, and more with the attitude they are likely to take to the very foundations of the social order.

More generally, Locke sees divine sanctions as key to the whole enterprise of morality and natural law. "[T]he true ground of Morality . . . can only be the Will and Law of a God, who sees Men in the dark, has in his Hand Rewards and Punishments, and Power enough to call to account the proudest Offender" (E: 1.3.6). True, in the *Essay* he acknowledges that God has, "by an inseparable connexion, joined virtue and public happiness together, and made the practice thereof necessary to the preservation of society, and visibly beneficial to all" (ibid.), so that in principle one might base one's whole morality on earthly convenience without any thought of God and his sanctions.[23] But elsewhere (particularly in *The Reasonableness of Christianity*), Locke insists on the inadequacy of a purely interest-based account of natural law. Though "[t]he law of nature, is the law of convenience too," yet so conceived, it can never really "rise to the force of a law" (RC: 142): "That could not be, without a clear knowledge and acknowledgment of the law-maker, and the great rewards and punishments for those that would, or would not obey him" (RC: 144). The idea of God is necessary for the idea of natural law to distinguish it from mere "conveniences of common life, and laudable practices" (ibid.), and to show "the strictness as well as obligation of its injunctions . . . with the inforcement of unspeakable rewards and punishments in another world" (RC: 122).

And it's not just divine sanctions; awareness of the existence of God also underpins people's ability to take seriously the idea of objective right answers to the moral questions to which their actions give rise. For example, think how important it is for Locke, in his theory of revolution, to be able to invoke the idea of an "appeal to Heaven,"[24] which is not at all the

---

[23] "[S]elf-interest, and the Conveniences of this Life, make many Men, own an outward Profession and Approbation of [moral principles], whose Actions sufficiently prove, that they very little consider the Law-giver, that prescribed these rules; nor the Hell he has ordain'd for the Punishment of those that transgress them" (E: 1.2.6). This is one of the grounds on which Leo Strauss has argued that Locke was some sort of crypto-Hobbesian himself, and not really a believer in a strong deontic notion of natural law at all: see Strauss, 'Locke's Doctrine of Natural Law,' pp. 499–501.

[24] See 2nd T: 21, citing the story of Jephtha from Judges 11:27.

same as an appeal for divine intervention, but a kind of acknowledgment that a person embarking on a course of active resistance makes to show that he understands there really is an objective right and wrong of the matter, and that he is ready to take the consequences at God's hands if it turns out that he is disturbing the peace and order of the realm for no good reason. In the chapters on resistance and revolution in the *Second Treatise*, Locke is evidently quite worried by the possibility (or at least by the criticism) that his doctrine will expose law and the state to disorder and ruin "as often as it shall please a busie head, or turbulent spirit, to desire the alteration of the Government" (2nd T: 230). He attempts to rebut the worry by insisting that such resistance will not happen as a matter of fact, unless tyranny is both genuine and general. But also he relies very much on the caution inspired by the idea of an appeal to heaven. "*God* in heaven... alone... is Judge of the Right (2nd T: 241). "[*F*]*orce* is to be *opposed* to nothing, but to unjust and unlawful *Force*; whoever makes any opposition in any other Case, draws on himself a just Condemnation both from God and Man" (2nd T: 204). Well, the atheist can't think in this way; this is not a way in which he can take his actions seriously. So, again, the apprehension would be that an atheist might be much more reckless in this regard, and thus politically and socially much more dangerous, than a God-fearing subject.

III

On the whole, I have opposed any interpretation of Locke that involved trying to read between the lines. But now I want to deviate from that practice and propose one additional line of argument about the intolerability of atheism, of which I can find only one or two hints in Locke's explicit argument in the *Letter Concerning Toleration*.

One aspect, it seems to me, of the general menace posed by the atheist in Locke's moral and political system, is that the atheist cannot really get hold of the notion of human equality. On Locke's account, the atheist doesn't have the wherewithal to make sense of that idea. He has no notion of human individuals as God's workmanship or God's property, let alone of their being "sent into the World by his order, and about his business... made to last during his, not one another's Pleasure" (2nd T: 6). His conception of the essence of the human species will be as chaotic and indeterminate as Locke's in Book III of the *Essay* – I mean the skepticism about species and their criteria and boundaries that we found in the *Essay*'s discussion of real and nominal essences. As we saw in Chapter 3, in order to get anything remotely approaching human equality out of that, there had to be some basis of interest or value that could rivet our attention on certain human attributes as range properties. Maybe the Hobbesian desire for survival could be the basis of a human equality founded on mutual fear.[25] But it would not be a *moralized* equality; it would not be the basis for a strong theory of natural rights of the sort that Locke insists upon. And my argument there was that no one who denied the being of a God or His interest or relevance to human affairs could be expected to come up with the sort of basis for equality that Locke came up with. Locke emphasized possession of a degree of rationality that consists in the power of abstraction and the power to relate an abstraction like God to the idea of one's own actions and one's own person. That particular moral capacity might strike an atheist as *interesting*, perhaps. But there is no reason to suppose that the atheist would think it made sense to draw any sort of important line at the threshold of that capacity, let alone think that beings endowed with such capacity were for that reason to be treated as special and sacred in the way Locke thought. Or if the atheist did just *stake a normative claim* on this threshold, one would be inclined to suspect that the reason for choosing this threshold rather than some other was that this was the one that has traditionally been identified – as it happens, on religious grounds – as the basis of human equality. Like someone using the cadences of the Book of Common Prayer to design his own "secular" marriage vows, the atheist would at best be taking advantage of a tradition that he pretended to repudiate, and doing so in a way that was quite disingenuous about the difficulties that have to be faced in this area.

Left entirely to his own devices, then, the atheist could not really be relied on to get hold of, or suffuse his actions and deliberations with, the principle of human equality – this principle that is so important in Locke's theories about consent, natural rights, slavery, property, the common good, and the basis of political representation. If he had a rights theory, it might be too radical a rights theory: for the atheist cannot really grasp the basis of the inalienability of human rights.[26] And if he cannot grasp that, he cannot grasp the point that a certain sort of respect is due to each one of God's human creatures *as such*, irrespective of what they have chosen or what their value is. The atheist, then, is not just a menace to society; he is, as John Dunn puts it, "an inherent menace to every other

---

[25] Hobbes, *Leviathan*, Ch. 13, p. 87. (Cf. Chapter 3, above, pp. 77–8.)
[26] Cf. Tuck, *Natural Rights Theories*, pp. 49–50.

human being" according to Locke.[27] True, acknowledging the existence of God is no *guarantee* that one will come up with the right view about equality or the right mode of respect for other persons as equals. Robert Filmer and the Anglican divines who republished his work are sufficient evidence of that. But at least in their case there is something to work on – if not the actual scriptures, then the *idea* of a God and his human creatures – which might provide some sort of leverage for arguments about equality and the implications of equality.

That's my hunch – or rather, that's my inference – for it seems to me that the notion of human equality is so essential to the fabric of Lockean politics and Lockean morality that there can be no question of allowing any person who does not grasp it, or who denies the main foundation of it, to play any sort of significant part in politics. Admittedly the textual basis for this inference is quite slim. I believe it follows as a particular instance of Locke's general assertion that "The taking away of God, tho but even in thought, dissolves all" (LCT: 51), i.e. dissolves the whole framework of natural law equality, and not just the fear of sanctions that motivates compliance with it. It can be discerned also in the sentence with which Locke concludes the passage on atheism in the *Letter Concerning Toleration*, where he says: "As for other Practical Opinions . . . *if they do not tend to establish Domination over others* . . . there can be no reason why they should not be tolerated" (LCT: 51). The tendency "to establish Domination over others" – that seems to be the hallmark of a religious view or a view about religion that is intolerable. And that's my clue: if the general issue of domination is regarded by Locke as the fallback criterion of intolerability, then it does look as though this issue of equality may rightly be regarded as a litmus test, and one reason for refusing toleration to the atheist is that he is in no position to maintain it, or teach it, or interpret it, or apply it, except by disingenuous imitation of those who own up to its real basis.

IV

My theme has been "Christian Equality" in Locke's political thought, but it is pretty clear that in all this stuff about dangers of denying the existence of God, Locke's main concern has been with theism (belief in God) as such, rather than specifically with Christian theism. Though much of the *Letter Concerning Toleration* is about "the mutual Toleration of *Christians*

---

[27] Dunn, "The Claim to Freedom of Conscience," p. 179.

in their different Professions of Religion" (LCT: 23 – my emphasis), still the *Letter* recognizes the sense in tolerating Jews, Muslims, and others, even though they accept little or nothing of the specifically Christian revelation.

Is this because they are at least monotheistic? It is never entirely clear whether atheism includes polytheism for Locke. There are some passages about tolerating pagans in the *Letters Concerning Toleration*, which seem to indicate that Greek and Roman polytheism gets under the bar.[28] But there are also passages about the ancients and the unsatisfactory state of their theories of morality, which seem to indicate that polytheism might lie beyond the pale.

There was no part of mankind, who had quicker parts, or improved them more; that had a greater light of reason, or followed it farther in all sorts of speculations, than the Athenians: and yet we find but one Socrates amongst them, that opposed and laughed at their polytheism, and wrong opinion of the Deity. (RC: 136)

The passage is not conclusive by any means, and Locke is mainly at pains to show that philosophy unaided often couldn't even get to first base so far as the derivation of morality was concerned. But it hints at a suggestion that, as long as there is no acknowledgment of "one invisible God" (RC: 137), there will always be serious moral deficiency. Maybe the fear of God subsides a little if you can play off one god against another; or maybe, as some have argued, polytheism sits uncomfortably with basic equality, since there might be different types of human being as there are different types and levels of god for them to be created in the image of.[29]

Anyway, leaving polytheism aside, Locke seems committed to the view that the main monotheistic religions are certainly within the pale. Their theologies do not threaten the foundations of social order, which I have interpreted to include, indeed to be pervaded by, the principle of basic equality. What does this do, then, to my argument in the preceding chapters that there is in fact a distinctively *Christian* content to Locke's own conception of equality? Well, it is hard to figure out, and Locke's views certainly have changed over time. Basically, I think there is supposed to be a difference between what is said to be required as a matter of elementary public safety, and what is required so far as the detailed elaboration of a particular theory is concerned. There may be something

[28] See Locke, *Third Letter for Toleration*, pp. 228–32.
[29] I am grateful to George Fletcher for some discussion of this issue.

like a distinction between *concept* and *conception* here.[30] A person with the idea of God can reason to the *concept* of equality and use that concept in his theorizing about social order and natural law; but he may need something more specific in the way of religious truth in order to develop a detailed *conception* of social policy. I don't think Locke believed one could get very far towards the truth about property and economy, for example, without attributing at least some specifically Judeo-Christian content to the evaluation of modes of subsistence. As I said in Chapter 6, he figures out some of the details of what equality requires in these contexts by reference to the meaning of biblical texts like "[b]e fruitful, and multiply, and replenish the earth, and subdue it."[31] Now admittedly that's a passage from the Old Testament and so it is something held in common among Christians, Jews, and Muslims also, who Locke thought "derived and borrowed" many of their doctrines from the Judeo-Christian heritage (RC: 137). But there may be elements that require a more particular elaboration – for example, elements of the doctrine of charity that can only be understood in light of the story of the good Samaritan or the parable of the sheep and the goats.[32]

Unfortunately, Locke does not say much about any monotheistic belief that exists entirely outside the Judeo-Christian framework. At one point in *The Reasonableness of Christianity*, he asks how those people in the world stand who were not the beneficiaries of God's revelation of Himself in ancient Israel. (We mentioned Socrates a moment ago: an isolated monotheist, but not a Judeo-Christian monotheist, in a culture of polytheism.) Locke's answer suggests that such people can get at least to the bare idea of God and of His moral significance by the fairly elementary processes of reasoning that I talked about in Chapters 3 and 4:

Many to whom the promise of the Messiah never came . . . were never in a capacity to believe or reject that revelation; yet God had, by the light of reason, revealed to all mankind, who would make use of that light, that he was good and merciful. The same spark of the divine nature and knowledge in man, which making him a man, showed him the law he was under, as a man; showed him also the way of atoning the merciful, kind, compassionate Author and Father of him and his being, when he had transgressed that law. He that made use of this candle of the Lord, so far as to find what was his duty, could not miss to find also the way to reconciliation and forgiveness, when he had failed of his duty: though if he used not his reason in this way, if he put out or neglected this light, he might, perhaps, see neither. (RC: 133)

---

[30] For the concept/conception distinction, see Dworkin, *Taking Rights Seriously*, pp. 134–6.
[31] Genesis 1:28.
[32] For the Good Samaritan, see Luke 10:25–37. For the parable of the sheep and goats, see Matthew 25:31–46, discussed by Locke at RC: 127.

On this basis, people outside the Judeo-Christian heritage might be able to share with those inside it some sort of consensus (like a Rawlsian "overlapping consensus")[33] on the broad outlines of divine rewards and punishments, on the requirement to keep one's promises, and on the basics of human equality. How much of the natural law theory you could get right on this basis, and how much would need the resources of a particular body of theological belief may have been something Locke vacillated about in the latter years of his life. Certainly there are passages in the *Reasonableness* which suggest that the specific teachings of Jesus Christ are indispensable; though there too, as we saw earlier in this chapter, a Christian orientation is no guarantee that you will get the details right.[34] Still, if someone cannot even reason his way to the *concept* of a religious foundation for morality and for our status as equals – if he does not have the elementary theistic premise, in the light of which moral responsibility and human equality become sensible and compelling ideas – then I think what Locke is saying is that he is not just likely to get the detail wrong, he becomes a general menace, who probably shouldn't be counted on for anything very much in social and political life.

v

What does Locke's refusal of toleration to the atheist amount to? What does he think should happen to an atheist by virtue of the fact that he is "not at all to be tolerated"?

These questions present something of an embarrassment for Locke's account. The most powerful argument in the *Letter Concerning Toleration* is that religion is a matter of authentic belief, and belief cannot be coerced by political power because belief is not subject to the will.[35] Now presumably this is as true of the elemental belief in the existence of God as it is of any of the detailed doctrines of any particular religion. An atheist cannot *choose* to believe in God, and so we cannot pressure his choices in order to get him to have the right beliefs. It is not just a point about the importance of respecting beliefs. If that were all, Locke might be able to get away with saying that "those that by their Atheism undermine and destroy all Religion, can have no pretence of Religion whereupon to challenge the Privilege of a Toleration" (LCT: 51). He might say they are not entitled to have their beliefs respected because they stake nothing in the way of their own salvation on the integrity of their beliefs. John

---

[33] Rawls, *Political Liberalism*, pp. xvii ff. and 133 ff.   [34] See above, p. 228.
[35] See LCT: 26–7. See also Waldron, "Locke, Toleration and the Rationality of Persecution," pp. 94–6.

Dunn makes much of this point in his interpretation.[36] But actually I don't think this argument works at all. What the atheists happen to think does not affect their accountability for their beliefs to God; nor does it change the complex mystery of the granting or withholding of His grace in belief or unbelief (LCT: 38). The fact that *in their own view* the atheists stake nothing in the way of their own salvation on the integrity of their beliefs does not except them from the benefit of the general point that Locke makes about the importance of the relation between man and God in respect of belief. In the case of believers, the point is supposed to be objective: it is not about the importance of respecting what the believer *thinks* is his relation to God in regard of his beliefs, it is a point about respecting what that relation actually is. And so it is not a point that can vary depending on whether you're dealing with a theist or an atheist. So, when Locke says in the *Letter* that "this at least is certain, that no Religion, which I believe not to be true, can either be true or profitable unto me" (LCT: 38), that has to be applied to the atheist as well. And it's not clear why the immediate inference does not also apply: "[a]nd therefore, when all is done, they must be left to their own Consciences" (ibid.).

The same is true of the point about coercion. "[S]uch is the nature of the Understanding, that it cannot be compell'd to the belief of any thing by outward force" (LCT: 27). The most that coercion can produce in an atheist, on Locke's account, is presumably a willingness to *say* that God exists and perhaps a willingness to act accordingly. But that's not enough to avoid the general Lockean argument in the *Letter* about the ineffectiveness of human penalties. Indeed Locke's argument that political power can produce only a hollow mockery of religion would apply as much to the atheist as it would to any other religious dissenter. If "[i]t is in vain for an Unbeliever," it is presumably also in vain for an atheist "to take up the outward shew of another mans [religious] Profession" purely to avoid the force of the magistrate's sword (LCT: 38).

These questions of what to *do* about the atheist go to the heart of our interest in equality. In order to treat other persons as one's equals, one has to view them in a certain light, i.e. in light of certain beliefs about their attributes and their relation to their Creator. But then there may be a problem enforcing the basis of this egalitarian orientation, for it involves enforcing beliefs. We might say that respect for equality can be enforced at the level of action even if the beliefs that are supposed to

---

[36] Dunn, "The Claim to Freedom of Conscience," p. 181.

ground equality are not enforced. But that is in some tension with the suggestion I made in Chapter 3 that one may not be able to get the actions right unless they are shaped in one's deliberations by the right beliefs. Another possibility is that equality may be secured in the basic structure of a Lockean society, i.e. in its laws and institutions, even if it cannot be enforced in the minds and ethics of the people. But doubts have been expressed in recent political philosophy about approaches of this general character. For example, G. A. Cohen has argued against Rawls that there cannot be a stable and effective basic structure dedicated to equality unless an egalitarian ethos is implicit in the lives and motivations of the citizens.[37] I suspect Locke would say something similar: atheists are a menace precisely because the integrity of the social and political structure is not independent of what ordinary people think. So we are left with the problem of what can be done about this menace in light of what the *Letter* says is possible and impossible so far as affecting people's beliefs is concerned.

Presumably the same difficulties would apply to the refusal of toleration to Catholics, if the common interpretation of Locke's views on that were correct. I don't think Richard Ashcraft would accept the argument that I made at the beginning of the lecture (though he should). But Ashcraft argues that to the extent that Locke *was* hostile to the toleration of Catholics, he

was prepared to argue not only that force employed against Catholics was a justifiable political policy . . . but also, and inconsistently with the presuppositions of his own general argument, he maintained that the application of force even carried with it the prospects that Catholics would abandon their religious beliefs and join the ranks of Protestantism. That a thinker such as Locke would tolerate such a glaring inconsistency can only be explained in terms of an attitude so deeply held that no reasoned argument against it . . . could overrule its explanatory status as an axiom of political life in seventeenth century England.[38]

Maybe the view that force can yield results when applied to Catholics becomes slightly more plausible if one accepts the Lockean claim that Catholic ceremonies and teachings are literally *absurd*. I guess the more absurd they are, the more indirect efficacy force might have in jolting somebody out of the corresponding beliefs. And maybe Locke thought something like that about atheism. Maybe he was thinking that the existence of God is so obvious that it's just a matter of forcing people to look

---

[37] Cohen, *If You're an Egalitarian, How Come You're So Rich?*, pp. 136–40.
[38] Ashcraft, *Revolutionary Politics*, pp. 100–1.

and see and consider. After all, we were all atheists once, says Locke: this is a fault "which we were every one of us once guilty of."[39] In the *Third Letter for Toleration*, Locke even suggested that the main obstacle to religion was ethical: if magistrates would only "interpose their power . . . against drunkenness, lasciviousness, and all sorts of debauchery . . . and by their administration, countenance, and example, reduce the irregularities of men's manners . . . and bring sobriety, peaceableness, industry, and honesty into fashion,"[40] then men would not turn against "the light of their reason, [and] do violence to their understandings and forsake truth, and salvation, too."[41] Certainly we know that Locke believed the argument for God's existence was elementary – not of course innate – but something which required no particularly abstruse reasoning and might be arrived at by the intellect of the plainest person.

Elsewhere, Locke takes a rather less sanguine view of the problem. He observed in the *Essay* that there have been many serious thinkers who denied the existence of God. (In *The Reasonableness of Christianity* he mentioned the rather casual polytheism of the Greek philosophers (RC: 136), a polytheism that came close to indifference as to whether or not there really was a God in a morally significant sense.) "Besides the Atheists, taken notice of amongst the Ancients, and left branded upon the Records of History, hath not Navigation discovered, in these later Ages, whole Nations, at the Bay of *Soldania*, in *Brazil*, . . . and in the *Caribbee* islands, etc., amongst whom there was to be found no Notion of a God, no religion" (E: 1.4.8). And he hazarded the suggestion – quite dangerous, one would have thought, to his own enterprise – that there may be more atheists around even in England than is generally believed. Close attention, says Locke, to "the lives and discourses of people not so far off" might reveal

that many, in more civilized Countries, have no very strong, and clear Impressions of a Deity upon their Minds; and that the Complaints of Atheism, made from the Pulpit are not without Reason. And though only some profligate Wretches own it . . . barefacedly now; yet perhaps, we should hear, more than we do, of it, from others, did not the fear of the Magistrate's Sword . . . tie up People's Tongues; which, were the Apprehension[ ] of Punishment . . . taken away, would as openly proclaim their *Atheism*, as their lives do. (E: 1.4.8)

However, this passage is interesting also in its suggestion that what law can do is *suppress* atheism – that is, prevent it from being proclaimed and ensure that it doesn't acquire the sort of wildfire popularity that

---

[39] Locke, *Third Letter for Toleration*, p. 233.   [40] Ibid., p. 469.   [41] Ibid., p. 470.

might follow if its public avowal did not have to be furtive. That may help a little with the problems we have been wrestling with for the last few paragraphs. Toleration, in Locke's system, is a multifaceted ideal. It includes not only refraining from attempts at the forcible imposition of beliefs, but also not prohibiting speech or gatherings or organizations, and not disqualifying those of minority religions from public life. Now even if it does not make sense for Locke to withdraw the benefit of the first of these elements of toleration from the atheist – since there is little prospect of forcible conversion – still the other aspects of toleration *can* sensibly be withdrawn, and atheist organizations crushed and atheists excluded from common and public life.

VI

It goes without saying that, as a bottom-line political position, this view – that atheists should be excluded from public life – is not an option for us. But the bottom-line is not everything.[42] And the fact that we don't buy the bottom-line does not mean we should not be exercised by Locke's reason for arriving at that bottom-line – namely, his conviction that a society inhabited by a significant number of people who deny the existence of God is running a grave risk with its public morality. We must not reason from rejection of Locke's solution to the non-existence of the problem he identified. Apart from anything else, there actually is continuing controversy in modern liberal philosophy about the foundations of equality and human rights and about the extent to which these can be sustained without religious belief. Some approach even the legal idea of equality in explicitly religious terms, and the most recent book-length treatment of equality as a political ideal is skeptical about any purely secular foundation.[43] We take equality seriously, and – at least for us theorists – it is an open question what that requires of us in the way of moral and philosophical foundations. Somewhere hard work has to be done on the question of whether basic equality can be made sense of, philosophically, in purely secular terms. John Locke's reasons for thinking that atheists should be excluded from public life may not be reasons of public policy for us; but they are still relevant to our philosophical enterprise of trying to arrive at a comprehensive grounding for and justification of our commitment to this ideal.

---

[42] See Waldron, "What Plato Would Allow."

[43] See e.g., Fletcher, "In God's Image," p. 1608, and also Coons and Brennan, *By Nature Equal*, pp. 145–214,

Beyond that, we have the debate surrounding John Rawls's "political" liberalism, and his views about public reason and the ability of public reason to accommodate arguments that proceed from religious premises.[44] Suppose – as I am inclined to believe – that a commitment to human equality is most coherent and attractive when it is grounded in theological truth, truths associated particularly with the Christian heritage. On Rawls's account, that is a comprehensive philosophical conception. It offers perhaps a path to an important principle that a political theory of justice must take seriously; Rawls, for example, recognizes that basic equality is crucial to justice.[45] But it is an undoubtedly sectarian path, for it appeals to considerations that many people in society claim they can make no sense of, or to considerations that make them acutely uncomfortable and require them to modify or rethink the basis of their own comprehensive convictions. Rawls is not saying that religious conceptions of equality or religious paths to equality are crazy or unreasonable. But there is no question of their representing a consensus for a well-ordered society under modern conditions. There is, he says, in modern society a diversity of comprehensive doctrines, some religious and some not, and since this diversity "is not a mere historical condition that may soon pass away," everyone has to recognize that the ascendancy of any one such comprehensive doctrine can be maintained only by "the oppressive use of state power."[46] Now, he says, it is a crucial presupposition of modern liberalism that state power is to be used to sustain only the political structure of liberalism, and citizens must be left to work out for themselves how this relates to their personal comprehensive convictions.[47] Rawls leaves us then with two conclusions, so far as the religious basis of equality is concerned. First, the religious basis of equality may not be adopted or established as the official ideology of equality; and second, even individual citizens are not to appeal to their own convictions about the religious basis of equality in deciding how to exercise their own political power, in deciding how to vote on the basics of justice, for example, or in influencing the votes of others.[48] The two conclusions are connected by the Rawlsian idea of *public reason*. The basic social and

[44] Rawls, *Political Liberalism*, pp. 212 ff.   [45] See ibid., pp. 19 and 79–81.   [46] Ibid., pp. 36–7.
[47] Ibid., p. 138: "When there is a plurality of reasonable doctrines, it is unreasonable or worse to want to use the sanctions of state power to correct, or to punish, those who disagree with us."
[48] Ibid., pp. 225–6. "In discussing constitutional essentials and matters of basic justice we are not to appeal to comprehensive religious or philosophical doctrines – to what we as individuals or members of associations see as the whole truth... [C]itizens are to conduct their fundamental discussions within the framework of what each regards as a political conception of justice based on values that the others can reasonably be expected to endorse."

political structure of a well-ordered society is sustained and elaborated through the deliberation and decisions of officials and citizens exercising various political powers. The medium of deliberation and decision is public reason, and since that is the medium through which state power is exercised, it must be kept free of any taint of sectarian philosophical conviction. There must be a commitment on the part of all who participate in public reason to offer up and to act upon only those reasons that it is reasonable to expect that others involved and others affected can accept.[49]

Much of the modern debate about Rawlsian public reason surrounds the second of his conclusions – that citizens may not appeal to their religious convictions in voting or in arguing for particular political positions.[50] And clearly the issues we have been studying are relevant to that. If the Lockean view that I have been outlining is correct, it may be impossible to articulate certain important egalitarian commitments without appealing to what one takes to be their religious grounds. If so, the Rawlsian exclusion seems unreasonable.[51] Rawls's view may seem appealing so long as we are assured that any reasonable political position can be defended within the confines of public reason, as he understands it; but if there are certain otherwise reasonable positions that cannot be defended in that way, than Rawls's view begins to look arbitrary, especially if the upshot is to remove the positions in question from the political agenda, rather than modify the constraints of public reason to accommodate them.[52]

But of course the Lockean position goes far beyond this debate. Locke is not just saying that religious argumentation about equality should be permitted in public life; he is arguing that it is indispensable. I emphasize "religious argumentation *about equality*." Locke in general is not inhospitable to something like Rawlsian constraints of public reason. He does not believe that religious considerations should be introduced willy-nilly

---

[49] Ibid., pp. 215 ff.
[50] In support of something like the Rawlsian position, see Audi, "Separation of Church and State"; Greenawalt, *Religious Convictions and Political Choice*; and Nagel, "Moral Conflict and Political Legitimacy." For the other side, see Raz, "Facing Diversity"; Connolly, *Why I am not a Secularist*; Perry, "Liberal Democracy and Religious Morality"; and McConnell, "Five Reasons to Reject the Claim that Religious Arguments Should be Excluded."
[51] In Waldron, "Religious Contributions to Political Deliberation," I argued that it may be impossible to articulate and defend certain positions on welfare and redistribution without appealing to religious grounds, and others have argued that this may be impossible too for certain positions on abortion and other issues concerning the boundaries of human life: see Finnis, "Public Reason, Abortion, and Cloning."
[52] For Rawls's vacillation on this with regard to the specific example of abortion, see Rawls, *Political Liberalism*, p. 243n, and the "correction" in a new preface at p. lv.

into public life. The upshot of his position on toleration is that most religious doctrines – particularly on issues about worship and creed – are
politically irrelevant, and those who exercise (or call for the exercise of)
political power should have nothing to do with them (LCT: 26 and 39).
But equality is different. The reasons why men are not permitted to
dominate and exploit one another are fundamental to politics and they
must be properly understood. They are matters *we must get to the bottom of,*
whether or not the bottom turns out to be controversial and philosophically sectarian. If we don't get to the bottom of these issues, if we shy
away from the foundations of equality because we are afraid of offending somebody or of requiring others to go somewhere in their thoughts
and deliberations where they would rather not go, then we risk making
our egalitarian political order more shallow and less articulate than it
ought to be.[53] There may have been a time, Locke says, when we could
afford to leave all this implicit (2nd T: 111–12). But basic equality is now
under attack by sophisticated bodies of theory, which have as their aim
the establishment of political power on an inegalitarian basis. So now
the implicit must become explicit, and what was vague must now be
carefully unpacked and expounded, even at the expense of the genial
consensus that vagueness guarantees. "To understand Political Power
right, and derive it from its Original, we must consider what State all
Men are naturally in" (2nd T: 4).

Rawls's arguments imply that if we move in this direction – if we
think it necessary publicly to explore the comprehensive foundations
of our egalitarianism – then we must accept the risk of sectarianism
and of being seen to exercise (and of actually exercising) state power
on a basis "about which citizens as reasonable persons are bound to
differ uncompromisingly."[54] It would be nice to be able to answer this
by saying, "Well if the Lockean argument about equality is right, then
those who hold non-religiously grounded conceptions of equality are
revealed to be unreasonable, for now they do not accept what is necessary
for a well-ordered egalitarian society." But I don't think that's the only
response. Apart from anything else, it fails to distinguish between what

---

53 And it's not just a matter of public *philosophy*. We may risk actually doing the wrong thing, so
   far as equality is concerned. Justice McLean in his dissent in *Dred Scot* v. *Sanford* thought the
   US Supreme Court did the wrong thing because they could not be convinced that the plaintiff
   slave was not just a chattel, but a person entitled to justice because "[h]e bears the impress of
   his Maker . . . and he is destined to an endless existence." See *Dred Scott* v. *Sandford* 60 US 393,
   550 (1856), McLean J. dissenting. I am grateful to Hadley Arkes for drawing this passage to my
   attention: see Arkes, "*Lochner v. New York* and the Cast of our Laws," p. 125.
54 Rawls, *Political Liberalism*, p. 138.

is a reasonable view in the sense of what view turns out to be necessary for a well-ordered egalitarian society, and what is a reasonable view in the sense of what turns out to be a reasonable exercise of human intellect under what Rawls refers to as the burdens of judgment.[55] It is patently true that secular or atheistic thought (including secular or atheist thought about the basis of social and political relations) is reasonable in the second sense. (Rawls uses both conceptions of reasonableness in *Political Liberalism*; and he either equivocates between them or assumes, quite without argument, that anything which is unreasonable in the first sense is also unreasonable in the second.)

A more sensible approach is to bear in mind that it is impossible to avoid commitment in political theory. If we try too hard to be non-sectarian, we will end up saying nothing. As things stand, not every ingredient even in a Rawls political liberalism is entirely comfortable for every member of the community. One of the basic foundations of Rawls's liberalism is a particular conception of the human person as a free agent, with certain moral powers. These powers are to be taken seriously and not simply regarded as reducible, psychologically, to various drives and rationalizations.[56] Rawls's view – in which I think he is quite correct – is that it is not possible to reason well or reliably about matters of justice without a conception of this kind – that is, without a serious moralistic conception of moral personality, the capacity for a conception of the good, and the capacity for a sense of justice.[57] Anyone who is skeptical about that will not see the point of a large part of Rawls's theory. Yet there *are* many people – mostly sophisticated people in our society – who are quite skeptical about all that, who indeed regard the notion of its significance and irreducibility as a myth, perhaps as much of a myth as the existence of God. So if you want to get a flavor of what Locke is saying about religious skepticism and the consequence of religion's exclusion from public reason, you can get a sense of it from the way in which John Rawls would be uncomfortable developing a theory of justice in the company of various Nietzscheans or radical Freudians who believed that all this moralistic talk of agency and moral personality was redundant and reducible nonsense.

The analogy – between John Locke on God and John Rawls on moral personality – is all the more striking, of course, when you realize that moral personality has to be able to do by itself in Rawls's theory all the work for equality that is done, for Locke, by the notion of our status in

---

[55] For the burdens of judgment, see ibid., pp. 54 ff.   [56] Ibid., pp. 47 ff.   [57] Ibid., pp. 81 ff.

the eyes of God. For Locke, the religious foundation is indispensable: we
have seen it do important work in political theory, as a premise and as
a constraint. For Rawls, the moral personality stuff is a similarly load-
bearing part of the theoretical structure, and similarly indispensable. Let
me be clear about this analogy. I am not saying that Rawls's political
liberalism fails and that eventually he has to reach down into the bowels
of some more comprehensive conception in order to establish his notion
of moral personality. All I am saying is that the overlapping consensus
that defines his political liberalism does have *indispensable content*, and some
of that content is controversial. In Rawls's case, the essential ingredient of
a recognition of moral personality is one of the controversial premises.
I think Rawls would say that anyone who proposes to participate in
discourse about justice while remaining skeptical about that is not, in
fact, being reasonable (in this first of the two senses of reasonableness
that I identified a moment ago).[58] And that is exactly what Locke is
saying, only about something slightly different. It is not reasonable, he
suggests, to think that you can proceed safely in public discourse or in
public life, without accepting the theism which in Locke's view is an
indispensable basis for equality and social stability. "The taking away of
God, though but even in thought, dissolves all."

VIII

Of course, our ability to grasp the Lockean position in this way, by
analogy with Rawls on moral personality, doesn't show that Locke is
right and that we *do* need the idea of God and of our relation to God
in order to establish the principle of basic human equality. Many deny
this – I am sure many of my readers deny this – and I want to end my
argument with some more general reflections on the position that I have
attributed to Locke.

The position I have foisted on him is that atheism is a menace, in
large part because it is impossible to arrive at, articulate, or defend a
deep and robust conception of basic human equality without some sort
of transcendent premise. What are we to make of this as a general thesis
in liberal theory, as opposed to one that is safely confined to the historical context in which John Locke thought about political philosophy? It
certainly seems counter-intuitive to us, and (as I said at the beginning

---

[58] See above, p. 239.

of section VI) the particular consequence Locke drew from it – that atheism is not to be tolerated, that atheists are to be disenfranchised – is quite out of the question as a practical conclusion for modern liberal theory. But how should we read this counter-intuitiveness? Is it simply confirmation of the verdict that John Dunn entered in 1969 – that one "cannot conceive of constructing an analysis of any issue in contemporary [i.e. present-day] political theory around the affirmation or negation of anything which Locke says about political matters"?[59] If so, this would confirm the central claim of the Cambridge school, that there is something inherently inappropriate about raiding Locke's work (or any other body of work so distant from us) for premises, conclusions, arguments, and insights to be recycled in twenty-first century political philosophy.

I am doubtful about this conclusion. I said in Chapter 1 that we should not be too quick to congratulate ourselves on having left the religious issues behind us, so far as the defense and elaboration of basic equality is concerned. And the point is relevant to the historicist concern. The issue, which in various ways is still familiar to us, of how much work can be done in moral and political theory without some specific religious premises was also perfectly familiar to John Locke and his contemporaries in seventeenth-century England. It is not a case of his assuming, as a matter of background world-view, that *of course* religion must be an ingredient, and our assuming, as a matter of a different background world-view, that *of course* it is not. Whatever our discomfort with Locke's particular conclusion about atheism, it turns out he is haunted by meta-ethical anxieties that are not dissimilar to our own (even if he is inclined to come down on a different side from that of the secularists among us). So it cannot sensibly be regarded as an offense against historical propriety to bring his reflections about religion and the basis of political morality into relation with our reflections about religion and the basis of political morality.

The Lockean discussion is clearest in *The Reasonableness of Christianity*. Locke is well aware that many people claim that we can reason through to important moral truths without religious authority. He believes that the currency of this claim reveals something of the arrogance of human reason:

[59] Dunn, *Political Thought of John Locke*, p. x. Cf. Dunn's partial revocation of this verdict almost twenty years later in Dunn, "What is Living and What is Dead in the Political Theory of John Locke," p. 9.

When truths are once known to us, though by tradition, we are apt to be favorable to our own parts; and ascribe to our understandings the discovery of what in reality we borrowed from others...A great many things which we have been bred up in the belief of, from our cradles (and are notions grown familiar, and, as it were, natural to us, under the gospel), we take for unquestionable obvious truths, and easily demonstrable; without considering how long we might have been in doubt or ignorance of them, had revelation been silent. (RC: 144–5)

It may seem to us now that we can make do with a purely secular notion of human equality; but as a matter of ethical history, that notion has been shaped and fashioned on the basis of religion. That is where all the hard work was done. To drive this point home, Locke introduces a wealth of imagery, emphasizing the labor that we take for granted as we squander our ethical inheritance:

Native and original truth is not so easily wrought out of the mine, as we, who have it delivered already dug and fashioned into our hands, are apt to imagine...He that travels the roads now, applauds his own strength and legs that have carried him so far in such a scantling of time; and ascribes all to his own vigor; little considering how much he owes to their pains, who cleared the woods, drained the bogs, built the bridges, and made the ways passable. (RC: 140 and 145)

The defense and elaboration of the principle of human equality, as we have seen in these chapters, has required no little effort in the way of bridge-building, wood-clearing, and bog-draining.

Still, at the end of the day, this is at most a genealogical point. It is a point about how we arrived at the concept of human equality, not a point about what the concept of human equality now implies or presupposes in a logical sense. The shape of the concept now may be inexplicable without reference to the religious traditions that fashioned it. But, some will say, modern egalitarians have simply given the lie to those like Locke who claim it is impossible to commit oneself to, or work with, or make great sacrifices for, something of this shape without a commitment to the forces that shaped it.[60] And maybe that is right. "It is," as Locke says, "no diminishing to revelation, that reason [now] gives its suffrage too, to the truths [that] revelation has discovered" (RC: 145).

Whether this concept of human equality, curiously shaped as it is (from reason's autonomous point of view), will retain its shape under the various

---

[60] I suspect that most of my readers believe that atheists are no more of a menace, probably much less of a menace, to society than various religious fanatics. Compare the response to Senator Joseph Lieberman's claims during the 2000 US Presidential Campaign about the sustainability of public morality in the absence of religious faith. See "Mr. Lieberman's Religious Words," *The New York Times*, August 31, 2000, p. 24.

pressures it faces, and how haphazardly it will grow once it takes on a life of its own, is of course another matter. Maybe the concept of equality will become more humane in various ways, for we have noticed one or two places in these lectures where Lockean equality seems to have quite a savage or unpleasant side by virtue of its place in Christian theology. Or maybe the notion of humans as one another's equals will begin to fall apart, under pressure, without the presence of the religious conception that shaped it. As we have seen, it is a very complex and elaborate idea and there is no reason to suppose that the complexity of basic human equality is not matched by its fragility when it – and we – are left to our own devices.

The final point in this regard that I think Locke would want to insist on is that equality is not just an idea for the intellectual. It is not an idea that can do its work on its own or in the academy. It is an idea, Locke thought, that can be trusted to do its best work in the hands of those who are its beneficiaries – the plain, unscholastic men and women, "the day-laborers, the tradesmen, the spinsters and the dairy-maids" (RC: 146) to whose intelligence the content of the idea plays tribute. Equality cannot do its work unless it is accepted among those whom it consecrates as equals. Locke believed this general acceptance was impossible apart from the principle's foundation in religious teaching. We believe otherwise. Locke, I suspect, would have thought we were taking a risk. And I am afraid it is not entirely clear, given our experience of a world and a century in which politics and public reason have cut loose from these foundations, that his cautions and suspicions were unjustified.

Bibliography

Abernethy, George L. (ed.) *The Idea of Equality: An Anthology* (Richmond: John Knox Press, 1959).

Ackerman, Bruce, *Social Justice in the Liberal State* (New Haven: Yale University Press, 1980).

Aquinas, Thomas, *Selected Political Writings*, ed. A. P. D'Entreves (Oxford: Basil Blackwell, 1959).

    Summa Theologica, excerpted in Aquinas, *Selected Political Writings*, ed. A. P. D'Entreves (Oxford: Basil Blackwell, 1959).

Arendt, Hannah, *On Revolution* (Harmondsworth: Penguin Books, 1977).

Aristotle, *The Politics*, ed. Stephen Everson (Cambridge: Cambridge University Press, 1988).

Arkes, Hadley, "*Lochner v. New York* and the Cast of our Laws," in R. P. George (ed.) *Great Cases in Constitutional Law* (Princeton: Princeton University Press, 2000).

Ashcraft, Richard, *Revolutionary Politics and Locke's "Two Treatises of Government"* (Princeton: Princeton University Press, 1986).

    Locke's Two Treatises of Government (London: Unwin Hyman, 1987).

    "Simple Objections and Complex Reality: Theorizing Political Radicalism in Seventeenth Century England," *Political Studies*, 40 (1992), 99–115.

Astell, Mary, *Reflections Upon Marriage* [1700], in M. Astell, *Political Writings*, ed. Patricia Springborg (Cambridge: Cambridge University Press, 1996), pp. 7–80.

    Political Writings, ed. Patricia Springborg (Cambridge: Cambridge University Press, 1996).

Audi, Robert, "The Separation of Church and State and the Obligations of Citizenship," *Philosophy and Public Affairs*, 18 (1989), 259–96.

Austin, J. L., *How to Do Things With Words*, 2nd edn (Cambridge, Mass.: Harvard University Press, 1975).

Ayers, Michael, *Locke: Epistemology and Ontology* (London: Routledge, 1991), 2 vols.

Berlin, Isaiah, "Equality," in I. Berlin, *Concepts and Categories*, ed. Henry Hardy (Princeton: Princeton University Press, 1999), pp. 81–102.

    Concepts and Categories, ed. Henry Hardy (Princeton: Princeton University Press, 1999).

Blackburn, Simon, "Reply: Rule-Following and Moral Realism," in S. Holtzman and C. Leich (eds.) *Wittgenstein: To Follow a Rule* (London: Routledge, 1981), pp. 163–87.

    Essays in Quasi-Realism (Oxford: Oxford University Press, 1993).

    Ruling Passions (Oxford: Clarendon Press, 1998).

Boucher, David and Kelley, Paul (eds.), *The Social Contract: From Hobbes to Rawls* (London: Routledge, 1994).

Boyd, Richard, "Homeostasis, Species, and Higher Taxa," in R. A. Wilson (ed.) *Species: New Interdisciplinary Essays* (Cambridge, Mass.: MIT Press, 1999), pp. 141–86.

Bracken, H. M., "Essence, Accident and Race," *Hermathena* 116 (Winter 1973), 81–96.

Brown, Stuart, "Hobbes: The Taylor Thesis," *Philosophical Review*, 68 (1959), 303–23.

Buchanan, Allen, "Justice and Charity," *Ethics*, 97 (1987), 558–75.

Burnet, Thomas, *Remarks on John Locke* (Doncaster: Brynmill, 1989).

Butler, Melissa, "Early Liberal Roots of Feminism: John Locke and the Attack on Patriarchy," *American Political Science Review*, 72 (1978), 135–50.

Clark, Lorenne M. G., "Women and Locke: Who Owns the Apples in the Garden of Eden?" in L. M. G. Clark and L. Lange (eds.) *The Sexism of Social and Political Theory: Women and Reproduction from Plato to Nietzche* (Toronto: University of Toronto Press, 1979), pp. 16–40.

Clark, Lorenne M. G. and Lange, Lynda (eds.) *The Sexism of Social and Political Theory: Women and Reproduction from Plato to Nietzche* (Toronto: University of Toronto Press, 1979).

Cohen, G. A., *Self-Ownership, Freedom and Equality* (Cambridge: Cambridge University Press, 1995).

    If You're an Egalitarian, How Come You're So Rich? (Cambridge, Mass.: Harvard University Press, 2000).

Colman, John, *John Locke's Moral Philosophy* (Edinburgh: Edinburgh University Press, 1983).

Connolly, William E., *Why I am not a Secularist* (Minneapolis: University of Minnesota Press, 1999).

Coons, John E. and Brennan, Patrick M., *By Nature Equal: The Anatomy of a Western Insight* (Princeton: Princeton University Press, 1999).

Coste, Peter, "The Character of Mr. Locke" [1720], in J. S. Yolton, *A Locke Miscellany: Locke's Biography and Criticism for All* (Bristol: Thoemmes, 1990), pp. 333–47.

Davie, George, *The Democratic Intellect: Scotland and her Universities in the Nineteenth Century* (Edinburgh: Edinburgh University Press, 1961).

Drescher, Seymour, "On James Farr's 'So Vile and Miserable an Estate,'" *Political Theory*, 16 (1988), 502–3.

Dunn, John, *The Political Thought of John Locke: An Historical Account of the Argument of the 'Two Treatises of Government'* (Cambridge: Cambridge University Press, 1969).

Locke (New York: Oxford University Press, 1984).

"What is Living and What is Dead in the Political Theory of John Locke," in J. Dunn, *Interpreting Political Responsibility: Essays 1981–1989* (Oxford: Polity, 1990), pp. 9–25.

Interpreting Political Responsibility: Essays 1981–1989 (Oxford: Polity, 1990).

"The Claim to Freedom of Conscience: Freedom of Speech, Freedom of Thought, Freedom of Worship?" in O. P. Grell, J. I. Israel and N. Tyacke (eds.) *From Persecution to Toleration: The Glorious Revolution and Religion in England* (Oxford: Clarendon Press, 1991).

The Cunning of Unreason: Making Sense of Politics (New York: Basic Books, 2000).

Dworkin, Ronald, *Taking Rights Seriously* (London: Duckworth, 1977).

"What is Equality? Part 1: Equality of Welfare," *Philosophy and Public Affairs*, 10 (1981), 185–246.

"What is Equality? Part 2: Equality of Resources," *Philosophy and Public Affairs*, 10 (1981), 283–345.

Law's Empire (Cambridge, Mass.: Harvard University Press, 1986).

Sovereign Virtue: The Theory and Practice of Equality (Cambridge, Mass.: Harvard University Press, 2000).

Farr, James, "'So Vile and Miserable an Estate': The Problem of Slavery in Locke's Political Thought," *Political Theory*, 14 (1986), 263–89.

"'Slaves Bought with Money': A Reply to Drescher," *Political Theory*, 17 (1989), 471–4.

Filmer, Robert, "The Anarchy of a Limited or Mixed Monarchy," in R. Filmer, *Patriarcha and Other Writings*, ed. Johann P. Sommerville (Cambridge: Cambridge University Press, 1991).

"Observations Concerning the Originall of Government, upon Mr Hobs *Leviathan*, Mr Milton against Salmasius, H. Grotius *De Iure Belli*," in R. Filmer, *Patriarcha and Other Writings*, ed. Johann P. Sommerville (Cambridge: Cambridge University Press, 1991).

Patriarcha and Other Writings, ed. Johann P. Sommerville (Cambridge: Cambridge University Press, 1991).

Finnis, John, *Natural Law and Natural Rights* (Oxford: Clarendon Press, 1980).

Aquinas (Oxford: Oxford University Press, 1998).

"Public Reason, Abortion, and Cloning," *Valparaiso University Law Review*, 32 (1998), 361–82.

Fish, Stanley, *The Trouble with Principle* (Cambridge, Mass.: Harvard University Press, 1999).

Fletcher, George P., "In God's Image: The Religious Imperative of Equality under Law," *Columbia Law Review*, 99 (1999), 1608–29.

Frankfurt, Harry G., "Equality and Respect," *Social Research*, 64 (1997), 3–15.

George, Robert P. (ed.) *Great Cases in Constitutional Law* (Princeton: Princeton University Press, 2000).

Gewirth, Alan, *Human Rights: Essays on Justification and Applications* (Chicago: University of Chicago Press, 1982).

Gorr, Michael, "Rawls on Natural Inequality," *Philosophical Quarterly*, 33 (1983), 1–18.

Grant, Ruth, *John Locke's Liberalism* (Chicago: University of Chicago Press, 1987).

Greenawalt, Kent, *Religious Convictions and Political Choice* (New York: Oxford University Press, 1988).

Grotius, Hugo, *The Rights of War and Peace*, trans. A. C. Campbell (New York: M. Walter Dunne, 1901).

Haksar, Vinit, *Equality, Liberty and Perfectionism* (Oxford: Clarendon Press, 1979).

Hare, R. M., *The Language of Morals* (Oxford: Oxford University Press, 1952).

Freedom and Reason (Oxford: Oxford University Press, 1963).

Sorting Out Ethics (Oxford: Clarendon Press, 1997).

Harris, Angela P., "Race and Essentialism in Feminist Legal Theory," *Stanford Law Review*, 42 (1990), 581–616.

Harris, Ian, *The Mind of John Locke: A Study of Political Theory in its Intellectual Setting* (Cambridge: Cambridge University Press, 1994).

"The Politics of Christianity," in G. A. J. Rogers (ed.) *Locke's Philosophy: Content and Context* (Oxford: Clarendon Press, 1994).

Hart, H. L. A., *The Concept of Law*, 2nd edn (Oxford: Clarendon Press, 1994).

Herzog, Don, *Happy Slaves: A Critique of Consent Theory* (Chicago: University of Chicago Press, 1989).

Hobbes, Thomas, *Leviathan*, ed. Richard Tuck (Cambridge: Cambridge University Press, 1988).

On the Citizen, ed. Richard Tuck and Michael Silverthorne (Cambridge: Cambridge University Press, 1998).

Holtzman, Steven and Leich, Christopher (eds.) *Wittgenstein: To Follow a Rule* (London: Routledge, 1981).

Hooker, Richard, *Of the Laws of Ecclesiastical Polity* [1593], ed. Arthur Stephen McGrade (Cambridge: Cambridge University Press, 1989).

Horne, Thomas A., *Property Rights and Poverty: Political Argument in Britain, 1605–1834* (Chapel Hill: University of North Carolina Press, 1990).

Hume, David, *A Treatise of Human Nature*, ed. L. A. Selby-Bigge and P. H. Nidditch, 2nd edn (Oxford: Clarendon Press, 1978).

Jolley, Nicholas, "Leibniz on Locke and Socinianism," *Journal of the History of Ideas*, 39 (1978), 233–50.

Johnston, David (ed.) *Equality* (Indianapolis: Hackett Publishing, 2000).

Kant, Immanuel, *Religion Within the Limits of Reason Alone* (New York: Harper, 1960).

Grounding for the Metaphysics of Morals, trans. James Ellington (Indianapolis: Hackett Publishing, 1981).

Kato, Takshi, "The *Reasonableness* in the Historical Light of the *Essay*," *Locke Newsletter*, 9 (1978), 45–59.

Kendall, Willmoore, *John Locke and the Doctrine of Majority-Rule* (Urbana: University of Illinois Press, 1965).

Kitcher, Philip, "Species," *Philosophy of Science*, 51 (1984), 308–33.

Kramer, Matthew, *John Locke and the Origins of Private Property: Philosophical Explorations of Individualism, Community, and Equality* (Cambridge: Cambridge University Press, 1997).

Laslett, Peter, "Introduction," to John Locke, *Two Treatises of Government*, ed. Peter Laslett (Cambridge: Cambridge University Press, 1988), pp. 3–126.

Lloyd Thomas, D. A., "Equality Within the Limits of Reason Alone," *Mind*, 88 (1979), 538–53.

Locke, John, *A Second Letter Concerning Toleration*, in *The Works of John Locke* (London: Thomas Tegg and others, 1823), vol. VI, 59–137.

A Third Letter for Toleration, in *The Works of John Locke* (London: Thomas Tegg and others, 1823), vol. VI, 139–546.

An Essay Concerning Human Understanding, ed. P. H. Nidditch (Oxford: Clarendon Press, 1971).

A Letter Concerning Toleration, ed. James Tully (Indianapolis: Hackett Publishing, 1983).

A Paraphrase and Notes on the Epistles of St. Paul, 2 vols., ed. Arthur W. Wainwright (Oxford: Clarendon Press, 1987).

Two Treatises of Government, ed. Peter Laslett (Cambridge: Cambridge University Press, 1988).

"The Last Will and Testament of John Locke, Esq.," in J. S. Yolton (ed.) *A Locke Miscellany: Locke's Biography and Criticism for All* (Bristol: Thoemmes Press, 1990), pp. 353–62.

Of the Conduct of the Understanding [1706], in John Locke, *Some Thoughts Concerning Education and Of the Conduct Of the Understanding*, ed. Ruth W. Grant and Nathan Tarcov (Indianapolis: Hackett Publishing, 1996), pp. 163–227.

Some Thoughts Concerning Education and Of the Conduct of the Understanding, ed. Ruth W. Grant and Nathan Tarcov (Indianapolis: Hackett Publishing, 1996).

"First Tract on Government" [1660], in John Locke, *Political Essays*, ed. Mark Goldie (Cambridge: Cambridge University Press, 1997), pp. 3–53.

"Second Tract on Government" [1662], in John Locke, *Political Essays*, ed. Mark Goldie (Cambridge: Cambridge University Press, 1997), pp. 54–78.

"Verses on Queen Catherine" [1662], in John Locke, *Political Essays*, ed. Mark Goldie (Cambridge: Cambridge University Press, 1997), pp. 209–11.

Essays on the Law of Nature [1663–64], in John Locke, *Political Essays*, ed. Mark Goldie (Cambridge: Cambridge University Press, 1997), pp. 79–133.

"An Essay on Toleration" [1667], in John Locke, *Political Essays*, ed. Mark Goldie (Cambridge: Cambridge University Press, 1997), pp. 134–59.

"The Fundamental Constitutions of Carolina" [1669], in John Locke, *Political Essays*, ed. Mark Goldie (Cambridge: Cambridge University Press, 1997), pp. 160–81.

"Virtue B" [1681], in John Locke, *Political Essays*, ed. Mark Goldie (Cambridge: Cambridge University Press, 1997), pp. 287–8.

"Of Ethic in General" [1686–8], in John Locke, *Political Essays*, ed. Mark Goldie (Cambridge: Cambridge University Press, 1997), pp. 297–304.

"*Homo ante et post Lapsum*" [1693], in John Locke, *Political Essays*, ed. Mark Goldie (Cambridge: Cambridge University Press, 1997), pp. 320–1.

"Law" [1693], in John Locke, *Political Essays*, ed. Mark Goldie (Cambridge: Cambridge University Press, 1997), p. 328.

"Liberty of the Press" [1693–4], in John Locke, *Political Essays*, ed. Mark Goldie (Cambridge: Cambridge University Press, 1997), pp. 330–9.

"An Essay on the Poor Law" [1697]," in John Locke, *Political Essays*, ed. Mark Goldie (Cambridge: Cambridge University Press, 1997), pp. 182–98.

Political Essays, ed. Mark Goldie (Cambridge: Cambridge University Press, 1997).

The Reasonableness of Christianity, as Delivered in the Scriptures (Bristol: Thoemmes Press, 1997).

A Second Vindication of the Reasonableness of Christianity, in John Locke, *The Reasonableness of Christianity, as Delivered in the Scriptures* (Bristol: Thoemmes Press, 1997).

Lovejoy, Arthur, *The Great Chain of Being* (Cambridge, Mass.: Harvard University Press, 1974).

Macdonald, Margaret, "Natural Rights," in J. Waldron (ed.) *Theories of Rights* (Oxford: Oxford University Press, 1984), pp. 21–40.

Macintyre, Alasdair, *After Virtue: A Study in Moral Theory* (London: Duckworth, 1981).

Whose Justice? Which Rationality? (Notre Dame, Ind.: University of Notre Dame Press, 1988).

Macpherson, C. B., *The Political Theory of Possessive Individualism: Hobbes to Locke* (Oxford: Oxford University Press, 1962).

Democratic Theory: Essays in Retrieval (Oxford: Clarendon Press, 1973).

Marshall, John, *John Locke: Resistance, Revolution, and Responsibility* (Cambridge: Cambridge University Press, 1994).

Martin, Josiah, *A Letter to the Author of Some Brief Observations on the Paraphrase and Notes of the Judicious John Locke, relating to the Womens Exercising their Spiritual Gifts in the Church* (London: [publisher unknown] 1716).

Masham, Damaris, "The Life and Character of Mr Locke," in J. S. Yolton (ed.) *A Locke Miscellany: Locke's Biography and Criticism for All* (Bristol: Thoemmes Press, 1990), pp. 348–52.

May, Kenneth, "A Set of Independent Necessary and Sufficient Conditions for Simple Majority Decision," *Econometrica*, 20 (1952), 680–4.

McClure, Kirstie M., *Judging Rights: Lockean Politics and the Limits of Consent* (Ithaca: Cornell University Press, 1996).

McConnell, Michael W., "Five Reasons to Reject the Claim that Religious Arguments should be Excluded from Democratic Deliberation," *Utah Law Review* (1999), 639–57.

McDowell, John, "Non-Cognitivism and Rule-Following," in Steven Holtzman and Christopher Leich (eds.) *Wittgenstein: To Follow a Rule* (London: Routledge, 1981), pp. 141–162.

McMurrin, S. M., *The Tanner Lectures on Human Values* (Salt Lake City: University of Utah Press, 1980).

Mill, John Stuart, *On Liberty*, ed. Currin V. Shields (Indianapolis: Bobbs Merrill, 1956).

　Considerations on Representative Government (Buffalo, N.Y.: Prometheus Books, 1991).

Milton, J. R., "John Locke and the Fundamental Constitutions of Carolina," *Locke Newsletter*, 21 (1990), 111–33.

Moore, J. T., "Locke on the Moral Need for Christianity," *Southwestern Journal of Philosophy*, 11 (1980), 61–8.

Nagel, Thomas, *The Possibility of Altruism* (Princeton: Princeton University Press, 1970).

　"Moral Conflict and Political Legitimacy," *Philosophy and Public Affairs*, 16 (1987), 215–40.

Norton, Mary Beth, *Founding Mothers: Gendered Power and the Forming of American Society* (New York: Alfred A. Knopf, 1996).

Nozick, Robert, *Anarchy, State and Utopia* (Oxford: Basil Blackwell, 1974).

Nuovo, Victor (ed.) *John Locke and Christianity: Contemporary Responses to "The Reasonableness of Christianity"* (Bristol: Thoemmes Press, 1997).

Parfit, Derek, *Equality or Priority?* (Lawrence: University of Kansas Press, 1995).

Parry, Geraint, *John Locke* (London: George Allen & Unwin, 1978).

Pateman, Carole, *The Sexual Contract* (Stanford: Stanford University Press, 1988).

Pears, Iain, *An Instance of the Fingerpost* (London: Jonathan Cape, 1997).

Perry, Michael J., "Liberal Democracy and Religious Morality," *DePaul Law Review*, 48 (1998), 1–49.

Pojman, Louis P. and Westmoreland, Robert (eds.) *Equality: Selected Readings* (New York: Oxford University Press, 1997).

Posner, Richard A., *The Problematics of Moral and Legal Theory* (Cambridge, Mass.: Harvard University Press, 1999).

Pufendorf, Samuel, *On the Duty of Man and Citizen According to Natural Law*, ed. James Tully (Cambridge: Cambridge University Press, 1991).

Rabieh, Michael S., "The Reasonableness of Locke, or the Questionableness of Christianity," *Journal of Politics*, 53 (1991), 933–57.

Rashdall, Hastings, *The Theory of Good and Evil: A Treatise on Moral Philosophy*, 2nd edn (Oxford: Oxford University Press, 1924), 2 vols.

Rawls, John, *A Theory of Justice* (Oxford: Oxford University Press, 1971).

　Political Liberalism (New York: Columbia University Press, 1993).

Raz, Joseph, *The Morality of Freedom* (Oxford: Clarendon Press, 1986).

　"Facing Diversity: The Case of Epistemic Abstinence," *Philosophy and Public Affairs*, 19 (1990), 3–46.

Ritchie, David G., *Natural Rights: A Criticism of Some Political and Ethical Conceptions* (London: Swan Sonnenschein, 1903).

Rogers, G. A. J. (ed.) *Locke's Philosophy: Content and Context* (Oxford: Clarendon Press, 1994).

Rorty, Richard, "Solidarity or Objectivity?" in R. Rorty, *Objectivity, Relativism and Truth: Philosophical Papers Vol. I* (Cambridge: Cambridge University Press, 1991), pp. 21–34.

    Objectivity, Relativism and Truth: Philosophical Papers Vol. I (Cambridge: Cambridge University Press, 1991).

    "Human Rights, Rationality and Sentimentality," in S. Shute and S. Hurley (eds.) *On Human Rights: The Oxford Amnesty Lectures 1993* (New York: Basic Books, 1993), pp. 111–34.

Ryan, Alan, 'Locke and the Dictatorship of the Bourgeoisie," *Political Studies*, 13 (1965), 219–30.

    Property and Political Theory (Oxford: Basil Blackwell, 1984).

Scanlon, T. M., *What We Owe to Each Other* (Cambridge, Mass.: Harvard University Press, 1998).

Schochet, Gordon, *Patriarchalism in Political Thought: The Authoritarian Family and Political Speculation and Attitudes Especially in Seventeenth-Century England* (Oxford: Blackwell, 1975).

    "Radical Politics and Ashcraft's Treatise on Locke," *Journal of the History of Ideas*, 50 (1989), 491–510.

Sen, Amartya, *Collective Choice and Social Welfare* (Amsterdam: Elsevier, 1969).

    "Equality of What?" in S. M. McMurrin, *The Tanner Lectures on Human Values* (Salt Lake City: University of Utah Press, 1980).

Shanley, Mary Lyndon, "Marriage Contract and Social Contract in Seventeenth-Century English Political Thought," *Western Political Quarterly*, 32 (1979), 79–91.

Shapiro, Ian, and DeCew, Judith Wagner, *Theory and Practice* Nomos XXXVII (New York: New York University Press, 1995).

Sharp, Andrew (ed.) *The English Levellers* (Cambridge: Cambridge University Press, 1998).

Shute, Stephen and Hurley, Susan (eds.) *On Human Rights: The Oxford Amnesty Lectures 1993* (New York: Basic Books, 1993).

Simmons, A. John, *The Lockean Theory of Rights* (Princeton: Princeton University Press, 1992).

Skinner, Quentin, "Meaning and Understanding in the History of Ideas," in James Tully (ed.) *Meaning and Context: Quentin Skinner and his Critics* (Princeton: Princeton University Press, 1988), pp. 29–67.

Skinner, Quentin, *Reason and Rhetoric in the Philosophy of Hobbes* (Cambridge: Cambridge University Press, 1996).

Spellman, W. M., *John Locke and the Problem of Depravity* (Oxford: Clarendon Press, 1988).

    John Locke (New York: St. Martin's Press, 1997).

Springborg, Patricia, "Mary Astell (1666–1731), Critic of Locke," *American Political Science Review*, 89 (1995), 621–33.

Squadrito, Kathy, "Locke on the Equality of the Sexes," *Journal of Social Philosophy*, 10 (1979), 6–11.

Sreenivasan, Gopal, *The Limits of Lockean Rights in Property* (New York: Oxford University Press, 1995).

Stevens, Jacqueline, "The Reasonableness of John Locke's Majority," *Political Theory*, 24 (1996), 423–63.

　Reproducing the State (Princeton: Princeton University Press, 1999).

Strauss, Leo, *Natural Right and History* (Chicago: University of Chicago Press, 1953).

　"Locke's Doctrine of Natural Law," *American Political Science Review*, 52 (1958), 490–501.

Taylor, A. E., "The Ethical Doctrine of Hobbes," *Philosophy*, 13 (1938), 406–24.

Taylor, Charles, *Sources of the Self: The Making of the Modern Identity* (Cambridge: Cambridge University Press, 1989).

Temkin, Larry, *Inequality* (Oxford: Oxford University Press, 1993).

Tuck, Richard, *Natural Rights Theories: Their Origin and Development* (Cambridge: Cambridge University Press, 1979).

Tully, James, *A Discourse on Property: John Locke and his Adversaries* (Cambridge: Cambridge University Press, 1980).

　"Rediscovering America: The *Two Treatises* and Aboriginal Rights," in J. Tully, *An Approach to Political Philosophy: Locke in Context* (Cambridge: Cambridge University Press, 1993), pp. 137–76.

　"Governing Conduct: Locke on the Reform of Thought and Behavior," in J. Tully, *An Approach to Political Philosophy: Locke in Context* (Cambridge: Cambridge University Press, 1993), pp. 179–241.

　An Approach to Political Philosophy: Locke in Contexts (Cambridge: Cambridge University Press, 1993).

　(ed.) *Meaning and Context: Quentin Skinner and his Critics* (Princeton: Princeton University Press, 1988).

Tyrrell, James, *Patriarcha Non Monarcha* (London: Richard Janeway, 1681).

　Of the Law of Nature [2nd edn, 1701] (Littleton, Colo.: Fred B. Rothman & Co., 1987).

Uzgalis, W. L., "The Anti-Essential Locke and Natural Kinds," *Philosophical Quarterly*, 38 (1988), 330–9.

Vlastos, Gregory, "Justice and Equality," in J. Waldron (ed.) *Theories of Rights* (Oxford: Oxford University Press, 1984), pp. 41–76.

Waldron, Jeremy, "Enough and as Good Left for Others," *Philosophical Quarterly*, 29 (1979), 319–28.

　"Locke's Account of Inheritance and Bequest," *Journal of the History of Philosophy*, 19 (1981), 39–51.

　"Two Worries About Mixing One's Labour," *Philosophical Quarterly*, 33 (1983), 37–44.

　"Locke, Tully and the Regulation of Property," *Political Studies*, 32 (1984), 98–106.

　(ed.) *Theories of Rights* (Oxford: Oxford University Press, 1984).

　The Right to Private Property (Oxford: Clarendon Press, 1988).

"John Locke: Social Contract versus Political Anthropology," *The Review of Politics*, 51 (1989), 3–28; reprinted in D. Boucher and P. Kelley (eds.) *The Social Contract: from Hobbes to Rawls* (London: Routledge, 1994).

"The Substance of Equality," *Michigan Law Review*, 89 (1991), 1350–70.

"Legislation and Moral Neutrality," in J. Waldron, *Liberal Rights: Collected Papers 1981–1991* (Cambridge: Cambridge University Press, 1993), pp. 143–67.

Liberal Rights: Collected Papers 1981–1991 (Cambridge: Cambridge University Press, 1993).

"Locke, Toleration and the Rationality of Persecution," in J. Waldron, *Liberal Rights: Collected Papers 1981–1991* (Cambridge: Cambridge University Press, 1993), pp. 88–114.

"Mill and the Value of Moral Distress," in J. Waldron, *Liberal Rights: Collected Papers 1981–1991* (Cambridge: Cambridge University Press, 1993), pp. 115–42.

"Property, Justification and Need," *Canadian Journal of Law and Jurisprudence*, 6 (1993), 185–215.

"Religious Contributions to Political Deliberation," *San Diego Law Review*, 30 (1993), 817–48.

"Special Ties and Natural Duties," *Philosophy and Public Affairs*, 22 (1993), 3–30.

"Theoretical Foundations of Liberalism," in J. Waldron, *Liberal Rights: Collected Papers 1981–1991* (Cambridge: Cambridge University Press, 1993), pp. 35–62.

"Welfare and the Images of Charity," in J. Waldron, *Liberal Rights: Collected Papers 1981–1991* (Cambridge: Cambridge University Press, 1993), pp. 225–49.

"What Plato Would Allow," in I. Shapiro and J. W. DeCew (eds.) *Theory and Practice* (New York: New York University Press, 1995), pp. 138–78.

The Dignity of Legislation (Cambridge: Cambridge University Press, 1999).

Law and Disagreement (Oxford: Clarendon Press, 1999).

"Ego-Bloated Hovel (Review of Richard A. Posner, *The Problematics of Moral and Legal Theory*)," *Northwestern University Law Review*, 94 (2000), 597–626.

"On the Road: Good Samaritans and Compelling Duties," *Santa Clara Law Review*, 40 (2000), 1053.

"Self Defense: Agent-Neutral and Agent-Relative Accounts," *California Law Review*, 88 (2000), 711–49.

"Three Essays on Basic Equality," unpublished draft, available from author.

Walker, William, "Locke Minding Women: Literary History, Gender, and the Essay," *Eighteenth-Century Studies*, 23 (1990), 245–68.

Welchman, Jennifer, "Locke on Slavery and Inalienable Rights," *Canadian Journal of Philosophy*, 25 (1995), 67–81.

Wikler, Daniel, "Paternalism and the Mildly Retarded," *Philosophy and Public Affairs*, 8 (1979), 377–92.

Wilkerson, T. E., "Species, Essences and the Names of Natural Kinds," *Philosophicals Quarterly*, 43 (1993), 1–19.

Natural Kinds (Aldershot: Avebury, 1995).

Williams, Bernard, "The Idea of Equality," in B. Williams, *Problems of the Self: Philosophical Papers 1956–1972* (Cambridge: Cambridge University Press, 1973), pp. 230–49.

   Problems of the Self: Philosophical Papers 1956–1972 (Cambridge: Cambridge University Press, 1973).

Wilson, Robert A. (ed.), *Species: New Interdisciplinary Essays* (Cambridge, Mass.: MIT Press, 1999).

Woltersdorff, Nicholas, *John Locke and the Ethics of Belief* (Cambridge: Cambridge University Press, 1996).

Wong, Jane, "The Anti-essentialism versus Essentialism Debate in Feminist Legal Theory," *William and Mary Journal of Women and the Law*, 5 (1999), 273–96.

Wood, Ellen Meiksins, "Locke Against Democracy: Consent, Representation and Suffrage in the *Two Treatises*," *History of Political Thought*, 13 (1992), 570–605.

Wood, Neal, *John Locke and Agrarian Capitalism* (Berkeley: University of California Press, 1984).

Wootton, David, "John Locke and Richard Ashcraft's *Revolutionary Politics*," *Political Studies*, 40 (1992), 79–98.

Yolton, Jean S., *A Locke Miscellany: Locke's Biography and Criticism for All* (Bristol: Thoemmes, 1990).

Index

Note: For John Locke's views on particular subjects (e.g. absolute monarchy), please refer to the individual subject headings (e.g. "absolutism" and "monarchy"). Entries listed under "Locke, John" are limited to Locke's life and career; his specific works are listed under "Locke's works."